CHART YOUR SUCCESS

ON THE

COMPASS

TEST

COMputer-adaptive Placement Assessment and Support System

SECOND EDITION

Nannette Commander
GEORGIA STATE UNIVERSITY

Walter Cotter
FLOYD COLLEGE

Carol Callahan
formerly FLOYD COLLEGE

CONTEMPORARY PUBLISHING COMPANY OF RALEIGH, INC.

6001-101 Chapel Hill Road, Raleigh, NC 27607 • (919) 851-8221

Publisher: Charles E. Grantham
Marketing Director: Sherri Powell
Production Manager: Erika Kessler
Cover Design: Contemporary Publishing Company of Raleigh, Inc.
Printer: Edwards Brothers, Inc.

ISBN: 0-89892-228-3

Printed in the United States of America

Printing 10 9 8 7 6 5 4 3 2

This book is in memory of Carol Callahan (1945-2000), our esteemed colleague. Her dedication to quality, generosity to others, and sense of humor will be sorely missed. Our friendship with Carol enriched our lives in countless ways, both professionally and personally.

This project would not have been possible without her efforts.

PREFACE

Computerized Adaptive Testing (CAT) is changing the way institutions test entering students. Computer testing provides shorter testing time with more accurate results. While there are attractive features to computerized testing, there are some differences that require a shift in the students' approach to testing. For example, because of the smaller number of items needed to place students, each item is critically important—a mini-test in itself. This book is designed to help students understand the COMPASS test, review the skills necessary to perform well on COMPASS, and take practice tests similar to the COMPASS test.

The book is divided into four parts—Introduction, Mathematics, Composition, and Reading. The first section relates information about adaptive testing, COMPASS features, and general test-taking hints. This section helps students become comfortable with adaptive testing and computer keyboard functions. Sections II, III, and IV provide content information based on the design of the COMPASS test. They are developed for a concise review of necessary skills. Practice tests designed to mimic items and responses in the COMPASS style complete each of these sections.

TABLE OF CONTENTS

INTRODUCTION TO COMPASS

WHAT IS COMPASS?

COMPASS (the computer-adaptive placement assessment and support system) is a test designed by the American College Testing Program. It tests reading, mathematics, and writing skills and is designed to help accurately place you in college courses. It may also, in some cases, be used as an exit test. **COMPASS** differs from many tests in that it is a computerized test. It is also adaptive. Adaptive means that the test administers questions based on your answers. If you answer easy questions correctly, the test will give you more difficult questions. The number of questions on your test will be determined by the answers you give. There is no time limit, so test takers will complete the test at their own rate. Your test will be different from everyone else's.

```
C
O
Mputer-adaptive
Placement
Assessment and
Support
System
```

This book is designed to help you prepare for the **COMPASS** test. Although it was originally written to accompany the DOS version, information pertaining to the newer Windows version has been added to the Introduction. *Chart Your Success on the COMPASS Test* will provide plenty of practice for students taking either version of the test.

The first chapter will help you to (a) prepare for tests in general, (b) understand features specific to the **COMPASS** test, (c) learn how the **COMPASS** test can work for you, and (d) know what your results mean. The subsequent chapters will give you basic instruction and sample items in the areas tested by **COMPASS**: mathematics, composition, and reading. Chapters 6, 9, and 12 provide practice tests in these subject areas that contain items similar to those on the test.

TEST–WISENESS

Many college students express worry and anxiety over tests and will often complain about the need for taking them. There is bad news and good news regarding tests. First, THE BAD NEWS—tests are a serious part of the business of being a successful student. You will at times feel like tests are coming at you from all directions. You may, because of negative test experiences in the past, view yourself as a poor "test-taker" and feel a great deal of apprehension regarding tests. Now, THE GOOD NEWS—through knowledge and application of a few simple techniques, you can significantly improve your ability to take tests. "Test-wiseness" is the ability to take a test as effectively and efficiently as possible. For the most part, your performance on a test reflects your mastery of a skill or your understanding of a body of knowledge. However, using "test-wiseness" techniques before, during, and after a test can improve your score. We recommend the following strategies for you to achieve your highest potential in any test situation.

Before the Test

1. **Eat right.**

   In the days and hours before a test, eat a diet high in protein and complex carbohydrates—meat (or protein substitute), vegetables, and fruits. Drink plenty of water and avoid overuse of caffeine. Avoid simple sugars, especially the day of the test. Sugar raises your blood sugar quickly, but the stress of the test can cause it to drop dramatically, leaving you weak and shaky.

2. **Get plenty of sleep.**

   It is often difficult to sleep well the night or two before an important test. You may need to "bank" your sleep by ensuring that you sleep well the week before the test. Then, if you cannot sleep well the night before the test, you still will have rested enough to stay alert throughout the test.

3. **Stick to your exercise schedule.**

   You should follow some regular exercise program several times a week. Don't skip this routine before a test. Exercise has an important effect on the body. It increases circulation, allowing more oxygen to feed your memory cells. Exercise also reduces stress, and it causes the body to release hormones that make you feel good.

4. **Plan to arrive at the test site early.**

   Allow plenty of time to arrive at the testing area. If you're unfamiliar with the location, plan a practice run ahead of time. Plan to arrive early and, if you are too early, take a walk around the area and relax as much as possible.

During the Test

1. **Concentrate on the test.**

   Focus on the test questions and tune out any external and internal distractions. If there is noise or movement in the room that is bothering you, discuss it with the test administrator. If you find that your mind is starting to wander, take a few deep breaths to relax. Tell yourself you will "think about that later," and reread the test question.

2. Follow directions.

Take your time reading the directions on any test. If there is any confusing information, ask the test administrator for clarification. Be sure you understand how the test is set up before you begin. A few minutes previewing the test and doing some practice items can pay off in accuracy.

3. Think.

In many test situations it is one's ability to persist on an item that results in the right answer. While you don't want to spend too long on any one item, don't give up too easily either. Use logic, knowledge, and common sense, and have confidence in your ability to reason through the question.

4. Don't pay attention to other test-takers.

Others may finish the test before you do for a variety of reasons. Don't allow students' leaving the test to intimidate you and cause you to feel anxiety about your performance. They may have finished more quickly at the expense of accuracy.

5. Have a plan to deal with stress.

Stress is not all bad. Without some stress we would not be motivated to do our best on tests. Harmful stress, however, is something that we need to learn to deal with since it can hinder our performance on tests. Learn to monitor your stress level at various times by asking yourself, "What things trigger my anxiety?" Consider what coping strategies would be helpful to you. For example, being late can cause stress. Some people learn to schedule their time better so they are not continually late, while others resist change and remain stressed unnecessarily. You also should have some plan in case of panic while taking a test. Positive statements such as "I know I will do well on this test" and "I've got the skills I need to achieve" can make a difference. Breathing exercises are proven to help deal with symptoms of stress. Try this: (a) breathe in deeply for a slow count of 3, (b) hold your breath for a slow count of 12, and (c) force the air out of your body for a slow count of 6 . . . Repeat this exercise seven times. Practice breathing exercises before the test situation.

After the Test

1. Review your results.

Analyze whether the results of your test reflect your knowledge and preparation. Discuss your performance with an academic advisor or a professor.

2. Modify your preparation.

As a student you will constantly be taking tests and analyzing your results. If you never make changes in the way you prepare for tests, your chances of improving are slim. Even if your score was extremely high on a test, improved test-taking skills may allow you to achieve the same high results with less preparation. On the other hand, you may need to spend more time preparing for the test. If you are unsure, discuss the way you prepared and your results with a learning specialist on your campus.

3. Pat yourself on the back.

Don't forget to reward yourself for your efforts. Academic achievement takes talent, hard work, and persistence. Positive reinforcement will keep you motivated.

DOS VERSION

FEATURES SPECIFIC TO COMPASS (DOS)

You have probably learned from experience that all tests differ. They all have features specific to them. There are features within **COMPASS** that are specific to each subtest: mathematics, writing, and reading. For example, there are some computer keys that have special functions. There are also different types of questions and rules for each area. Here is a list of rules, features, and important keys that apply to the DOS version of the COMPASS Test.

Mathematics

► You are not allowed to use a calculator on the mathematics portion of the test. (This applies to the DOS version only.)

► All of the mathematics items are multiple choice.

► Once you choose an answer you cannot go back and change it.

► You may not skip any problems and come back to them.

► Paper and pencil will be provided for the mathematics subtest.

Writing

► The writing test requires you to edit an essay.

► You may have to move a pointer to a place in the text and then choose an answer from a list of items.

► You may have to highlight a portion of text and then edit it.

► You will be asked to press F when you finish editing the essay. After doing so, you will not be allowed to make any changes.

► You may not use paper and pencil on the writing subtest.

Reading

► On the reading test you have to toggle (go back and forth) between the passage and the questions. You cannot see the passage and the questions on the same screen.

► When you have responded to all of the questions for a particular passage, you may go back and revise your answers before continuing.

► You may not use paper and pencil for the reading subtest.

DOS VERSION

COMPUTER KEYBOARD FUNCTIONS

Following is a list of keys on the computer keyboard that you need to be familiar with for the DOS version of the COMPASS Test.

Arrow Keys   These keys have several uses on the test. For one, they are used to move to the letter (A, B, C, D, or E) that you think is the correct answer to the question on the screen. They are also used to indicate where you would insert a mark of punctuation or to indicate what part of the text you wish to highlight. Finally, the arrow keys are used to scroll up or down in the text.

Y for Yes & N for No   You will be prompted to verify your name and social security number, to begin or end a test, and to confirm an answer before moving on to the next question. At all of these points, you will type Y for "yes" and N for "no."

Letters A through E   You can choose the letter of the best answer for a multiple-choice question by pressing that key and *enter* (or *return* on some keyboards) or by using the arrow keys.

S for Toggling   The S key is used for toggling back and forth between screens. This feature is used in the reading section of the test where a passage and the related set of questions are on separate screens.

H for Help   Throughout the entire test you may press the H key to reach a help screen.

Home & End   The Home key places the cursor at the beginning of a line. The End key places it at the end of a line.

Enter   The COMPASS test prompts you to use this key to verify your answer choice.

Space Bar   This key is used to move the highlighter to positions in the text.

Esc   This key is used when you want to change an answer you have just entered.

The most important thing to remember is always READ the screen, since COMPASS will tell you which keys are presently active.

WINDOWS VERSION

FEATURES SPECIFIC TO COMPASS (Windows)

The COMPASS Test is now available for Windows. The format of this version is different from the DOS version. For example, the DOS screens are dark with light text, whereas the Windows screens are white with black text. The Windows version has squares beside each answer choice instead of circles. Certain rules have been changed as well, such as the use of calculators. Find out if your institution has adopted the Windows version, so you will know what to expect on the day of the test. The more familiar you are with the content, rules, and format, the more confident you will be.

Mathematics

You ARE allowed to use calculators on the Windows version of COMPASS. You may use the on-screen pop-up calculator or bring your own. If you choose to bring your own, make sure it is an approved model. Calculators with a QWERTY keypad (like a keyboard) are not allowed. Graphing and scientific models are allowed, provided they meet all guidelines. For a list of calculator guidelines, visit the following website: *www.act.org/compass/sample/calc.html* . Or, you can call ACT (the test publisher) at 1-800-498-6481 to get a recorded message about approved models.

Before you plan on bringing a calculator, make certain that your institution is using the Windows version of COMPASS. Also, make sure yours is an approved model. Nothing will shake your confidence more than showing up on test day and being told you cannot use a calculator when you were planning on it.

Writing

Note: This is the only section of the test that *requires* the use of a mouse. If you are not accustomed to using a mouse, ask the testing center at your institution for some practice.

On the Writing Skills Test, you will be able to see the essay and test item on the same screen. Your task is to edit the essay that appears in a box on the left. Any time you use the mouse and click on a part of the passage, a portion of that text will become highlighted. A box on the right will then display five options. Choice **A** is always the same as the highlighted text. The next four choices will rewrite that portion of the essay.

When you think you have corrected all the errors in the passage, click on the button labelled "Finished editing the passage." Next, you will be asked several questions concerning strategy, organization, and style. This section of the Writing Skills Test will look similar to the Reading Test screen.

Reading

In this section of the Test, a passage will appear on the left and a question on the right. Only one question will be displayed at a time. To move to a different question, click on the square with the question number you wish to move to. Or, simply press the that number on the keyboard. You will not be allowed to go on to the next passage until you have answered all the questions for that current passage.

WINDOWS VERSION

SAMPLE SCREEN

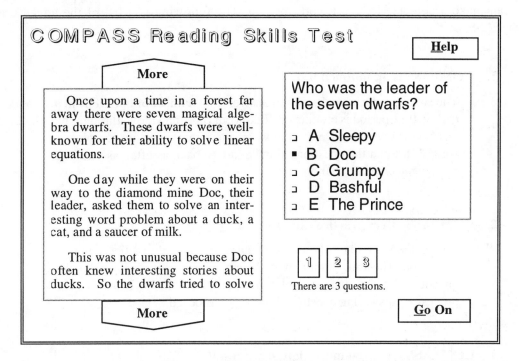

COMPUTER KEYBOARD FUNCTIONS

KEY	FUNCTION	SECTION
A, B, C, D, E	selects answer A, B, C, D, or E	M, W, R
F	indicates you have finished editing the essay	W
G	confirms the selected answer and moves you to the next question	M, W, R
H	activates the Help screen	M, W, R
L	activates the pop-up calculator	M
1, 2, 3...	moves you to a different numbered question	W, R
Up and Down arrow keys	scrolls through the essay/passage	W, R
Left and Right arrow keys	moves you to a different numbered questions	W, R

M = Math   W = Writing   R = Reading

The mouse can be used to perform all of these functions. It is up to you which way you wish to enter your answers. Once you press G or click the "Go On" button, your answer to the Math question on the screen or to all the questions relating to a single essay/passage are confirmed. COMPASS will then move you to the next Math question, Writing essay, or Reading passage. Remember, there is no going back once you "Go On."

7

HOW THE COMPASS TEST CAN WORK FOR YOU

Because **COMPASS** is a computerized test, it will be a different experience for every student. It may be a challenge. If you are aware of what material is covered and the best approach to the test, you can make a computerized test work for you. The following is a list of the advantages of **COMPASS**.

1. **COMPASS is an untimed test**.

   The stress produced by having to answer a set number of questions in a certain time period is eliminated. Take your time, and move through the test at your own pace. Do not choose an answer until you are completely sure of it. Read the questions slowly and go back as often as you like before you confirm your answer.

2. **COMPASS offers practice exercises**.

   Before the beginning of each test, there are several practice items to allow you to become familiar with the mechanical part of answering the questions. Be sure that you feel comfortable with the keyboard and the process of answering questions before you proceed.

3. **COMPASS gives you immediate score results**.

   Your results are available right after you take the test, and they are easy to interpret. You may receive them at the testing center or shortly after from a professional who can interpret the results with you. Be sure you understand the decisions that will be made based on your results. What course placement is recommended? Are there areas of weakness you can improve or strengths that you can build on?

4. **COMPASS is a personalized test**.

   The test you take is unlike anyone else's. You will not be answering the same questions as the person next to you. If you take the test more than once, you will not be answering the same set of questions each time. You will receive an individualized report of your skill level. Ask the person who gives you the results to explain every part of your score report. Because **COMPASS** is a personalized test, it is a more accurate estimate of your ability than a paper-and-pencil test.

5. **COMPASS operates at your comfort level**.

   The **COMPASS** test adjusts to your responses and comfort level instead of your frustration level. It is unlikely you will feel bored or impatient during the test. By tailoring the items to your skill level, the test will challenge but not discourage you.

6. **COMPASS requires different tasks**.

    This test does not rely only on multiple-choice questions, so you have different opportunities for communicating your knowledge. For instance, in the reading test there are text-highlighting items that ask a question and then require you to locate within a passage a specific segment of text that answers the question. You may also be asked questions that are not about the content of the passage but about your prior knowledge regarding the subject.

7. **COMPASS can be taken when you want to take it**.

    In place of the traditional paper-and-pencil test given only during certain times on certain dates to a large group, computerized adaptive testing allows you to take the test when you want, in a relatively small group, in a comfortable setting.

8. **COMPASS is a short test**.

    You will have to answer fewer items than on a traditional paper-and-pencil test. This is good because sometimes on a long test students may become tired and lose their concentration.

9. **COMPASS prompts you to remember the things you should do on a test**.

    You are told to go back and reread the essay you have edited. It prompts you to check each answer before going on.

10. **COMPASS does not penalize you for guessing**.

    If you are not sure of an answer, make your best guess. You can only benefit from guessing.

WHAT YOUR RESULTS MEAN

Again, there is good news and bad news. The good news is that as soon as you finish the test your results are ready. The results will be immediate, accurate, and fair. The bad news is that we cannot guarantee you will pass the test. However, the fact that you are taking the time to read this book and prepare means you are doing your best to do well on the test. This preparation will give you an advantage on test day.

How your results are reported to you depends entirely on where you take the test. Some testing sites will give you your results before you leave the room. Other sites will have you meet with a counselor to review your results. Another site might mail you the results at a later date. It all depends on how your testing site is set up.

The most common way to get your scores is from the **COMPASS** Standard Individual Report. This report is usually printed out before you leave the testing center.

► The first section will have your name, ID#, location of the test, test date and test session.

► The next section may show your answers to the demographic questions that you answered before the actual test began. (Often, this demographic section is not included.)

► The next section of the report will describe the Administration Mode and the Placement Group used to give you your test. These facts are rarely of any importance to you.

► The next section(s) contains your test scores, times, and recommendations. If your test was taken for placement your score will be given as a range. For example, a range of 69-100 would mean you scored somewhere between 69 and 100. If your test was taken for a score then you will get a number (for example, 73). The test will also report how long it took you to take the test (for example, 19 mins, 17 sec). This time has no effect on your grade or placement. Recommendations are the last portion of this section. Recommendations are messages to you about your test score. These messages will help you and an advisor determine what courses you should take. If you are taking the test as an exit exam, then whether or not you passed or failed will be written here.

► The last section of the report is a release that allows the testing center to share your results with other educational institutions.

Whoever is proctoring your test will be able to explain your results or direct you to an academic advisor who will be able to tell you more about your test scores and how they affect your plans.

RESOURCES ON THE WEB

American College Testing (ACT), the publisher of the COMPASS Test, maintains a website that you can visit for additional information on COMPASS. The site address is: *www.act.org/ compass/index.html* . For additional support in preparing for the mathematics test on COMPASS, please visit the website: *www.fc.peachnet.edu/wcotter/compass.htm* .

ADAPTIVE TESTING

The following graphs explain how questions adapted to your skill level are used to arrive at your score.

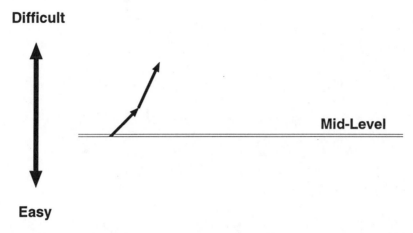

An adaptive test starts with a mid-level question. If you get the question right, you will be asked a harder question.

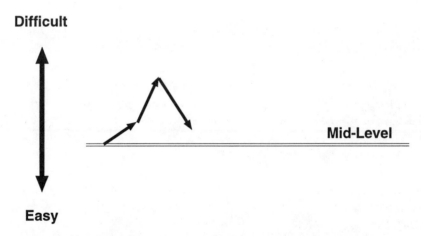

If you answer incorrectly, the test will give you an easier question.

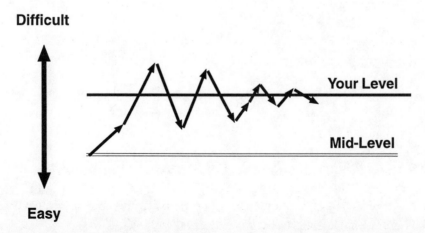

This process continues until the computer is confident that it has found your level of performance. This is your score.

SECTION II

INTRODUCTION TO MATHEMATICS

COMPASS Mathematics Sections:

Pre–algebra/Numerical Skills
Algebra
College Algebra
Geometry
Trigonometry

INTRODUCTION

The mathematics portion of the **COMPASS** test has five sections: pre-algebra/numerical skills, algebra, college algebra, geometry, and trigonometry. Each section has a pool of about 200 test items. **COMPASS** will select problems from this pool for you according to how well you do. If you answer questions correctly, **COMPASS** will give you harder questions. If you answer incorrectly, **COMPASS** will give you easier questions. Because the selection process is based on how well you do, the test you take will be different from those taken by other test-takers, even on the same day. Most people will answer fewer than 17 questions in a particular section.

If you do very well in one section, **COMPASS** will move you to the next section. If you do poorly in a section, **COMPASS** will move you back a section. This process continues until **COMPASS** finds the hardest section of the test that you can do well. **COMPASS** will not tell you when you move from one section to the next. Some people will only see one section, others two. Very few people will see more than two, but it is possible.

KNOW WHAT TO STUDY

Some schools will not use certain sections of the test. For example, some schools use the geometry section of the test, some do not, and others let the **COMPASS** program decide. Make sure that you know what sections of the test you might be tested on. There is no point in spending test preparation time on something you will not be tested over. If you have very limited time to study, start with the Algebra chapter, chapter number three.

KNOW HOW TO ANSWER

Before you take the test you will be given a chance to practice inputting answers on some example items that do not count towards your test score. Each item has five options just like the real test. You can select your answer in one of three ways:

1) Use the space bar until your choice is highlighted, then press enter.

2) Press the key (A, B, C, D, or E), then press enter.

3) Use the pointer/arrow to select your answer by moving the mouse, then press enter.

After you select your answer **COMPASS** will ask you to confirm your answer by pressing enter again. Once you confirm your answer, you cannot go back and change it later.

FORMAL LANGUAGE

Mathematics is its own language. Every language has different styles. People from England speak a very different English than the people from the Southeastern United States. The mathematical language on this test is a little different from the everyday mathematical language spoken in most classrooms. The language on the test is much more formal and "correct." Do not let this formal style distract or intimidate you. For the most part this language can be ignored, and you can focus on the real questions.

Here are a few examples of phrases which you may or may not be familiar with.

▶ For all x such that ...   (meaning: x can be anything)

▶ For $x \neq 4$...   (meaning: x can be anything BUT 4, because 4 is not in the domain, probably because it would cause a zero to be in the denominator)

▶ If $i^2 = -1$, then...   (meaning: this problem deals with complex numbers)

Usually you can ignore most prepositional phrases. These phrases provide a context for the problem. Once you recognize the context, concentrate on the rest of the information provided.

CALCULATORS

Calculators are not permitted on the DOS version of the COMPASS Test. However, they are allowed on the Windows version. If your school is using the Windows version of COMPASS, make sure that you have an approved calculator. The following web page lists which are approved and which are not: *www.act.org/compass/sample/calc.html* . The site is updated as new models become available. Or, call ACT (the Test publisher) at 1-800-498-6481 for current information.

TEST HINTS

► **TIME** is the number one thing. This test is not timed. The longer you take on the test the better for you. Relax and do your best on each question.

► On the test day make sure you have several hours to take the test. Do not plan anything after your test that could make you rush. Some people will take the test in 20 minutes; others may take over three hours. Give yourself the time to do your best.

► Each question is its own test. Concentrate only on the question that is on the screen. Forget about questions you have already answered. Don't worry about the next question. Once you have answered and confirmed your answer, it is gone. Forget about it, and move on to the new question that is now on the screen.

► Even if you feel very confident about an answer, make sure you check and recheck your answer. Time is not important.

► When you get a question right, a harder question is your reward. Eventually you will get one that is too hard. Do not let this worry you. Some questions will be too hard for you. That is the way that the test is designed.

► Touch the screen. Use your finger, the eraser of your pencil, or the mouse to help you read and concentrate on parts of the problem. This is especially important on graphs, where you may need to count the location of different points.

► Most people who take **COMPASS** start in the algebra section. Do most of your studying here, as colleges use this information to help them decide what math course to place you in.

► Make sure you are answering the question asked. Sometimes the question will ask for the value of x^2, not of x.

► The number one mistake is a sign (+/–) error. The test will have the right answer, and it will also have the right answer with the wrong sign.

► Memorize the first 16 perfect squares. They show up often, especially in factoring.

N	1	2	3	4	5	6	7	8	9	10	11	12	13	14	15	16
N^2	1	4	9	16	25	36	49	64	81	100	121	144	169	196	225	256

► Become familiar with the perfect cubes:

N	1	2	3	4	5	6	7	8
N^3	1	8	27	64	125	216	343	512

► Do **not** bring a watch. Time is **not** important.

HELP ON THE WEB

For more information on preparing for the mathematics test on COMPASS, visit the following website: *www.fc.peachnet.edu/wcotter/compass.htm* .

CHAPTER TWO

PRE-ALGEBRA/NUMERICAL SKILLS

The pre-algebra section covers these topics:

P1	Basic Operations with Integers
P2	Basic Operations with Fractions
P3	Basic Operations with Decimals
P4	Exponents
P5	Order of Operations
P6	Ratios and Proportions
P7	Percentages
P8	Averages (Means)

• •

P9	Multiples and Factors of Integers
P10	Absolute Values of Numbers
P11	Greater Than / Less Than
P12	Conversions Between Fractions and Decimals

Over 85% of the pre-algebra section will come from the first 8 topics. Concentrate your studies on these.

P1 BASIC OPERATIONS WITH INTEGERS

Basic operations with integers include addition, subtraction, multiplication and division. These problems are the most basic on the test, but do not rush through these items. Make sure you spend enough time to get the problem correct. The number one mistake a person will make on a problem in this section is to get a + or − sign wrong.

ADDITION

$$7 + (-9) = -2 \qquad -5 + (-8) = -13 \qquad 18 + (-12) = 6$$

In an addition problem like $7 + (-9) = -2$, 7 and −9 are called **addends.** The answer −2 is called the **sum**.

SUBTRACTION

$$16 - (-5) = 21 \qquad -8 - (-12) = 4 \qquad 13 - 22 = -9$$

In a subtraction problem $16 - (-5) = 21$; 16 is called the **minuend** and −5 is called the **subtrahend**. The answer 21 is called the **difference**. If you are not good at subtracting signed numbers, try changing the sign of the subtrahend and adding.

$$16 - (-5) = 16 + (5) = 21 \qquad -8 - (-12) = -8 + (12) = 4 \qquad 13 - 22 = 13 + (-22) = -9$$

MULTIPLICATION

When multiplying $8 \times 7 = 56$, 8 and 7 are called **factors**. The answer 56 is called the **product**. Multiplication can be written many different ways. In the following examples, notice what happens to the sign of the product when we change the signs of the factors.

With an x

$8 \times 7 = 56$	$8 \times –7 = –56$	$–8 \times 7 = –56$	$–8 \times –7 = 56$

With a •

$8 • 7 = 56$	$8 • –7 = –56$	$–8 • 7 = –56$	$–8 • –7 = 56$

With juxtaposition (placing two factors next to each other)

$(8)(7) = 56$	$(8)(–7) = –56$	$(–8)(7) = –56$	$(–8)(–7) = 56$

DIVISION

When dividing $20 \div 4 = 5$, 20 is called the **dividend** and 4 is called the **divisor**. The answer 5 is called the **quotient**.

$$20 \div 4 = 5 \qquad (–35) \div 7 = –5 \qquad \frac{42}{–7} = –6$$

SIGNS OF TERMS

For multiplication and division only, if there is just one term in an expression (no addition or subtraction), then count the number of negative signs. If there is an odd number of negative signs, then your answer is negative. If there is an even number of negative signs, then the result will be positive.

P1   Practice simplifying.

a. $33 + (–13) + 22 + (–9) + 15$

b. $23 + (–15) + 22 + (–17) + 16$

c. $43 – (–23) + 25 – (9) + 33$

d. $38 – (–22) + 30 – (–17) + 24$

(*Answers* to all practices in
Chapter Two are found on p. 28.)

P2 BASIC OPERATIONS WITH FRACTIONS

Basic operations with fractions include addition, subtraction, multiplication and division. These are the same operations that were discussed in P1.

COMMON DENOMINATOR

In a fraction, the top is called the **numerator,** and the bottom is called the **denominator**. When adding or subtracting fractions with different denominators, the fractions must first be converted to make their denominators the same. Suppose we wanted to add $5/6$ and $3/8$. Since 6 and 8 are unlike denominators, we must first convert these fractions into two fractions with a common denominator. The smallest number that both 6 and 8 will divide into is 24. Multiply $5/6$ by $4/4$ and $3/8$ by $3/3$. When we multiply by $4/4$ and $3/3$, we are actually multiplying by the number 1 so the value of $5/6$ and $3/8$ is not changed, just the way that they look.

$$\frac{\textit{numerator}}{\textit{denominator}} = \frac{5}{6} = \left(\frac{5}{6}\right)\left(\frac{4}{4}\right) = \frac{20}{24} \qquad \frac{\textit{numerator}}{\textit{denominator}} = \frac{3}{8} = \left(\frac{3}{8}\right)\left(\frac{3}{3}\right) = \frac{9}{24}$$

With a common denominator, we can now combine the fractions and then add the numerators:

$$\frac{20}{24} + \frac{9}{24} = \frac{20+9}{24} = \frac{29}{24}$$

If you are able to reduce the resulting fraction, the denominator will change again. Section **P9** has more information about finding common denominators.

Caution. When you are adding and subtracting fractions you must find a common denominator, but do not forget about signs. If you forget about signs, you will get the problem just as wrong as the person who could not find the common denominator.

ADDITION

Example 1

$$\frac{7}{10} + \frac{3}{8} = \frac{28}{40} + \frac{15}{40} = \frac{28+15}{40} = \frac{43}{40}$$

Example 2

$$\frac{2}{5} + \frac{6}{11} = \frac{22}{55} + \frac{30}{55} = \frac{22+30}{55} = \frac{52}{55}$$

SUBTRACTION

Subtraction has the same rules about common denominator that addition has. Just subtract after you find the common denominator.

Example 3

$$\frac{7}{12} - \frac{3}{10} = \frac{35}{60} - \frac{18}{60} = \frac{35-18}{60} = \frac{17}{60}$$

MULTIPLICATION

Multiplication and division are much easier than addition and subtraction since a common denominator is not required. Just multiply numerator by numerator and denominator by denominator.

Example 4

$$\frac{2}{5} \times \frac{3}{14} = \frac{6}{70} = \frac{3}{35}$$

You may find it easier to cancel before multiplying in order to get the answer in lowest terms:

$$\frac{2}{5} \times \frac{3}{14} = \frac{1}{5} \times \frac{3}{7} = \frac{3}{35}$$

The answer to a multiplication problem is called a **product.** Consider what is necessary for the product of a pair of fractions to equal 1. For example, $\frac{2}{3} \times \frac{3}{2} = \frac{6}{6} = 1$. $\frac{3}{2}$ is the **reciprocal** of $\frac{2}{3}$. Every number except 0 has a reciprocal. A number multiplied by its reciprocal will always equal 1. To find the reciprocal of a number, simply flip the number over: The reciprocal of $\frac{5}{2}$ is $\frac{2}{5}$; the reciprocal of $\frac{15}{14}$ is $\frac{14}{15}$; the reciprocal of 8 is $\frac{1}{8}$.

DIVISION

To perform division take the reciprocal of the divisor and then multiply. (Don't ask why . . . just flip and multiply.)

Example 5

$$\frac{4}{7} \div \frac{9}{5} = \frac{4}{7} \times \frac{5}{9} = \frac{20}{63}$$

COMBINATIONS

Do multiplications and divisions in order from left to right **before** performing addition and subtraction in order from left to right.

Example 6

$$\frac{2}{5} + \frac{7}{10} \cdot \frac{-3}{2} - \frac{4}{15}$$

$$= \frac{2}{5} + \frac{-21}{20} - \frac{4}{15}$$

$$= \frac{24}{60} + \frac{(-63)}{60} - \frac{16}{60}$$

$$= \frac{24 + (-63) - 16}{60}$$

$$= \frac{-55}{60} = \frac{-11}{12}$$

Example 7

$$\frac{3}{4} \div \frac{1}{15} + \frac{2}{3} \div \frac{-2}{7}$$

$$= \frac{3}{4} \cdot \frac{15}{1} + \frac{2}{3} \cdot \frac{-7}{2}$$

$$= \frac{45}{4} + \frac{-7}{3}$$

$$= \frac{135}{12} + \frac{-28}{12}$$

$$= \frac{135 + -55}{12} = \frac{107}{12}$$

P2 Practice. Simplify.

a. $\left(\dfrac{-18}{14}\right)\left(\dfrac{49}{-6}\right)$

b. $\dfrac{2}{5} + \dfrac{3}{7}$

c. $\dfrac{3}{4} + \dfrac{4}{9} \cdot \dfrac{-5}{2} - \dfrac{3}{4}$

20

P3 BASIC OPERATIONS WITH DECIMALS

ADDITION AND SUBTRACTION

When adding and subtracting decimal numbers, don't forget to line up the decimals.

$$3.85 + 1.2 + (-0.15) = 4.9$$

$$
\begin{array}{r}
3.85 \\
1.2 \\
+ \quad (-0.15) \\
\hline
4.9
\end{array}
$$

MULTIPLICATION

When multiplying decimals, count the number of digits behind the decimal in the factors. This is where you will place the decimal point in the answer.

$$3.6 \times 4 = 14.4 \qquad\qquad 2.1 \times 0.63 = 1.323$$

When multiplying, the numbers that are multiplied together (3.6 and 4) are called **factors.** The answer (14.4) is called a **product.** A product is the result of multiplying two factors.

DIVISION

In the following division problem, 20.5 is called the **dividend,** 0.5 is the **divisor,** and 41 is the **quotient.**

$$20.5 \div 0.5 = 41$$

When dividing, if the divisor has a decimal, move it to the end of the number. 0.5 would become 5. For this to be legal, you must make a corresponding move in the dividend; therefore, 20.5 becomes 205. Now just divide as usual.

$$0.5\overline{)20.5} \quad \rightarrow \quad 5\overline{)205} \quad = \quad 41$$

Another way of writing this problem would be as a fraction. The dividend becomes the numerator, and the divisor becomes the denominator. We move the decimal point by multiplying the top and the bottom by the same number.

$$\frac{20.5}{0.5} = \left(\frac{20.5}{0.5}\right)\left(\frac{10}{10}\right) = \frac{205}{5} = 41$$

P3 Practice. Simplify.

a. $12.5 + 3.7 - 13.002$ b. $1.2 \bullet 3.0$ c. $36 \div 0.4$ d. $\dfrac{6.5}{0.13}$

P4 EXPONENTS

2^3 2 is called the **base**. 3 is called the **exponent**. 2^3 is read as "2 raised to the third power" or "2 to the third." The meaning of 2^3 is "use 2 three times as a factor."

Here is a mathematical way of writing that definition.

$2^3 = 2 \cdot 2 \cdot 2 = 8$

What is the exponential notation for $5 \cdot 5 \cdot 5 \cdot 5$?   Answer: 5^4

Notice what happens to the sign of our product when the exponent is odd or even.

$(-3)^2 = (-3)(-3) = 9$

$(-3)^3 = (-3)(-3)(-3) = -27$

$(-3)^4 = (-3)(-3)(-3)(-3) = 81$

$(-3)^5 = (-3)(-3)(-3)(-3)(-3) = -243$

$(-3)^6 = (-3)(-3)(-3)(-3)(-3)(-3) = 729$

Whenever the exponent is an even number, the answer is positive. If the exponent is an odd number, the sign will be the same one that you started with.

Here are two expressions that look alike, but are very different.

$(3x^2)$ $(3x)^2$

The difference between these two expressions is what the exponent affects. The square on the left affects only the x. The square on the right applies to the 3 *and* the x because of the parentheses.

$(3x^2) = 3x^2$ $(3x)^2 = 9x^2$

P4   Practice.

Write the exponential notation.

a. $x \cdot x \cdot x \cdot x \cdot x$ b. $7 \cdot 7 \cdot 7 \cdot 7 \cdot 7$ c. $5 \cdot 5 \cdot 5 \cdot A \cdot A \cdot A \cdot B \cdot B$

Simplify.

d. 4^3 e. $(-1)^{83}$ f. $(4a)^2$ g. 1^8

P5   ORDER OF OPERATIONS

When evaluating mathematical expressions, it is important that you perform operations in the correct order. Consider 3 + 4 x 5 − 8. What should be done first?

Correct

3 + 4 x 5 − 8	Multiply first
= 3 + 20 − 8	Add
= 23 − 8	Subtract
= 15	

Incorrect

3 + 4 x 5 − 8	(addition done before
= 7 x (− 3)	multiplication)
= − 21	

Because the incorrect way looks correct, we must guard against doing the problem that way. The **order of operations** is the method you use to make sure that you are doing everything in the correct order.

THE ORDER OF OPERATIONS

1. **P**   Do everything inside **Parentheses** ( ) or any other grouping symbol, such as brackets [ ], first.
2. **E**   Do all **Exponents**.
3. **MD** Do all **Multiplications** and **Divisions** in order from left to right.
4. **AS** Do all **Additions** and **Subtractions** in order from left to right.

Here is a silly way to remember the Order of Operations:

1. **P**   Please   **Parentheses**
2. **E**   Excuse   **Exponent**
3. **MD**   My Dear   **Multiplication** and **Division**
4. **AS**   Aunt Sally **Addition** and **Subtraction**

Example 1

$8 − 10 \div 2 + 4 \bullet 3$	Divide
$= 8 − 5 + 4 \bullet 3$	Multiply
$= 8 − 5 + 12$	Subtract
$= 3 + 12$	Add
$= 15$	

Example 2

$3^2 + 5 \bullet 2 − (8 + 9)$	Parentheses
$= 3^2 + 5 \bullet 2 − 17$	Exponent
$= 9 + 5 \bullet 2 − 17$	Multiply
$= 9 + 10 − 17$	Add
$= 19 − 17$	Subtract
$= 2$	

P5   Practice. Simplify.

a. $7 − 4 \times 3 + 5$

b. $2^2 + 9 \times 3^3 + 4 − 6$

c. $\dfrac{12 − 7}{3^2 + 4^2}$

d. $\dfrac{4(6 − 2) + 5(2 + 6)}{33 − (−2)}$

P6 RATIOS AND PROPORTIONS

A **ratio** is an expression of the relationship between two or more things. Fractions are ratios. Here are some examples of how ratios are written.

$$\frac{a}{b} \qquad\qquad a\ to\ b \qquad\qquad a{:}b$$

A **proportion** is a statement of equality about two ratios.

$$\frac{3}{4} = \frac{9}{12} \qquad\qquad \frac{A}{B} = \frac{C}{D} \qquad\qquad \frac{20}{4} = \frac{5}{1}$$

If a proportion is true then you can cross multiply and get a true answer. **Cross multiplication** means multiplying the denominator of one fraction by the numerator of the other. This method can be used to determine if two fractions are equal.

$$\frac{3}{4} = \frac{9}{12} \qquad \rightarrow \qquad 3 \bullet 12 = 9 \bullet 4 \qquad \rightarrow \qquad 36 = 36$$

When we have a proportion with one part missing or unknown we can use cross multiplication to find the missing part.

$$\frac{x}{3} = -\frac{8}{12}$$

$$x \bullet 12 = -8 \bullet 3$$

$$12x = -24$$

$$\frac{12x}{12} = -\frac{24}{12}$$

$$x = -2$$

P6 Practice.
Solve these proportions.

a. $\dfrac{w}{5} = \dfrac{7}{10}$

b. $\dfrac{8}{13} = \dfrac{X}{39}$

c. $\dfrac{36}{8} = \dfrac{9}{Y}$

d. $\dfrac{-1.2}{Z} = \dfrac{4}{5}$

P7 PERCENTAGES

Per means part and **cent** means 100, therefore percentage means "part of 100." In other words, what would the numerator be if the denominator were 100?

Example 1   What percent of 25 is 8?

$$\frac{8}{25} = \frac{8}{25} \cdot \left(\frac{4}{4}\right) = \frac{32}{100} = 32\%$$

Example 2   What percent of 225 is 27?

"Of" means multiply and "is" means =, therefore

W% of 225 *is* 27

$$\frac{W}{100} \cdot 225 = 27$$

$$\frac{W}{100} = \frac{27}{225}$$

$$W = \frac{27 \cdot 100}{225} = \frac{27 \cdot 4}{9} = 3 \cdot 4 = 12$$

$$W = 12\%$$

Example 3   What is 30% of 45?

"Of" means multiply and "is" means =, therefore

30% *of* 45 *is W*

$$\frac{30}{100} \cdot 45 = W$$

$$\frac{3}{10} \cdot 45 = W$$

$$\frac{3}{2} \cdot 9 = \frac{27}{2} = 13.5 = W$$

Example 4   80% of what number is 36?

Just divide 0.8 into 36.

$$\frac{36}{0.8} = \frac{360}{8} = 45$$

P7   Practice.

a. 8 is what percent of 32?

b. What number is 85% of 360?

c. 22 is 20% of what number?

P8 AVERAGES (MEANS)

Finding the **mean** of a group of numbers is exactly like finding the average grade for a group of tests. First add all of the test grades. Then divide by the number of tests.

Example 1
Find the mean of these tests grades: 78, 83, 85, and 75.

$$\frac{78 + 83 + 85 + 75}{4} = \frac{321}{4} = 80.25$$

P8   Practice.

a. Find the mean of 17, 22, 19, and 30.

b. Find the mean of 7, 12, 39, 4, and 3.

c. Find the mean of 16, 0, and 11.

P9   MULTIPLES AND FACTORS OF INTEGERS

MULTIPLES

Consider all the numbers that 4 will divide evenly. For example, 16 is divisible by 4, as is 484 and 4,444,444. Because these numbers are divisible by 4, they are considered **multiples** of 4. To list all the multiples of 4, you would begin with 4, 8, 12, 16, 20, . . . To list all of the multiples of 6, you would begin 6, 12, 18, 24, 30, 36, 42, . . . Comparing the two lists of multiples we find some numbers in common.

Multiples of 4: 4, 8, **12,** 16, 20, **24,** 28, 32, **36,** 40
Multiples of 6: 6, **12,** 18, **24,** 30, **36,** 42, . . .

The numbers which occur in both lists—12, 24, and 36—are common multiples. Since 12 is the smallest common multiple in this group it is called the **least common multiple (LCM).** The least common denominator (LCD) is sometimes referred to as the LCM. Thus, the LCM is very important for adding fractions. In the following addition of fractions problem, the LCM of 4 and 6 is used to solve the problem.

$$\frac{1}{4} + \frac{1}{6} = \frac{3}{12} + \frac{2}{12} = \frac{3+2}{12} = \frac{5}{12}$$

FACTORS

A factor is both a noun (thing) and a verb (action). Factor (noun) means the numbers that are multiplied together to get a product. When we factor (verb), we start with the product and find numbers that will divide into the product. For example, in the equation $36 = 9 \cdot 4$, 36 is the product of the factors 9 and 4. Also, $9 \cdot 4$ is a **factorization** of 36. Since neither 4 or 9 is a prime number, $9 \cdot 4$ is not a **prime factorization** of 36. A prime factorization is a list of prime factors of a number such that when you multiply them all together you get the product you are interested in. For 36 the prime factorization is $2 \cdot 2 \cdot 3 \cdot 3$. More often it is written $36 = 2^2 \cdot 3^2$. Every number has its own unique prime factorization.

FACTORS AND LCMS

Prime factorization is a powerful tool we can use to find the LCM of a group of numbers. For example, let's find the LCM of 12, 18 and 24.

$$12 = 2 \cdot 2 \cdot 3 \qquad 18 = 2 \cdot 3 \cdot 3 \qquad 24 = 2 \cdot 2 \cdot 2 \cdot 3$$

Now use each factor the <u>most</u> times it was used in any of the three factorizations.

$$LCM = 2 \cdot 2 \cdot 2 \cdot 3 \cdot 3 = 72$$

Therefore, 72 is the smallest number that 12, 18, and 24 will all divide into evenly.

P9   Practice.

a. Find the LCM of 8 and 12.

b. Find the LCM of 9, 12, and 4.

c. Find the prime factorization of 96.

d. Find the prime factorization of 360.

P10   ABSOLUTE VALUES OF NUMBERS

The **absolute value** of a number is the distance that number is away from zero.

$$|-8| = 8$$

Read this as "the absolute value of negative 8 is 8."

$$|-8| = 8 \qquad |5| = 5 \qquad |-3.8| = 3.8 \qquad |0| = 0$$

One of the few guarantees in life is that a negative value will never come out of an absolute value sign.

P11   GREATER THAN / LESS THAN

Sometimes we want to compare numbers that we know are not equal to each other. To do this we use an inequality sign. The small end of the **greater than / less than sign** always points towards the smaller value. The larger end always opens towards the largest value.

$$3 < 5 \qquad 5 > 3 \qquad -1.02 < -1.01 \qquad -7 < 5$$

P12 CONVERSIONS BETWEEN FRACTIONS AND DECIMALS

To change a fraction to a decimal, divide the numerator by the denominator.

$$\frac{7}{8} = 0.875$$

To change a decimal to a percent, move the decimal point two places to the right.

0.875 = 87.5%

To change a percent to a decimal, move the decimal point two places to the left.

112% = 1.12

To change a decimal to a fraction, place the number over 1.0 and then multiply the top and the bottom by whatever it takes (10, 100, 1000) to move the decimal point to the last significant digit of the numerator. In this example we want to move the decimal point two spots, so we will use 100 over 100 as the multiplier.

$$1.15 = \frac{1.15}{1.0} \cdot \left(\frac{100}{100}\right) = \frac{115}{100} = \frac{23}{20}$$

P12 Practice. Complete this table.

Fraction	Decimal	Percent
³⁄₈		
	0.35	
		8%

ANSWERS TO PRACTICES

P1 Answers
a. 48
b. 29
c. 115
d. 131

P2 Answers
a. $21/_2$
b. $29/_{35}$
c. $-{}^{10}/_9$

P3 Answers
a. 3.198
b. 3.6
c. 90
d. 50

P4 Answers
a. x^5
b. 7^5
c. $5^3A^3B^2$
d. 64
e. −1
f. $16a^2$
g. 1

P5 Answers
a. 0
b. 245
c. $^1/_5$
d. $^8/_5$

P6 Answers
a. w = 3.5
b. X = 24
c. Y = 2
d. Z = −1.5

P7 Answers
a. 25%
b. 306
c. 110

P8 Answers
a. 22
b. 13
c. 9

P9 Answers
a. 24
b. 36
c. $96 = 2^5 \cdot 3$
d. $2^3 \cdot 3^2 \cdot 5$

P12 Answers
$^3/_8 = .375 = 37.5\%$
$^7/_{20} = .35 = 35\%$
$^2/_{25} = .08 = 8\%$

CHAPTER THREE

ALGEBRA

The content of the Algebra section falls into three major categories: Elementary Algebra, Intermediate Algebra, and Coordinate Geometry.

Elementary Algebra (about 60%)
A1 Substituting values into algebraic expressions
A2 Setting up equations for given situations
A3 Basic operations with polynomials
A4 Factorization of polynomials
A5 Solving polynomial equations by factoring
A6 Formula manipulation and field axioms
A7 Linear equations in one variable
A8 Exponents
A9 Linear inequalities in one variable

Intermediate Algebra (about 20%)
A10 Rational Expressions
A11 Exponents
A12 Systems of linear equations in two variables
A13 Quadratic formulas
A14 Absolute value equations and inequalities

Coordinate Geometry (about 20%)
A15 Linear equations in two variables
A16 Distance formula in the plane
A17 Graphing conics (parabolas, circles)
A18 Graphing systems of equations and rational functions
A19 Midpoint formula

A1 SUBSTITUTING VALUES INTO ALGEBRAIC EXPRESSIONS

This is also known as "plug and chug." You are going to plug values into equations, and then chug along until the expression is simplified. You must be careful to keep track of signs and to follow the order of operations. (The order of operations was discussed in P5.)

Evaluate $x^3 + 2(x + 1)^2 + x - 5$ when x = 3. Whenever you substitute into an equation, use parentheses for each substitution. This will help you keep track of signs.

$$= (3)^3 + 2((3)+1)^2 + (3) - 5 \qquad \text{substitute}$$
$$= (3)^3 + 2(4)^2 + (3) - 5 \qquad \text{add inside the parentheses}$$
$$= 27 + 2(16) + 3 - 5 \qquad \text{calculate the exponents}$$
$$= 27 + 32 + 3 - 5 \qquad \text{multiply}$$
$$= 57 \qquad \text{add and subtract}$$

When substituting values into algebraic expressions, it is extremely important to keep track of signs. You can do all of the multiplication, division, addition, and subtraction exactly right, but if you miss just one sign you will get the problem just as wrong as the person who could not do the simplest addition. Perhaps the most dangerous substitution is plugging a negative value into an expression that has subtraction:

Find the value of the expression $2x^2 - 4x + 5$ when x = − 6.

$$= 2(-6)^2 - 4(-6) + 5 \qquad\qquad = 2(-6)^2 - 4(-6) + 5$$
$$= 2(36) - 4(-6) + 5 \qquad\qquad = 2(36) - 4(-6) + 5$$
$$= 72 - 24 + 5 \qquad\qquad\qquad = 72 + 24 + 5$$
$$= -43 \quad \text{INCORRECT} \qquad\qquad = 96 + 5 = 101 \quad \text{CORRECT}$$

Also, pay careful attention to signs when calculating exponents:

What is the difference between -2^2 and $(-2)^2$?

$$-2^2 = -(2)(2) = -4 \qquad\qquad (-2)^2 = (-2)(-2) = 4$$

A1 Practice.

1. Evaluate $2X^2 + 9X - 5$ for X = −2.

2. Evaluate $y^2 - 10y + 25$ for y = 5.

3. Evaluate $z^2 + 5z - 8$ for z = −3.

4. Evaluate $a^2 - 3a + 2ab - 6b$, for a = −3 and b = 2.

(*Answers* to all practices in Chapter Three are found on pp. 65-66.)

A2 SETTING UP EQUATIONS FOR GIVEN SITUATIONS

Some questions will be word problems. But, rather than coming up with the "answer," you will have to determine an equation to solve the problem. In translating a word problem into algebra, it is useful to know that some words are associated with particular operations.

+ Addition	− Subtraction	• x ( ) Multiplication	÷ / Division	= Equal
sum more than together and	difference less than fewer than	product of times twice	divided quotient	is was will be (any form of be)

Usually you will have to use more than one operation in combination. When doing this you must pay attention to the difference between the algebraic order of operation (**PEMDAS**) and the order of operations called for in the word problem. For example, the *sum of the products* means something different than the *product of the sums*.

The sum of the products of a times b and d times c $ab + dc$
The product of the sums of a and b times d and c $(a + b)(d + c)$

If we substitute values of $a = 2$, $b = 3$, $c = 4$, and $d = 5$, we see how different these two similar things actually are.

$$ab + dc = (2)(3) + (4)(5) = 6 + 20 = 26$$
$$(a + b)(d + c) = (2 + 3)(4 + 5) = (5)(20) = 100$$

Once you come up with what you think is the correct equation, try plugging in some values to see if your equation gives you what you think it should.

A2   Practice. Select the best answer.

1. Find the sum of the product of 2 times x and 3 times y.

    a) $(2 + x)$
    b) $6(x + y)$
    c) $6xy$
    d) $2x + 3y$
    e) $6x + 6y$

2. What is the sum of three consecutive integers?

    a) $x + y + z$
    b) $x + (x + 1) + (x + 2)$
    c) $x + 1 + 2$
    d) $x + (x + 2) + (x + 4)$
    e) $x + 2x + 3x$

3. Susan gets paid a salary of D dollars a week, plus a commission of 6%, based on her sales total (S). Which expression below best describes Susan's pay?

    a) $D + S$
    b) $6D + S$
    c) $D + 6S$
    d) $D + .06S$
    e) $.06(D + S)$

4. A piece of rope 135 feet long is cut into three pieces. The second piece is twice as long as the first piece. The third piece is 3 times as long as the second.

    a) $x + (x + 2) + (x + 3) = 135$
    b) $x + 2(x + 3) = 135$
    c) $x + 2x + 6x = 135$
    d) $3x + 2x + x = 135$
    e) $6x = 135$

A3 BASIC OPERATIONS WITH POLYNOMIALS

POLYNOMIALS

Poly means many and **nominal** means terms. Therefore, polynomial means many terms. Even though the name literally means many terms, polynomials can have just one term. If it is just a one-term polynomial, it has a special name, **monomial**. Terms are always separated from each other by addition or subtraction signs.

1 term Monomials	2 terms Binomials	3 terms Trinomials	4 or more (no special name)
a	a + b	a + b + c	a + b + c + d
−2x	c − 5	$x^2 - 8x + 15$	$x^3 - x^2 + 2x + 9$
$4y^2$	$x^2 - y^2$	$x^4 - x + y$	5a − 4b + 3c − 2d − 5e + 8f − 9

ADDITION

When adding polynomials, drop parentheses and combine like terms.

$$(x^2 - 8x + 15) + (x^3 - x^2 + 2x + 9) = x^2 - 8x + 15 + x^3 - x^2 + 2x + 9 = x^3 - 6x + 24$$

SUBTRACTION

When subtracting, make sure to change all of the signs in the subtrahend, then add.

$$(a + b + c) - (a - b) = a + b + c - a + b = 2b + c$$

$$(x^2 - 8x + 15) - (x^3 - x^2 + 2x + 9) = x^2 - 8x + 15 - x^3 + x^2 - 2x - 9 = -x^3 + 2x^2 - 10x + 6$$

MULTIPLICATION

Distribution is the basis for multiplication of polynomials.

$$a(b + c) = ab + ac$$

$$2(x + 5) = 2x + 10$$

When multiplying polynomials be aware of how many terms you are multiplying together. In the example above, a(b + c) = ab + ac, we multiplied a binomial by a monomial, so 1 x 2 = 2 multiplications had to be performed. If you are multiplying a binomial times a binomial, you will have 2 x 2 = 4 multiplications to perform. If you are multiplying a trinomial by a binomial, you will have 3 x 2 = 6 multiplications to perform.

FOIL

When multiplying a binomial by a binomial remember the acronym **FOIL** (First Outside Inside Last).

$$(x + 4)(x - 3) = (x + 4)(x - 3)$$

F	First	Multiply the **First** terms of both binomials	$x \bullet x = x^2$
O	Outside	Multiply the **Outside** terms of both binomials	$x \bullet (-3) = -3x$
I	Inside	Multiply the **Inside** terms of both binomials	$4 \bullet x = 4x$
L	Last	Multiply the **Last** terms of both binomials	$4 \bullet (-3) = -12$

$$(x + 4)(x - 3) = x^2 - 3x + 4x - 12 = x^2 + x - 12$$
$$\text{F} \quad \text{O} \quad \text{I} \quad \text{L}$$

When squaring a binomial just write the binomial down twice and **FOIL**.

$$(a + 3)^2 = (a + 3)(a + 3) = a^2 + 3a + 3a + 9 = a^2 + 6a + 9$$

When multiplying a trinomial by a binomial, think of it as two monomials being **distributed** through a trinomial, then combine like terms.

$$(b + 3)(b^2 - 2b - 15) = (b^3 - 2b^2 - 15b) + (3b^2 - 6b - 45) = b^3 + b^2 - 21b - 45$$

DIVISION

When dividing a polynomial by a monomial, just divide each term by the monomial.

$$\frac{4x^3 + 16x^2 - 10x}{2x} = \frac{4x^3}{2x} + \frac{16x^2}{2x} - \frac{10x}{2x} = 2x^2 + 8x - 5$$

Division of polynomials by binomials will require factorization, which is the next topic (**A4**).

A3   Practice.

1. Add $(3x^5 + 5x^3 - 5x^2 + 6x - 7) + (3x^4 + 2x^2 - 9x + 5)$

2. Subtract $(7x^5 + 3x^3 - 5x^2 + 5x - 7) - (2x^4 - 2x^3 + 7x^2 - 7x + 6)$

3. Multiply $(A + 7)(A + 2)$

4. Multiply $(B - 4)(B + 2)$

5. Multiply $(2C + 3)(C - 4)$

6. Multiply $(4D^3 + 3D^2 - 4D + 5)(-5)$

A4 FACTORIZATION OF POLYNOMIALS

In the previous section, A3, we reviewed multiplication of polynomials. In this section, we will reverse the process and factor polynomials. When a polynomial is factored, it changes from being addition and subtraction to multiplication. Thus, it changes from being a polynomial to being a monomial. This process is essential for solving many types of equations.

GREATEST COMMON FACTOR (GCF)

The first tool to use when attempting to factor a polynomial is to find the **Greatest Common Factor** (GCF). The GCF is the largest factor that will divide evenly into all of the terms of the polynomial. Consider $4x + 10$. The largest factor that will divide evenly into both 4 and 10 is 2. Therefore, 2 is the GCF.

$$4x + 10 = 2(2x + 5)$$

Whenever you want to check a factorization, just multiply. You should get what you started with.

$$2(2x + 5) = 4x + 10$$

Here is another expression that can be factored.

$$42x^2 + 30x$$

Notice that the binomial could be factored several different ways:

$$42x^2 + 30x = 2(21x^2 + 15x)$$
$$42x^2 + 30x = 3(14x^2 + 10x)$$
$$42x^2 + 30x = 2x(21x + 15)$$
$$42x^2 + 30x = 3x(14x + 10)$$
$$42x^2 + 30x = 6x(7x + 5)$$

While none of these factorizations are incorrect, the best factorization is the last one. It is the one that pulls out the GCF.

FACTORING BINOMIALS

If you are factoring a binomial, check to see if it is the **difference of squares**.

Example 1 $X^2 - 25 = (X + 5)(X - 5)$

Example 2 $a^2 - 16 = (a + 4)(a - 4)$

Example 3 $m^2 - 144 = (m + 12)(m - 12)$

This will only work when there is subtraction. $A^2 + B^2$, the sum of squares, will not factor in the real number system.

Sometimes there can be a problem within a problem. After the first factorization in the problem below there is a factor, $(B^2 - 4)$, which can be factored further.

Example 4 $(B^4 - 16) = (B^2 + 4)(B^2 - 4) = (B^2 + 4)(B + 2)(B - 2)$

If the binomial is a **sum of cubes** or a **difference of cubes** it can be factored according to these formulas.

Sum of Cubes Formula: $\boxed{a^3 + b^3 = (a + b)(a^2 - ab + b^2)}$

Example 3 $x^3 + 8 = (x + 2)(x^2 - 2x + 4)$

Example 4 $27y^3 + 64 = (3y + 4)(9y^2 - 12y + 16)$

Difference of Cubes Formula: $\boxed{a^3 - b^3 = (a - b)(a^2 + ab + b^2)}$

Example 5 $x^3 - 8 = (x - 2)(x^2 + 2x + 4)$

Example 6 $8y^3 + 125 = (2y + 5)(4y^2 - 10y + 25)$

Notice how similar the formulas are; the only difference is the signs.

FACTORING TRINOMIALS

When you are faced with factoring a trinomial, check first to see if it is a **perfect square trinomial** by answering these three questions:

$$x^2 + 10x + 25$$

Is the first term a perfect square?	Yes	$\sqrt{x^2} = x$
Is the last term a perfect square?	Yes	$\sqrt{25} = 5$
Is the middle term equal to twice the product of the roots of the first and last terms?	Yes	$10x = 2 \bullet x \bullet 5$

Since we answered yes to all three questions, we know that we have a perfect square trinomial. The factorization of any perfect square trinomial will be a binomial squared.

$$x^2 + 10x + 25 = (x + 5)(x + 5) = (x + 5)^2$$

Here are some more examples. Notice that the sign of the last term must always be positive, and the sign used in the factor is always the same as the middle term.

Example 7 $x^2 - 8x + 16 = (x - 4)(x - 4) = (x - 4)^2$

Example 8 $x^2 + 12x + 36 = (x + 6)(x + 6) = (x + 6)^2$

Example 9 $4x^2 + 12x + 9 = (2x + 3)(2x + 3) = (2x + 3)^2$

Example 10 $9x^2 - 30x + 25 = (3x - 5)(3x - 5) = (3x - 5)^2$

To verify any of these results, **FOIL** out the binomial.

If a trinomial is not a perfect square trinomial, then a different approach to factoring is required. We shall consider two: **inspection** and **grouping**.

INSPECTION

The inspection method of factoring trinomials requires you to consider two things. First, what are all the factors of the last term? Second, which of these factors add up to equal the number, or **coefficient,** of the middle term? The inspection method is easiest when the coefficient of the first term is 1. In Examples 11 and 12, since no number is written in front of the x^2 we know that the coefficient is 1.

Example 11   Factor $x^2 + 7x + 12$ by inspection.

To solve by inspection, we need the factors of 12 that add together to equal 7.

What are the factors of 12?	What is the sum of each set of factors?
$12 = 1 \cdot 12$	$1 + 12 = 13$
$12 = 2 \cdot 6$	$2 + 6 = 8$
$12 = 3 \cdot 4$	**$3 + 4 = 7$**

Since $3 + 4 = 7$, the middle term of the trinomial, we use the factors 3 and 4 to write the factorization of $x^2 + 7x + 12$: $x^2 + 7x + 12 = (x + 3)(x + 4)$. As with all factorizations, check by multiplying. These problems can become quite complex, especially when we mix signs.

Example 12   Factor $x^2 + 2x - 48$ by inspection.

What are the factors of –48?	What is the sum of each set of factors?
$48 = -1 \cdot 48$	$-1 + 48 = 47$
$48 = -2 \cdot 24$	$-2 + 24 = 22$
$48 = -3 \cdot 16$	$-3 + 16 = 13$
$48 = -4 \cdot 12$	$-4 + 12 = 8$
$48 = -6 \cdot 8$	$-6 + 8 = 2$

Since $-6 + 8 = 2$, the middle term of the trinomial, we use those factors to write the factorization of $x^2 + 2x - 48$: $x^2 + 2x - 48 = (x - 6)(x + 8)$.

Factoring by inspection is another way of saying *guess the factorization* until you come up with the correct factors. Factoring by inspection is a skill that requires some practice. The more you factor, the better you will get at it. It is essential that you check your factorization by FOIL.

GROUPING

Factoring by grouping requires less skill than inspection, but it usually takes more time. In grouping, we are going to split the middle term into two terms and pull out the GCF three times. First let's consider the general form of a trinomial written in descending order: $ax^2 + bx + c$

STEPS FOR FACTORING BY GROUPING

Step 1.   Multiply $(a \cdot c)$. Pay attention to the sign.

Step 2.   List all the factors of $a \cdot c$.

Step 3.   If the sign of $(a \cdot c)$ is *positive,* ADD all the pairs of factors of $(a \cdot c)$ until you find a pair that will sum to b.

If the sign of $(a \cdot c)$ is *negative,* find the DIFFERENCE of all the pairs of factors $(a \cdot c)$ until you find a pair that has a difference of b.

Step 4.   Rewrite the trinomial into a four term polynomial using the factor pair found in step 3 to replace the bx term.

Step 5.   Factor out the GCF of the first two terms. Factor out the GCF of the last two terms. The result is two terms. Each term is a monomial times a binomial.

Step 6.   Factor out the GCF of the two terms, and you are finished.

Example 13 $3x^2 - 13x - 10$

Step 1.   Multiply (a • c): $3(-10) = -30$

Steps 2 and 3.   Since (a • c) is a negative, we will look for a difference:

Factors of −30		Difference
1	30	29
2	15	13
3	10	7
5	6	1

Step 4.   Since the difference of 2 and 15 is 13, this is the pair of factors we use to rewrite the trinomial. Since we want to replace a −13, we let the 15 be negative and the 2 be positive.

$$3x^2 - 13x - 10 = 3x^2 - 15x + 2x - 10$$

Step 5.   Now we pull the GCF (3x) of the first group $(3x^2 - 15x)$ and then the GCF (2) of the second group $(2x - 10)$. This is where the name of this method, **factor by grouping**, comes from.

$$3x^2 - 15x + 2x - 10 = (3x^2 - 15x) + (2x - 10)$$
$$= 3x(x - 5) + 2(x - 5)$$

Step 6.   Now we have a binomial with two terms. The first term is $3x(x - 5)$ and the second term is $2(x - 5)$. The GCF is $(x - 5)$. Factor out the GCF.
$$= 3x(x - 5) + 2(x - 5)$$
$$= (x - 5)(3x + 2)$$

Factoring is complete. Check by multiplying, using the FOIL method.

Example 14   Factor $6x^2 - x - 40$ by grouping.

Find the factors of $6 • (40) = -240$ that have a difference of −1.

Factors of 6 • (40) = −240		Difference
1	240	239
2	120	118
3	80	77
4	60	56
5	48	43
6	40	34
8	30	22
10	24	14
12	20	8
15	16	1

Since 15 and 16 differ by 1, we can rewrite the trinomial into a four term polynomial ready for factoring. Since we want a negative 1, 16 will be negative and 15 will be positive ($-16 + 15 = -1$). The order you write −16 and 15 in does not matter.

$$6x^2 - x - 40 = 6x^2 - 16x + 15x - 40 = (6x^2 - 16x) + (15x - 40)$$
$$= 2x(3x - 8) + 5(3x - 8) = (2x + 5)(3x - 8)$$

Check by multiplication, using FOIL.

FACTORING OTHER POLYNOMIALS

If you have more than three terms, try factoring by grouping.

Example 15

$ac + ad + bc + bd$
$= (ac + ad) + (bc + bd)$
$= a(c + d) + b(c + d)$
$= (a + b)(c + d)$

Example 16

$2cd + 16c - 3d - 24$
$= (2cd + 16c) + (-3d - 24)$
$= 2c(d + 8) + -3(d + 8)$
$= (2c - 3)(d + 8)$

Example 17

$x^3 - 2x^2 + 3x - 6$
$= (x^3 - 2x^2) + (3x - 6)$
$= x^2(x - 2) + 3(x - 2)$
$= (x^2 + 3)(x - 2)$

Some problems call for a combination of methods:

Example 18

$x^3 + 7x^2 - 4x - 28$
$= (x^3 + 7x^2) + (-4x - 28)$ Begin with grouping.
$= x^2(x + 7) + -4(x + 7)$
$= (x^2 - 4)(x + 7)$ Notice the difference of squares.
$= (x + 2)(x - 2)(x + 7)$

PRIME POLYNOMIALS

Consider the polynomial $x^2 + 8x + 10$. If we were to try to factor this polynomial by inspection, we would need to find factors of 10 that would also add up to 8. The factors of 10 are (1, 10) and (2, 5). Since neither of these factor pairs will produce the required sum of 8, we know that $x^2 + 8x + 10$ cannot be factored. If a polynomial cannot be factored, it is called a **prime polynomial.**

FACTORING SURVIVAL

Factoring is a skill that you can get better at with practice. Whenever you must factor a polynomial and cannot decide where to start, try these steps.

A) **GCF**: Always try to factor out a **GCF**. If this is possible, the rest of the problem will be easier.

B) Count the number of terms. This will tell you what to do next.

- *One Term* – no need to factor

- *Two Terms* – check for the **difference of squares, sum of cubes, or difference of cubes**, and follow these formulas. Remember, the sum of squares will not factor in the real number system.

prime polynomial (will not factor)	$a^2 + b^2$
difference of squares	$a^2 - b^2 = (a + b)(a - b)$
sum of cubes	$a^3 + b^3 = (a + b)(a^2 - ab + b^2)$
difference of cubes	$a^3 - b^3 = (a - b)(a^2 + ab + b^2)$

- *Three terms* – Check for a **perfect square trinomial**.

  $$a^2 + 2ab + b^2 = (a + b)(a + b) = (a + b)^2$$
  $$a^2 - 2ab + b^2 = (a - b)(a - b) = (a - b)^2$$

  If that does not work, try **inspection** or **grouping**.

- *Four terms* – Grouping

FACTORING SURVIVAL, continued

C) Factor completely. Watch out for combinations of two or more methods.

D) Check by multiplying. With this type of test, you have time to work backwards from the answers that are given on the test.

An important thing to remember about a test like the COMPASS is that you can often work backwards from the answers to determine the correct response. For example, suppose you were given an item like this:

For all x, $x^2 + 3x - 40$

    a) $(x + 5)(x + 8)$
    b) $(x + 5)(x - 8)$
    c) $(x - 5)(x + 8)$
    d) $(x - 5)(x - 8)$
    e) $(x - 4)(x + 10)$

If you did not have any idea about how to factor this polynomial, you could multiply each of the answers out until you found the one that matched the question.

For all x, $x^2 + 3x - 40$

    a) $(x + 5)(x + 8) = x^2 + 8x + 5x + 40 = x^2 + 13x + 40$
    b) $(x + 5)(x - 8) = x^2 - 8x + 5x - 40 = x^2 - 3x - 40$
    c) $(x - 5)(x + 8) = x^2 + 8x - 5x - 40 = \mathbf{x^2 + 3x - 40}$
    d) $(x - 5)(x - 8) = x^2 - 8x - 5x + 40 = x^2 - 13x + 40$
    e) $(x - 4)(x + 10) = x^2 + 10x - 4x - 40 = x^2 + 6x - 40$

So, choice "c" is the correct answer. Because COMPASS is not a timed test, you are free to work problems like this the long way.

A4 Practice.
Factor completely. If a polynomial is prime, state so.

1.	$2X^2 + 9X - 35$	2.	$X^2 - 10X + 25$
3.	$X^4 - 81$	4.	$X^2 + 5X - 8$
5.	$a^2 - 3a + 2ab - 6b$	6.	$A^2 - 13A + 42$
7.	$2B^2 - 3B - 20$	8.	$12C^2 + 46C + 40$
9.	$12D^3 + 22D^2 - 70D$	10.	$X^2 - 16X + 64$
11.	$3y^3 + 27y + 18y^2$	12.	$A^8 - 256$
13.	$4b^2 - 16c^2$	14.	$36c^2 - 12c + 1$

A5 SOLVING POLYNOMIAL EQUATIONS BY FACTORING

In this section we will see how factoring is used to solve equations.

THE PRINCIPLE OF ZERO PRODUCTS

What types of multiplication problems have zero as an answer? Only those that use zero as a factor. For example: $0 \cdot 0 = 0$; $0 \cdot -7 \cdot 4.238 = 0$; $110 \cdot 0 \cdot 82 \cdot 2 \cdot 5 = 0$. So, if we see a multiplication problem like this: $25 \cdot x \cdot 53 \cdot 7 \cdot 205 = 0$, we know that x has to be equal to 0. The reasoning that supports this claim is known as the **Principle of Zero Products:**

$$\boxed{\textbf{If a} \cdot \textbf{b = 0, then either a = 0 or b = 0.}}$$

The Principle of Zero Products allows us to look at a multiplication problem like $(x = 8)(x - 5) = 0$ and reason that either $(x + 8) = 0$ or $(x - 5) = 0$. Thus, x = –8 or x = 5. These are the only values that will produce a zero factor, hence a zero product.

If you are given a polynomial such as $2x^2 = 16x - 30$ to solve, you can use the Principle of Zero Products to find the solutions:

$2x^2 = 16x - 30$	First, set the polynomial equal to 0.
$2x^2 - 16x = 30 = 0$	Now factor out the GCF, which is 2.
$2(x^2 - 8x = 15) = 0$	Try to factor the remaining polynomial.
$2(x - 3)(x - 5) = 0$	Set each of the three factors equal to 0.
$2 = 0$	Since 2 = 0 will never be true, this factor will not make a contribution to the solution set.
$x - 3 = 0$	
$x = 3$	So 3 is a member of the solution set.
$x + 5 = 0$	
$x = -5$	So –5 is a member of the solution set.
$x = \{-5, 3\}$	The solution set is $\{-5, 3\}$.

Example 1   Solve $x^2 + 5x + 6 = 0$.

This equation is a trinomial. We will factor, which will change it into a multiplication problem. Then use the Principle of Zero Produts to find solutions.

$x^2 + 5x + 6 = 0$	
$(x + 3)(x + 2) = 0$	Set each factor = 0
$(x + 3) = 0 \qquad (x + 2) = 0$	
$x = -3 \qquad\quad x = -2$	The solution set is x = $\{-3, -2\}$

Example 2   Solve $2X^2 + 9X = 35$.

Sometimes problems are not set equal to zero. Therefore, you must set the equation equal to zero before you factor. That is always the first step.

$2X^2 + 9X = 35$	
$2X^2 + 9X - 35 = 0$	
$(2X - 5)(X + 7) = 0$	Set each factor = 0
$(2X - 5) = 0 \quad (X + 7) = 0$	
$2X = 5 \qquad\quad X = -7$	
$X = \dfrac{5}{2}$	The solution set is X = $\left\{\dfrac{5}{2}, -7\right\}$

Example 3   Solve $12x^3 + 22x^2 = 70x$.

In this problem, first set the equation equal to zero. Then, factor out the GCF, which is 2x. Next, factor the trinomial, which gives us three factors. Finally, set each factor equal to zero to find the solution set.

$$12x^3 + 22x^2 = 70x$$
$$12x^3 + 22x^2 - 70x = 0$$
$$2x(6x^2 + 11x - 35) = 0$$
$$2x(2x + 7)(3x - 5) = 0$$

$2x = 0$	$2x + 7 = 0$	$3x - 5 = 0$
$2x = 0$	$2x = -7$	$3x = 5$
$x = \dfrac{0}{2}$	$x = -\dfrac{7}{2}$	$x = \dfrac{5}{3}$

$$x = \left\{ 0, -\frac{7}{2}, \frac{5}{3} \right\}$$

Example 4   Solve $X^2 + 8X = -16$.

Sometimes quadratic equations have only one solution. For example, $X^2 + 8X = -16$ is a perfect square trinomial. Whenever the equation is a perfect square trinomial, you will only have one solution.

$$X^2 + 8X = -16$$
$$X^2 + 8X + 16 = 0$$
$$(X + 4)(X + 4) = 0$$
$$(X + 4)^2 = 0 \qquad\qquad \text{Set each factor} = 0$$
$$X + 4 = 0 \qquad X + 4 = 0$$
$$X = \{-4\}$$

Example 5   Solve $3x^2 + 6x = 0$.

If you have a quadratic but no "c" term, then factor out the common factor of x.

$$3x^2 + 6x = 0$$
$$3x(x + 2) = 0 \qquad\qquad \text{Set each factor} = 0$$

$3x = 0$	$x + 2 = 0$
$x = 0$	$x = -2$

$$x = \{0, -2\}$$

Whenever you have a monomial factor that contains the variable, then you will have a zero in the solution set. See Example 3: 2x and Example 5: 3x.

Example 6   Solve $X^2 = 5X + 8$.

Sometimes equations will have no rational solution. This is one such equation.

$$X^2 = 5X + 8 \qquad\qquad X^2 - 5X - 8 = 0$$

The factors of 8 are (1, 8) and (2, 4). There is no way to combine these factors and come up with a −5; therefore, this quadratic is not factorable. This means it has no rational solutions. Later we will see how to find irrational solutions to this type of equation.

A5   Practice. Solve.

1.	$X^2 = 36$	2.	$X^2 = 5X$
3.	$(X + 2)(X - 3) = 0$	4.	$X^2 = 7X - 12$
5.	$X^2 - X = 6$	6.	$A^2 - 13A = -42$
7.	$B^2 + 3B + 20 = 0$	8.	$X^3 + 2X^2 - 9X - 18 = 0$

A6 FORMULA MANIPULATION AND FIELD AXIOMS

Formula manipulation means solving for a particular variable. When solving for a variable, let's call that variable the **target.** What you want to do is get everything away from the target and have the target alone on either side of the equal sign.

When dealing with a target that has no exponents, try this procedure:

Step 1. Remove all grouping symbols.

Step 2. Move all terms containing the target on one side of the equation.

Step 3. Move all other terms to the other side of the equation.

Step 4. If you have two or more unlike terms with the target in them, factor out the target.

Step 5. Multiply by the reciprocal of the coefficient of the target.

Example 1   Solve for x. $C + 2x = a(x + 3) + x$

$C + 2x = a(x + 3) + x$	
$C + 2x = ax + 3a + x$	1. Remove all grouping symbols.
$C = ax + 3a - x$	2. Collect the target variable terms on one side.
$C - 3a = ax - x$	3. Move everything else to the other side.
$C - 3a = x(a - 1)$	4. Factor.
$\dfrac{C - 3a}{a - 1} = x$	5. Divide by the coefficient.

Example 2   Solve for b_2. $A = \dfrac{1}{2}(b_1 + b_2)H$

$A = \dfrac{1}{2}(b_1 + b_2)H$	1. Remove all grouping symbols. Distribute $\frac{1}{2}$. Distribute the H.
$A = (\dfrac{1}{2}b_1 + \dfrac{1}{2}b_2)H$	
$A = \dfrac{1}{2}b_1 H + \dfrac{1}{2}b_2 H$	2. Collect the target variables on one side. (Not needed)
$A - \dfrac{1}{2}b_1 H = \dfrac{1}{2}b_2 H$	3. Move everything else to the other side.
	4. Factor. (Not needed)
	5. Multiply by the reciprocal of the coefficient.
$\dfrac{2}{H} \cdot \left(A - \dfrac{1}{2}b_1 H\right) = \left(\dfrac{1}{2}b_2 H \cdot \dfrac{2}{H}\right)$	
$\dfrac{2A}{H} - b_1 = b_2$	

Sometimes it is easier to follow a different procedure to get the same result.

$A = \dfrac{1}{2}(b_1 + b_2)H$	1. Multiply both sides by 2.
$2A = (b_1 + b_2)H$	2. Divide by H.
$\dfrac{2A}{H} = (b_1 + b_2)$	3. Subtract b_1.
$\dfrac{2A}{H} - b_1 = b_2$	

FIELD AXIOMS

In field axioms, you will be given a made-up rule and then be asked to apply it.

Example 3   Choose the best answer.

The operation a ∘ b means "take 3a and add it to 2b." Find (6x) ∘ (7y) when x = 4 and y = 5.

A. 72   B. 70   C. 2   D. 5040   E. 142

Plug in 6x for a and 7y for b: $3(6x) + 2(7y) = 3(6(4)) + 2(7(5)) = 3(24) + 2(35) = 72 + 70 = 142$. Therefore, the correct answer is E. 142. Notice that the incorrect answers all have something to do with the correct solution. This is very common on multiple choice tests. Often the incorrect answers you are given are only wrong by a sign or some other simple error.

This type of problem is not very common. If you work carefully and check your answer against those provided with the problem it should not be too difficult.

K PROBLEMS

Another type of problem will involve "k".   "K" will be the missing part of some situation. You will need to figure out the value of "k" before you can do anything else with the problem.

Example 4   Choose the best answer.

If x = 4 and y = kx + x, then y = 5. What is *the value of y when x = 8?*

A. 8   B. 10   C. 16   D. 20   E. 24

To find the solution, we must first find the value of k. Then we will use that k value and x = 8 to find *the value of y when x = 8.*

$y = kx + x$ Solve for k.
$(5) = k(4) + (4)$
$5 - 4 = 4k$
$1 = 4k$
$\frac{1}{4} = k$ Now, substitute 8 for x and $\frac{1}{4}$ for k.
$y = \left(\frac{1}{4}\right)(8) + (8) = 2 = 8 = 10$ Therefore, the answer is B.

A6   Practice.

1. Solve $A = \pi rs + \pi r^2$ for s.

3. Solve $\frac{1}{x} + \frac{1}{y} = \frac{1}{z}$ for x.

2. Solve $P = 2l + 2w$ for l.

4. If x = 4 and y = kx + 2x, then y = 9. What is the value of y when x = 2?

5. If x = 6 and y = kx + x, then y = 18. What is the value of y when x = 8?

6. If x = 9 and y = kx + x, then y = 12. What is the value of y when x = 6?

A7 LINEAR EQUATIONS IN ONE VARIABLE

This section is very similar to the first half of the previous section, A6. We have added step 6 (Check your answer). Often there will be other, more efficient ways to solve particular problems, but this way will always work.

Step 1. Remove all grouping symbols.

Step 2. Collect all terms containing the target on one side of the equation.

Step 3. Move all other terms to the other side of the equation.

Step 4. If you have two or more unlike terms with the target in them, factor out the target.

Step 5. Multiply by the reciprocal of the coefficient of the target.

Step 6. Check by plugging your answer into the original equation.

Example 1

$3(x + 5) = 21 + x$
$3x + 15 = 21 + x$
$3x - x + 15 = 21$
$3x - x = 21 - 15$
$2x = 6$
$x = 3$

1. Remove all grouping symbols.
2. Collect the target variable terms on one side.
3. Move everything else to the other side.
4. It is not necessary to Factor this example.
5. Divide by the coefficient.

$3((3) + 5) = 21 + (3)$
$3(8) = 21 + 3$
$24 = 24$ Correct.

6. Check.

Whenever you encounter a fraction in an equation, you can get rid of it by multiplying by the LCD of all the denominators.

Example 2

$$\frac{2x}{3} + \frac{x}{2} = x + 3$$

$$(6) \bullet \left(\frac{2x}{3} + \frac{x}{2}\right) = (x + 3) \bullet (6)$$

$$\frac{12x}{3} + \frac{6x}{2} = 6x + 18$$

$$4x + 3x = 6x + 18$$

$$7x = 6x + 18$$

$$x = 18$$

The numbers 3 and 2 are the denominators so 6 is the LCD.

Check:

$$\frac{2(18)}{3} + \frac{18}{2} = 18 + 3$$

$$12 + 9 = 21$$

$$21 = 21$$

Correct!

A7   Practice.   Solve.

a. $X + 6 = -19$

b. $66 = 6Y$

c. $6A - 4 = 41$

d. $-67 = 7B - 4$

e. $9C - 5 = 4C + 20$

f. $D + \dfrac{D}{4} = 20$

44

A8 EXPONENTS

PRODUCT RULE OF EXPONENTS

$a^4 \bullet a^3 = a^{4+3} = a^7$ When **multiplying** like bases, **add** the exponents. (Multiplication becomes addition)

Examples:

$(X^5 Y^2)(X^4 Y^3) = X^9 Y^5$ $(s^2 t)(s^3 t^4) = s^5 t^5$ $(5z^2)(3z^3) = 15z^5$

QUOTIENT RULE OF EXPONENTS

$\dfrac{a^9}{a^3} = a^{9-3} = a^4$ When **dividing** like bases, **subtract** exponents. (Division becomes subtraction)

Examples

$\dfrac{X^6 Y^4}{X^4 Y^3} = X^2 Y$ $\dfrac{s^4 t}{s^3} = st$ $\dfrac{5z^{10}}{3z^3} = \dfrac{5z^7}{3}$

ZERO EXPONENT RULE

$C^0 = 1$ Anything (except zero) raised to the zero power is 1.

Examples

$5^0 = 1$ $X^0 = 1$ (assume $X \neq 0$) $0^0 =$ undefined

THE POWER RULE OF EXPONENTS

$(D^4)^3 = D^{4 \bullet 3} = D^{12}$ When taking a power to a power, multiply the exponents.

$(X^5 Y^2)^3 = X^{15} Y^6$ $(s^2 t)^4 = s^8 t^4$ $(3z^3)^2 = 9z^6$

Raising a product or a quotient to a power: $\left(\dfrac{C}{D}\right)^3 = \dfrac{C^3}{D^3}$ $(AB)^3 = A^3 B^3$

What is the difference between the product rule and the power rule?

Product Rule
$a^4 \bullet a^3 = a^7$ Notice there are two "a" bases and two exponents.
ADD   aaaa $\bullet$ aaa = aaaaaaa = a^7

Power Rule
$(D^4)^3 = D^{12}$ Notice there is only one "D" base and two exponents.
MULTIPLY $(D^4)(D^4)(D^4) =$ (DDDD)(DDDD)(DDDD)
      = DDDDDDDDDDDD = D^{12}

What about regular addition?

$a^4 + a^3 = a^4 + a^3$ Addition will not change exponents.
We cannot combine unlike terms.

What about signs? Does $-3^2 = (-3)^2$?

No! $-3^2 = -(3)(3) = -9$ $(-3)^2 = (-3)(-3) = 9$

A8   Practice. Simplify.

1. $K^5 \cdot K^3$ 2. $\dfrac{X^7Y^8}{X^2Y^3}$ 3. $(M^3N^4)^5$ 4. 13^0

A9 LINEAR INEQUALITIES IN ONE VARIABLE

The basic difference between a linear equality and a linear inequality is that an equality has one answer and an inequality has an infinite number of answers.

Equality

$x + 2 = 7$

$x = 7 - 2$ Subtract 2 from both sides

$x = 5$

Inequality

$x + 2 \geq 7$

$x \geq 7 - 2$

$x \geq 5$

Graph.

$x = 5$

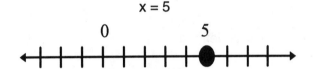

$x \geq 5$

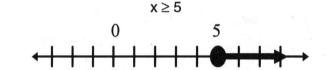

To solve a linear inequality, do everything exactly as you would with a linear equality; however, if you ever have to multiply or divide by a negative number, you must reverse the sign of the inequality.

Example 1

$-7Y + 5 \leq 33$ The act of dividing by −7 reverses the direction of the inequality.

$7Y \leq 33 - 5$

$-7Y \leq 28$

$\dfrac{-7Y}{-7} \geq \dfrac{28}{-7}$

$Y \geq -4$

Check this problem by inserting any number greater than −4 into the original equation and see if it true. For example, let y = 3.

$-7(3) + 5 \leq 33$

$-21 + 5 \leq 33$

$-16 \leq 33$ True.

A9   Practice.

1. $3x + 8 \leq 35$ 2. $12 - 4y > 2y + 18$

3. $9(z + 3) - 18 \geq -9$ 4. $14C - 5 \leq 4C + 20$

A10 RATIONAL EXPRESSIONS

Rational expressions have variables in the denominator. All of the rules about fractions apply to rational expressions. One of the most important rules in algebra is that denominators can never equal zero. Consider the following expression:

$$\frac{20}{x - 3}$$

If x were 8, we could plug it in and get a value of 4 for the expression. However, if we tried to plug in a 3 for x, we would get a zero in the denominator. And a zero in the denominator is the worst thing that can ever happen in your life! To find the value(s) for which a rational expression is undefined, set the denominator equal to zero and solve for x:

$$x - 3 = 0$$
$$x = 3$$

In other words, x = 8 is a meaningful replacement, but the expression is undefined for x = 3.

ADDITION AND SUBTRACTION

Adding or subtracting rational expressions requires a common denominator. Then the operation can be performed on the numerators.

$$\frac{4}{x^2 + x - 6} - \frac{2}{x^2 + 3x - 10}$$

$$= \frac{4}{(x + 3)(x - 2)} - \frac{2}{(x + 5)(x - 2)}$$

$$= \frac{4(x + 5)}{(x + 3)(x - 2)(x + 5)} - \frac{2(x + 3)}{(x + 3)(x - 2)(x + 5)}$$

$$= \frac{4(x + 5) - 2(x + 3)}{(x + 3)(x - 2)(x + 5)}$$

$$= \frac{4x + 20 - 2x - 6}{(x + 3)(x - 2)(x + 5)}$$

$$= \frac{2x + 14}{(x + 3)(x - 2)(x + 5)}$$

Sometimes finding the LCD requires factoring. In this example, after the denominators are factored, we only have three factors: (x + 3), (x − 2), and (x + 5). The LCD is the smallest number that contains these factors. Thus, the LCD is (x + 3)(x − 2)(x + 5). Once found, the LCD will not change for the rest of the problem.

Notice that the negative 2 is distributed all the way through the (x + 3) numerator to become − 2x − 6 in the next to last step.

MULTIPLICATION

When multiplying rational expressions, just multiply numerator by numerator and denominator by denominator.

When you are instructed to simplify the multiplication of rational expressions, you need to factor and then cancel. Do not multiply.

$$\frac{x^2 + x - 6}{x^2 - x - 12} \cdot \frac{x^2 - 16}{x^2 + 3x - 10}$$

$$= \frac{(x + 3)(x - 2)}{(x + 3)(x - 4)} \cdot \frac{(x + 4)(x - 4)}{(x + 5)(x - 2)}$$

$$= \frac{(x + 4)}{(x + 5)}$$

DIVISION

When dividing, multiply by the reciprocal of the divisor. (When dividing, *don't ask why just flip and multiply.*)

$$\frac{a}{b} \div \frac{c}{d} = \frac{a}{b} \cdot \frac{d}{c} = \frac{ad}{bc}$$

A10 Practice.

1. For what values of x is the expression undefined? $\dfrac{3}{2x + 8}$

2. For what values of y is the expression undefined? $\dfrac{-5}{2y}$

3. Add

$$\frac{x}{2} + \frac{3}{x}$$

4. Subtract

$$\frac{3}{x^2 + 5x + 6} - \frac{2}{x^2 - 4}$$

5. Multiply

$$\frac{x^2 + 10x + 25}{x^2 - x - 2} \cdot \frac{x^2 + x - 6}{x^2 - 25}$$

6. Divide

$$\frac{x^2 + x + 2}{x^2 + 4x + 3} \div \frac{x + 2}{x + 3}$$

48

A11 EXPONENTS

Negative exponents have nothing to do with whether a number is positive or negative. Negative exponents tell us to switch the position of the base from the numerator to the denominator or from the denominator to the numerator. In other words, if a base in the numerator has a negative exponent, move it to the denominator, and the exponent is positive. For example: $x^{-2} = \dfrac{1}{x^2}$

Example 1   Simplify.

$$\dfrac{a^{-2}b^3}{c^4d^{-5}} \qquad \dfrac{b^3d^5}{a^2c^4}$$

Example 2   The power rule is used to "distribute" an exponent across a term.

$$\left(\dfrac{3}{2}\right)^{-2} = \left(\dfrac{2}{3}\right)^2 = \dfrac{2^2}{3^2} = \dfrac{4}{9}$$

Example 3

$$(2a^2b^{-3}c^4d^{-5})^{-2} = 2^{-2}a^{-4}b^6c^{-8}d^{10} = \dfrac{b^6d^{10}}{4a^4c^8}$$

Example 4

Notice the difference in what the exponent touches in A and B.

A) $\dfrac{3}{(4x)^{-3}} = 4^3x^3 \cdot 3 = 64x^3 \cdot 3 = 192x^3$

B) $\dfrac{3}{4x^{-3}} = \dfrac{3x^3}{4}$

SCIENTIFIC NOTATION

Negative exponents are very important in scientific notation. We use negative exponents to describe very small numbers.

$$0.00000123 = \dfrac{1.23}{1000000} = 1.23 \times 10^{-6}$$

On the other hand, positive exponents are used to indicate very large numbers.

$$123000000000 = 1.23 \times 100000000000 = 1.23 \times 10^{11}$$

A11 Practice.
Simplify. Leave all exponents positive.

1. $\dfrac{a^{-2}b^{-3}}{a^{-4}b^{-5}}$

2. $\left(\dfrac{3a^2}{2a}\right)^{-2}$

3. $(3x^3y^{-2}c^5d^{-3})^{-2}$

4. $\dfrac{2a^{-2}}{(2a)^{-3}}$

5. $\left(\dfrac{3a^{-1}}{5a^{-2}}\right)^{-2}$

6. $\dfrac{s^{-2}t^8}{s^3t^{-8}}$

A12 SYSTEMS OF LINEAR EQUATIONS IN TWO VARIABLES

A linear equation is a line. We will find out more about graphing lines in section A16. A system of linear equations in two variables consists of two lines. If you have two lines in a plane there are three possibilities for how they touch each other. First, they could be the same line. In such cases they are said to be **collinear** and they intersect at infinitely many points. Second, they could be **parallel**; these lines never intersect. Third, they could intersect at one point.

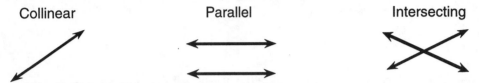

Collinear   Parallel   Intersecting

This section is about finding the one point of intersection if it exists. We will discuss two methods to find the point of intersection. One is called **substitution**, and the other is called **elimination**. Before using either method to find a solution, we need to discuss how to determine if your answer is correct.

CHECKING

First, what is an ordered pair? An **ordered pair** is two numbers arranged in order. Ordered pairs will always be in alphabetical order. So, if the system has a's and b's, the ordered pair (4, 9) means a = 4 and b = 9.

Example 1   Is the ordered pair (3, 2) a solution to this system?

x + y = 5
x − y = 1

Plug the ordered pair into each equation. If it is true for both, then it is a true solution for the system of equations. If it is false for either, it is false for the system.

x + y = 5   x − y = 1
(3) + (2) = 5   (3) − (2) = 1
5 = 5   1 = 1
True   True

Therefore, (3, 2) is a solution for the system.

Example 2   Is the ordered pair (8, 4) a solution to this system?

2x − 3y = 4
x + y = 10

Like before, we plug the ordered pair into each equation. It must be true for both to be a true solution for the system of equations.

2(8) − 3(4) = 4   x + y = 10
16 − 12 = 4   (8) + (4) = 10
4 = 4   12 = 10
True   False

Therefore, (8, 4) is not a solution for the system.

SUBSTITUTION

In substitution, we first solve for one variable in either equation. Then, we substitute that information back into the other equation. That will tell us what the value of one of the variables is. Finally, we plug that value into either of the equations, and that will reveal the value of the other variable.

Example 3

$2x + 3y = 5$

$x + 3y = 7$

$\Rightarrow x = 7 - 3y$

Solving for x in the second equation is the easiest variable to solve for in this system.

$2(7 - 3y) + 3y = 5$

$14 - 6y + 3y = 5$

$14 - 3y = 5$

$-3y = 5 - 14$

$-3y = -9$

$\dfrac{-3y}{-3} = \dfrac{-9}{-3}$

$y = 3$

Plug the value obtained for x back into the other equation, and then solve for y.

$\Rightarrow x = 7 - 3y$

$x = 7 - 3(3)$

$x = 7 - 9$

$x = -2$

Now that you have a y value, plug it back into either of the original equations to find x.

$2(-2) + 3(3) = 5$

$-4 + 9 = 5$

$5 = 5$

Plug back into an original equation to check. Since the check is true, we know (–2, 3) is the solution to this system.

ELIMINATION

In substitution, one equation communicates with the other by the act of the substitution. In elimination, the communication takes place by adding the two equations together. The reason this method is called elimination is that we will alter the equations such that when we add them together one of the variables is eliminated.

Example 4 $2x - 3y = 5$ $x + 3y = 7$

$\quad 2x - 3y = 5$

$+ \quad x + 3y = 7$

$\overline{\quad 3x \qquad = 12}$

$x = \dfrac{12}{3} = 4$

Since $(-3y) + (3y) = 0$ we are already ready to eliminate y by adding the two equations.

Solve for x and then substitute the value back into either equation to find the y value.

$x + 3y = 7$

$(4) + 3y = 7$

$3y = 7 - 4 = 3$

$\dfrac{3y}{3} = \dfrac{3}{3}$

$y = 1$

$2x - 3y = 5$

$2(4) - 3(1) = 5$

$8 - 3 = 5$

$5 = 5$

Check the ordered pair in the other equation.

Sometimes when you try substitution or elimination, you get what appears to be nonsense.

Example 5   Solve using elimination.

$-x + 3y = 5$
$2x - 6y = 4$

$(2) \bullet (-x + 3y) = (5) \bullet (2)$ Multiply both sides of the first equation by (2).
$-2x + 6y = 10$

$-2x + 6y = 10$ Add the two equations together.
$+\ 2x - 6y = 4$
_____
$\quad\quad 0 = 14$ False!

The procedure was executed correctly, but we got an obviously **false** result. This means that the system is inconsistent, parallel, and has no solution.

Example 6   Solve using substitution.

$2x - 8y = 16$
$x = 4y + 8$
$2(4y + 8) - 8y = 16$ Since the second equation is already solved for x just substitute (4y + 8) into the first equation for x.

$8y + 16 - 8y = 16$
$16 = 16$ True

True, but all of the variables are gone. This means that the system is collinear. It has an infinite number of answers. Any ordered pair that works for one equation will also work for the other.

If you are using one of these methods and all of the variables disappear, then the last statement will either be true or false, as in the last two examples. If the statement is false, then the system is inconsistent—parallel—no solution. If the statement is true, then the system is consistent–collinear—infinite solutions.

Collinear   **Parallel**   **Intersecting**
Consistent   Inconsistent   Consistent
Dependent   Dependent   Independent
∞ solutions   No solutions   One solution

Consistent or inconsistent means "do the lines touch?"
Dependent or independent means "do the lines go in the same direction?"

A12   Practice. Solve, using any method.

1. $x + y = 13$ 2. $2x - 4y = 3$ 3. $y = 2x - 3$
$x - y = 1$ $3x + 5y = 10$ $4x - 5y = 9$

4. $x = 3y + 5$ 5. $y - 5 = x$ 6. $4x - 2y = -4$
$3x - 9y = 4$ $2x + 2y = 10$ $x + 3y = -15$

A13 QUADRATIC FORMULA

Memorize this formula. As soon as you begin the test, before you answer the first question, write the formula down on the provided scrap sheet of paper. Then, when you need to use it during the test, you won't have to worry about recalling it—you will already have it in front of you.

$$x = \frac{-b \pm \sqrt{b^2 - 4ac}}{2a}$$

Any equation of the form $ax^2 + bx + c = 0$ is called a quadratic equation. The quadratic formula will solve any quadratic equation. Any time you have a quadratic equation all you have to do is to identify a, b, and c and plug them into the formula.

Example 1   Solve $x^2 - 8x + 15 = 0$

$a = 1 \quad b = -8 \quad c = 15$ First identify a, b, and c. Pay attention to signs.

$x = \dfrac{-(-8) \pm \sqrt{(-8)^2 - 4(1)(15)}}{2(1)}$ Plug into the Quadratic Formula, then simplify.

$x = \dfrac{8 \pm \sqrt{64 - 60}}{2} = \dfrac{8 \pm \sqrt{4}}{2} = \dfrac{8 \pm 2}{2}$ The $\pm$ sign means work the problem twice.

$= \dfrac{8 + 2}{2} \qquad = \dfrac{8 - 2}{2}$

$= 5 \qquad\qquad = 3$ Thus, our equation $x^2 - 8x + 15 = 0$ has a solution set of $x = \{5, 3\}$.

When you get integer answers like these then you know that the equation would have factored. But, if you do not like to factor, you can always use the quadratic formula. It will always work, even with quadratics that will not factor—like the next one.

Example 2   Solve $x^2 + 5x + 3 = 0$

$a = 1 \quad b = 5 \quad c = 3$ Identify a, b, and c.

$x = \dfrac{-(5) \pm \sqrt{(5)^2 - 4(1)(3)}}{2(1)}$ Plug into the formula.

$= \dfrac{-5 \pm \sqrt{25 - 12}}{2} = \dfrac{-5 \pm \sqrt{13}}{2}$

$x = \left\{ \dfrac{-5 + \sqrt{13}}{2} , \dfrac{-5 - \sqrt{13}}{2} \right\}$ The square root of 13 will not simplify, so it shows up in your answer.

Sometimes the equation is not in standard form. Always write the equation in standard form before you identify a, b, and c.

Example 3   Solve $33 = 5x + 2x^2$

$33 = 5x + 2x^2$ First, set the equation equal to zero. Write

$0 = 2x^2 + 5x - 33$ the equation in descending order.

$a = 2 \quad b = 5 \quad c = -33$ Identify a, b, and c.

$x = \dfrac{-5 \pm \sqrt{5^2 - 4(2)(-33)}}{2(2)}$ Plug the values for a, b, and c into the Quadratic equation.

$x = \dfrac{-5 \pm \sqrt{25 + 264}}{4} = \dfrac{-5 \pm \sqrt{289}}{4} = \dfrac{-5 \pm 17}{4}$

$x = \dfrac{-5 - 17}{4} = \dfrac{-22}{4} = \dfrac{-11}{2} = -5.5$ or $x = \dfrac{-5 + 17}{4} = \dfrac{12}{4} = 3$

$x = \{-5.5, 3\}$

1. $x^2 + 6x + 8 = 0$ 2. $y^2 + 5y = 24$ 3. $7 - 11z = 3z^2 + 8z - 33$

4. $50 + 2x^2 = 20x$ 5. $0 = x^2 + 4x - 7$ 6. $0 = 2x^2 + x - 5$

A14   ABSOLUTE VALUE EQUATIONS AND INEQUALITIES

When variables are included within absolute value signs in an equation, you must work the equation twice, once for the positive case and once for the negative case.

Example 1 $|x| = 3$

   $x = 3$ and $x = -3$ The solution set for x = {3, –3}.

Example 2 $|x + 5| = 7$
   $x + 5 = 7$ $x + 5 = -7$
   $x = 2$ and $x = -12$ The solution set for x = {2, –12}.

ABSOLUTE VALUES IN INEQUALITIES

Consider $|x| \le 3$. What integer values would make this inequality false? Clearly, {4, 5, 6...} would not satisfy the inequality. Neither would {...-6, -5, -4}. The integers in between these two sets will solve the inequality. So, {-3, -2, -1, 0, 1, 2, 3} is part of the solution set.

These seven values are only the integer solutions. The complete answer to $|x| \le 3$ would have to take into account all of the fractions and irrational numbers between 3 and -3. We would write the answer as (-3, 3). Note that this is the same notation used for ordered pairs. The only way to tell the two apart is by the context.

To solve this type of inequality algebraically, we must work the problem twice, just as we did with the absolute value equations in Examples 1 and 2 above. Recall that we work the equation once as it is written, but without the absolute value signs. The second time we work an equality, we introduce a negative sign. The procedure for working inequalities is similar. The only difference is that when a negative sign is introduced, the direction of the inequality sign must change.

Example 3 $3 \ge |x|$

         $3 \ge x$ Work the problem once without the absolute value signs.
AND $-3 \le x$ Work the problem a second time with a negative sign and a reversed inequality sign.

The final answer might be expressed in any of three ways:

Set notation $\{-3 \le x \le 3\}$

Interval notation $[-3, 3]$

Graphing

Note that the sign of the inequality was pointing towards the absolute value sign. Also note that the solution consists of one zone that runs from -3 to 3, inclusive. Suppose the sign pointed the other way?

Example 4 $5 \leq |x|$

$5 \leq x$ Work the problem once without the absolute value signs.

OR $-5 \geq x$ Work the problem a second time with a negative sign and a reversed inequality sign.

Again, the final answer might be expressed in three different ways:

Set notation $\{ x \leq -5 \cup x \geq 5 \}$

Interval notation $(-\infty, -5) \cup (5, \infty)$

Graphing

The symbol $\cup$ stands for "union." This means that the answer is one of the two sets described on either side of the $\cup$ symbol.

Note that the sign of the inequality was pointing away from the absolute value sign. Also note that the solution consists of two zones that run from $-\infty$ to -5 or from 5 to ∞, where ∞ stands for "infinity."

A14   Practice. Solve.

a. $|w + 3| = 6$ b. $|2x - 2| = 10$ c. $7 < |y - 3|$ d. $|z| - 2 < 0$

A15   LINEAR EQUATIONS IN TWO VARIABLES

A linear equation with one variable usually has one answer.

   x + 2 = 5   So, x = 3. There are no other solutions to this equation.

A linear equation with two variables has an infinite number of answers.

   x + y = 5   (2, 3) is an ordered pair that means x = 2 and y = 3

How many answers can you think of?

   . . .(–2, 7), (–1, 6), (0, 5), (1, 4), (2, 3), (3, 4), (4, 1), (5, 0), (6, –1), (7, –2) . . .

How about decimals?

   . . . (1.5, 3.5), (1.6, 3.4), (1.7, 3.3) . . .

Rather than write all of these answers out, we can represent the solutions with a line. Any point in our list is included in the line, and any point on the line will fit into the equation.

Slope is the direction of a line. The line on the graph below goes down one unit for every unit it goes to the right. It is said to have a slope of negative one. Slope is defined by the formula:

$$m = \frac{y_2 - y_1}{x_2 - x_1} = \frac{\Delta y}{\Delta x} = \frac{\text{RISE}}{\text{RUN}}$$

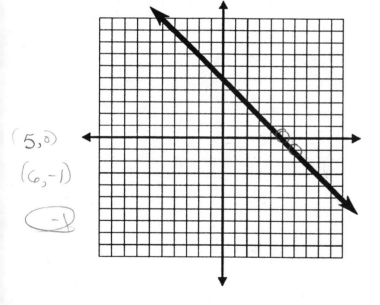

(5, 0)

(6, –1)

–1

Memorize the formula above. Slope is m. The small numbers after the x's and y's are called subscripts. Subscripts are used to tell one ordered pair from another. x_2 and y_2 come from point two and x_1 and y_1 come from point one. Δy , pronounced "delta y," is the change in y. Δy is sometimes called "rise" because it describes how much a line changes in the up and down direction. Δx, "delta x," is the change in x. Δx is called "run" because it describes how much a line changes from left to right. The change, or Δ, is found by subtracting the x and y values of one point from another point.   Slope is the change in y over the change in x, or rise over run.

Example 1   Find the slope of the line containing (7, 8) and (3, 5).

$$m = \frac{y_2 - y_1}{x_2 - x_1} = \frac{5 - 8}{3 - 7} = \frac{-3}{-4} = \frac{3}{4}$$

Remember that the *worst thing* that can ever happen in your life is to have zero in your denominator. If that situation occurs while you are computing the slope of a line, then what you have is an undefined slope. This happens with a vertical line.

Example 2   Find the slope of the line containing (2, 8) and (2, 5).

$$m = \frac{y_2 - y_1}{x_2 - x_1} = \frac{5 - 8}{2 - 2} = \frac{-3}{0} \quad \text{Undefined}$$

If a linear equation is solved for y, then the coefficient of x is the slope. So, to find the slope of any given equation, just solve for y.

Example 3   Find the slope of the line 2x + 3y = 6.

2x + 3y = 6

3y = -2x + 6

$$\frac{3y}{3} = \frac{-2x}{3} + \frac{6}{3}$$

$$y = \frac{-2}{3} x + 2$$

Move everything except the y term to the other side of the equation.

Divide by the coefficient of y.

Now you have the form y = mx + b. The coefficient of the x term is –2/3. Therefore, –2/3 is the slope.

Example 4   Graph.

$$y = \frac{-2}{3} x + 2$$

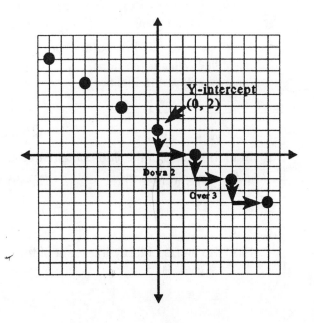

y = mx + b is called the **slope intercept** form of the line. It is the most useful form for graphing equations quickly.

The b term is where the line intersects the y–axis. Since 2 is the b term then the y-intercept is (0, 2).

The m coefficient gives the direction of the line. y = mx + b is all you need to graph a line. Just go to the intercept, then make the slope move down 2 and over 3. This will give you another point on the graph.

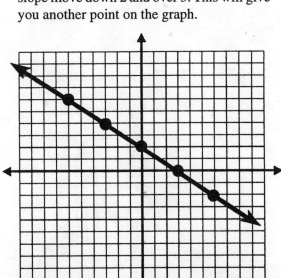

After you have found enough points, usually three, connect them, and you have a graph of the line.

57

Example 5　　4x − y = 8

Another way of graphing a line is to just make a chart and find ordered pairs that fit into the equation until you have enough points to make a graph. Each row in the chart means that the problem was worked again.

　　4x − y = 8　　　　Plug in values for x and solve for y.

x	y
0	−8
1	−4
2	0
3	4
4	8

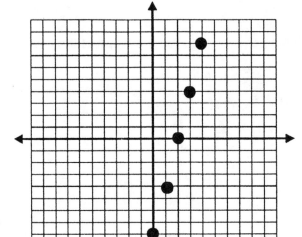

When you have enough points, connect them for a graph.

Is the slope of this line positive or negative? What is the slope? (answer below A15 Practice)

A15 Practice.

Find the slope of the line containing the given points.

1. (3, −5) and (−4, 7)　　　　2. (3, −5) and (3, 7)　　　　3. (3, −5) and (−4, −5)

Find the slope of the y-intercept of the line.
4. 5x − 3y = 9　　　　　　5. 2x = 3y + 3　　　　　　6. −4x − 7y = −9

Graph.
8. y = 3x　　9. 2x − 8y = 16　　10. x = 3y + 9　　7. Find the slope and y-intercept of the line on the graph below.

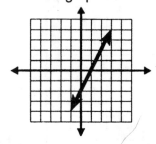

Answer to Example 5: positive $\dfrac{4}{1}$

A16   DISTANCE FORMULA IN THE PLANE

Pythagorean Theorem

$$a^2 + b^2 = c^2$$

Distance Formula

$$d = \sqrt{(x_2 - x_1)^2 + (y_2 - y_1)^2}$$

The distance formula in the plane is based on the Pythagorean Theorem. The distance formula is used to find the distance between two points in the plane.

Example 1   Find the distance between (4, -4) and (-2, 4)

$$d = \sqrt{(x_2 - x_1)^2 + (y_2 - y_1)^2}$$

$$d = \sqrt{(-2 - 4)^2 + (4 - (-4))^2}$$

$$d = \sqrt{(-6)^2 + (8)^2}$$

$$d = \sqrt{36 + 64}$$

$$d = \sqrt{100}$$

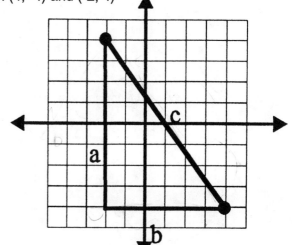

The Pythagorean Theorem can also be used to compute this distance.

$$a^2 + b^2 = c^2$$

$$8^2 + 6^2 = c^2$$

$$64 + 36 = c^2$$

$$100 = c^2$$

$$\sqrt{100} = \sqrt{c^2}$$

$$10 = c$$

a = the absolute value of the difference in the y values of the two points.

$$a = |4 - (-4)| = 8$$

b = the absolute value of the difference in the x values of the two points.

$$b = |(-2) - 4| = 6$$

A16   Practice.
Find the distance between the two points.

1. (0, 0), (5, 12)   2. (-1, 2), (3, 5)   3. (2, 7), (11, –5)

A17 GRAPHING CONICS (PARABOLAS, CIRCLES)

PARABOLAS

$$y = ax^2 + bx + c$$

Here is a four-step method for graphing parabolas.

Step 1.   When graphing equations of the form $y = ax^2 + bx + c$, the most important point is the **vertex**. This is where the parabola changes directions. The x value of the parabola can be found with this formula:

$$x = \frac{-b}{2a}$$

If this formula looks familiar, it should. It is the beginning of the quadratic formula. Once you find the x value, plug that into the original equation to find the corresponding y value.

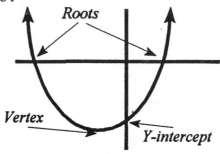

Step 2.   Find the y-intercept. Just plug in a 0 for x. The y-intercept will be (0, c).

Step 3.   Find the "roots" of the equation. The **roots** are another name for x-intercepts. Find the roots by factoring or the quadratic formula. This will give you either two, one, or no real answers.

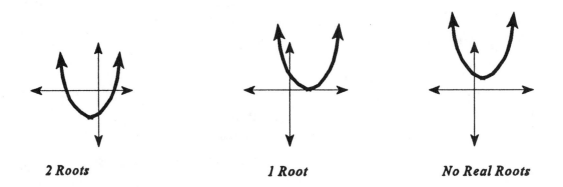

2 Roots   *1 Root*   *No Real Roots*

Step 4.   Connect the points. If ax^2 is positive, then the parabola will point up (Smiley Face ☺). If ax^2 is negative, the parabola will point down (Frowny Face ☹). If you need more points plug values into the equation and make a xy chart.

60

Example 1

   Graph y = x² - 2x -3

   This equation is in the form of $y = ax^2 + bx + c$. We know immediately that this is a parabola. Let's find the vertex, the y-intercept, and the roots so that we will have enough points to graph the equation.

$$x = \frac{-b}{2a} = \frac{-(-2)}{2(1)} = 1$$

1. Find the vertex.

$$y = (1)^2 - 2(1) - 3 = 1 - 2 - 3 = -4$$

$$\text{vertex } (1, -4)$$

$$y = (0)^2 - 2(0) - 3 = -3$$
$$y-\text{intercept } (0, -3)$$

2. Find the y-intercept.

$$0 = x^2 - 2x - 3$$
$$0 = (x - 3)(x + 1)$$
$$x = [3, -1]$$
$$\text{roots } (3, 0), \quad (-1, 0)$$

3. Find the roots.

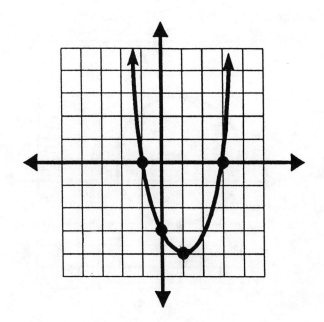

4. Now, plot the points and connect them to graph the parabola.

   (1, –4)

   (0, –3)

   (3, 0)

   (–1, 0)

CIRCLES

$$(x - h)^2 + (y - k)^2 = r^2$$

A circle is all of the points that are the same distance, r, the **radius**, from a particular point, called the **center**, in a plane. The circle formula is very similar to the distance formula. Circles are written in the form $(x - h)^2 + (y - k)^2 = r^2$, where (h, k) is the center of the circle and r is the radius.

Equation	Center	Radius
$(x - h)^2 + (y - k)^2 = r^2$	**(h, k)**	**r**
$(x - 3)^2 + (y + 5)^2 = 16$	(3, - 5)	4
$(x + 8)^2 + (y + 5)^2 = 25$	(-8, -5)	5

To graph a circle:

Step 1. Identify the center and the radius.

Step 2. Plot points North, South, East and West the specified distance away from the center. Add the radius to the y value of the center to get the North point. The x value for the North point will be the same as the centerpoint x value. Subtract to get the South point. Do the same with the x values to find the East point (add the radius to the centerpoint x value) and the West point (subtract). Use the centerpoint y value for the East and West points.

North (h, k+r)   South (h, k–r)
East   (h+r, k)   West (h–r, k)

Step 3. Connect the points in a smooth arc.

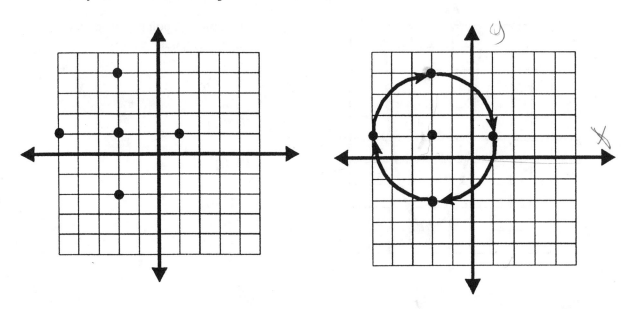

Example 1   Graph $(x + 2)^2 + (y - 1)^2 = 9$

1. The center is at (-2, 1). Remember to change the signs. The radius is $\sqrt{9}$, which equals 3.
2. By adding and subtracting 3 from the center (-2, 1), we find the values for the compass points: North (-2, 4), South (-2, -2), West (-5, 1), East (1, 1).
3. Now, connect the points in an arc.

A17   Practice.

Find the vertex, y-intercept, and roots of the parabolas.

1. $y = x^2 - 6x + 8$

2. $y = 4 - x^2$

3. $y = 2x^2 - 4x - 6$

Find the center, radius, and North, South, East, and West points of the circles.

4. $(x + 3)^2 + (y - 2)^2 = 4$

5. $x^2 + y^2 = 36$

6. $(x - 4)^2 + (y + 3)^2 = 4$

A18   GRAPHING SYSTEMS OF EQUATIONS

To graph a system of equations, just graph one of the equations and ignore the other. When that one is done, graph the other. Make sure that you know where they intersect. Because finding the exact intersection by graphing is tricky, sometimes you should remember that you can always find this intersection algebraically by elimination or substitution.

Example 1   Solve by graphing.

$x + 2y = 5$
$x - 2y = 1$

$x + 2y = 5$

x	y
1	2
2	1.5
3	1

$x - 2y = 1$

x	y
1	0
2	0.5
3	1

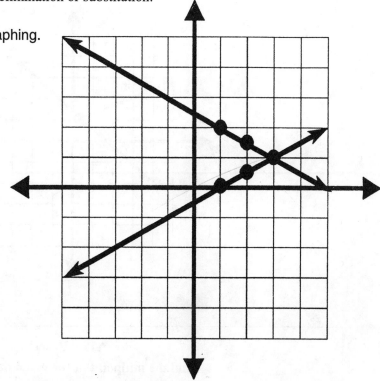

The solution for this system is (3, 1). (Just a reminder: substitution or elimination would have been a more efficient way of finding this intersection.)

A18   Practice.

Find the solution (the point of intersection) if such exists for each system.

1. $2x + 3y = 12$
   $4x - 2y = 8$

2. $y = 2x$
   $5x - 2y = 2$

3. $x + 3y = 2$
   $6y = 8 - 2x$

A19 MIDPOINT FORMULA

The **midpoint formula** will give the location of the center of a line segment. This point is the **midpoint**.

$$\left(\frac{x_2 + x_1}{2} \quad , \quad \frac{y_2 + y_1}{2}\right)$$

Another way to think about it is that the midpoint is the "average" point on the line.

Example 1

Find the midpoint of the line segment that has (3, 4) and (-4, -2) as endpoints.

$$\left(\frac{3 + -4}{2} \quad , \quad \frac{4 + -2}{2}\right) = \left(\frac{-1}{2}, \frac{2}{2}\right) = \left(\frac{-1}{2}, 1\right)$$

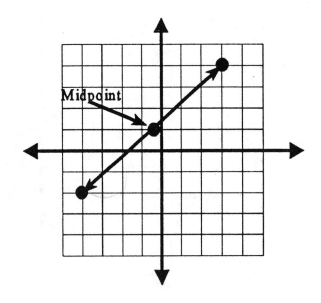

Midpoint

A19 Practice.

Find the midpoint of the given line segments.

1. (3, 8) and (-9, 2)

2. (-5, 7) and (-3, 2)

3. (0, 0) and (−10, 20)

4. (−8, 3) and (−9, 3)

ANSWERS TO PRACTICES

A1 Answers
1. -15
2. 0
3. -14
4. -6

A2 Answers
1. d
2. b
3. d
4. c

A3 Answers
1. $3x^5 + 3x^4 + 5x^3 - 3x^2 - 3x - 2$
2. $7x^5 - 2x^4 + 5x^3 - 12x^2 + 12x - 13$
3. $A^2 + 9A + 14$
4. $B^2 - 2B - 8$
5. $2C^2 - 5C - 12$
6. $8D^4 - 14D^3 - 23D^2 + 30D - 25$

A4 Answers
1. $(X + 7)(2X - 5)$
2. $(X - 5)^2$
3. $(X^2 + 9)(X + 3)(X - 3)$
4. Prime
5. $(a + 2b)(a - 3)$
6. $(A - 6)(A - 7)$
7. $(B - 4)(2B + 5)$
8. $2(2C + 5)(3C + 4)$
9. $2D(2D + 7)(3D - 5)$
10. $(X - 8)^2$
11. $3y(y + 3)^2$
12. $(A^4 + 16)(A^2 + 4)(A + 2)(A - 2)$
13. $4(b + 2c)(b - 2c)$
14. $(6c - 1)^2$

A5 Answers
1. $X = \{6, -6\}$
2. $X = \{0, 5\}$
3. $X = \{-2, 3\}$
4. $X = \{3, 4\}$
5. $X = \{-2, 3\}$
6. $A = \{6, 7\}$
7. No Solution
8. $X = \{-2, -3, 3\}$

A6 Answers
1. $s = \dfrac{A - \pi r^2}{\pi r}$
2. $l = \dfrac{p - 2w}{2}$
3. $x = \dfrac{yz}{y - z}$
4. $k = \dfrac{1}{4}$ $y = \dfrac{9}{2}$
5. $k = 2$ $y = 24$
6. $k = \frac{1}{3}$ $y = 8$

A7 Answers
a. $X = -25$
b. $Y = 11$
c. $A = 7.5$
d. $B = -9$
e. $C = 5$
f. $D = 16$

A8 Answers
1. K^8
2. $X^5 Y^5$
3. $M^{15} N^{20}$
4. 1

A9 Answers
1. $x \le 9$
2. $-1 > y$
3. $z \ge -2$
4. $c \le 2.5$

A10 Answers
1. $x \ne -4$
2. $y \ne 0$
3. $\dfrac{x^2 + 6}{2x}$
4. $\dfrac{x - 12}{(x + 2)(x + 3)(x - 2)}$
5. $\dfrac{(x + 5)(x + 3)}{(x + 1)(x - 5)}$
6. 1

A11 Answers
1. $a^2 b^2$
2. $\dfrac{4}{9a^2}$
3. $\dfrac{y^4 d^6}{9x^6 c^{10}}$
4. $16a$
5. $\dfrac{25}{9a^2}$
6. $\dfrac{1}{s^5}$

A12 Answers
1. $(7, 6)$
2. $(2.5, .5)$
3. $(1, -1)$
4. Parallel, no solution

ANSWERS TO PRACTICES (CONTINUED)

A13 Answers
1. x = {−2, −4}
2. y = {3, −8}
3. z = {⁵/₃, −8}
4. x = {5}
5. $-2 \pm \sqrt{11}$
6. $\dfrac{-1 \pm \sqrt{41}}{4}$

A14 Answers
a. w = {−9, 3}
b. x = {−4, 6}
c. (−∞, −4) U (10, ∞)
d. −2 < z < 2

A15 Answers
1. m = −12/7
2. m = undefined
3. m = 0
4. m = 5/3   b = −3
5. m = 2/3   b = −1
6. m = −4/7   b = 9/7
7. m = 2   b = −2

8.
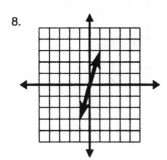

9.
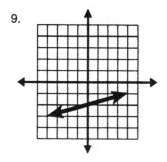

10.
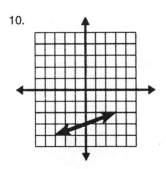

A16 Answers
1. 13
2. 5
3. 15

A17 Anwers
1. Vertex (3, −1), Y-int (0, 8)
    Roots (4,0), (2, 0)
2. Vertex (0, 4), Y-int (0, 4)
    Roots (−2,0), (2, 0)
3. Vertex (1, −8), Y-int (0, −6)
    Roots (3,0), (-1, 0)
4. Center (−3, 2) radius 2, North (−3, 4),
    South (−3, 0), East (−1, 2), West (−5, 2)
5. Center (0, 0) radius 6, North (0, 6),
    South (0, −6), East (6, 0), West (−6, 0)
6. Center (4, −3) radius 2, North (4, −1),
    South (4, −5), East (6, −3), West (2, −3)

A18 Answers
1. (3, 2)
2. (2, 4)
3. No solution

A19 Answers
1. (−3, 5)
2. (−4, 4.5)
3. (−5, 10)
4. (−8.5, 3)

CHAPTER FOUR

COLLEGE ALGEBRA

About 80% of the College Algebra portion of the **COMPASS** exam is concerned with functions, exponents, and complex numbers. The remaining 20% covers a wide variety of topics including: sequences and series, factorials, matrices, systems of equations, and roots of polynomials. Consequently, this chapter is divided into four sections corresponding to the weight **COMPASS** places on them.

C1 **Functions** (About 40%)

C2 **Exponents** (About 25%)

C3 **Complex numbers** (About 15%)

Other topics not included in this book (About 20%): arithmetic and geometric sequences and series, factorials, matrices (basic operations, equations and determinants), systems of linear equations in three or more variables, and logic and proof techniques.

C1 FUNCTIONS

Functions are extremely important during the freshman year of college mathematics. An understanding of functions is essential for calculus. But before we understand functions we must first understand what a correspondence is.

ORDERED PAIRS (DOMAIN, RANGE)

An ordered pair (x, y) is a partnership between two sets. The first is always the domain. The second is always the range. Notice how domain and range are in alphabetical order. Domain is usually x, and range is usually y.

CORRESPONDENCE

A correspondence is a rule that assigns one element from the domain to another element from the range. For example:

Two sets where D = the domain and R = the range: D = { a, b, c, d} R = {1, 3, 5, 8}

Let F be a correspondence, a rule, that links D and R. F tells what happens when we input an element from the domain and which element we end up with from the range.

$F = \{(a, 1), (b, 5), (c, 3), (d, 8)\}$

(a, 1) is an ordered pair. It tells us that for an input "a" that "1" is the output. "a" and "1" are partners. The order they occur in tells us which is from the domain and which is from the range. Now if we have an input of d into the correspondence F we know that the output will be 8. This is the way we write an input of d and an output of 8:

$F(d) = 8$

Read this as, "F of d is 8." What is $f(g)$? Look at the domain. There is no "g"; therefore, the mathematical way to answer this type of question is to say that "g" is not in the domain of F.

FUNCTION

A **function** is a special type of correspondence that assigns exactly one member of the range to a member of the domain.

Function	Not a Function
$G = \{(a,1), (b, 2), (c, 3), (d, 2)\}$	$H = \{(a,1), (b, 2), (a, 3), (d, 2)\}$

- 2 can occur twice as output
- Ranges can repeat with new partners

- a is listed with two domain elements
- Domains cannot repeat with new partners

A **function** is a relation in which no two ordered pairs have the same first coordinate with different second coordinates.

VERTICAL LINE TEST

If the graph of a relation is intersected more than once by any vertical line, that relation is not a function.

Function   **Not a Function, fails the vertical line test**

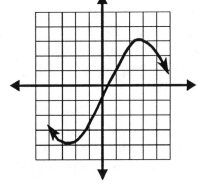 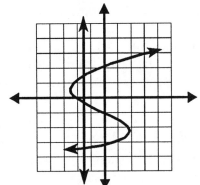

FUNCTIONAL NOTATION

In functional notation $y = 2x + 3$ could be written as $F(x) = 2x + 3$. $F(x)$ does **not** mean multiply $F \cdot x$. $F(x)$ does mean plug in an x value and find the y value. $F(x)$ is the same as y.

Functional notation is shorthand for writing down instructions about algebra.

For example,   Find the value of y when $y = 2x + 3$ and $x = 3$.
Can be written: $F(3) = 2x + 3$

When working with functions it is often useful to make an x-y chart. The headings of these charts can be different, but they all mean the same thing.

Input	Output
Independent	Dependent
x	F(x)
x	y
0	3
2	7
8	19

$F(x) = 2x + 3$

Different Possible Headings that mean exactly the same thing.

For each row, pick an x value and then calculate the F(x).

DIFFERENT TYPES OF FUNCTIONS

POLYNOMIAL FUNCTIONS

There are actually an infinite number of different types of polynomial functions. We will consider the first four types: constant, linear, quadratic, and cubic.

CONSTANT FUNCTIONS $\boxed{F(x) = c}$

A constant function always stays the same no matter what the input is. For example:

$F(x) = 3$

Input	Output
x	y
x	F(x)
3	3
2	3
1	3
0	3
−1	3
−2	3

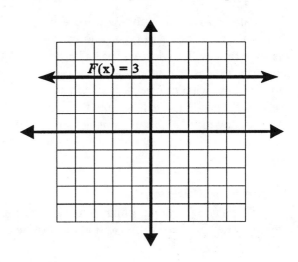

LINEAR FUNCTIONS $\boxed{F(x) = mx + b}$

(See also A7 and A16)

The simplest type of linear function is the constant function we just talked about. The slope of a constant function is 0. Usually when we think of linear functions we think of lines with slopes other than zero. $3x + 2y = 12$ is a linear equation in standard form. If we solve for y we get the equation into the slope intercept form of the line, $y = mx + b$. Recall that the coefficient of the x variable, m, is called the slope. Slope tells exactly the direction a line will take. Now, if we just replace y with functional notation, we will have a linear function.

Example 1   Write $3x + 2y = 12$ as a function.

$3x + 2y = 12$
$2y = -3x + 12$
$$\frac{2y}{2} = \frac{-3x}{2} + \frac{12}{2}$$
$$y = \frac{-3x}{2} + 6$$
$$G(x) = \frac{-3x}{2} + 6$$

Linear functions are always straight lines when graphed. Calculate at least three points to graph.

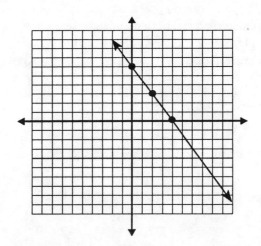

x	G(x)
0	6
2	3
4	0

69

QUADRATIC FUNCTIONS
(See also A14 and A18)

Quadratic functions are second degree polynomials. The most important point of a quadratic function is the vertex. The vertex is the point where the parabola will change direction. This is also where the maximum or minimum value of the parabola will occur.

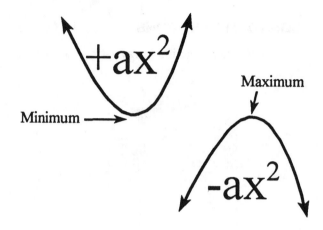

$$F(x) = ax^2 + bx + c$$

Direction

Parabolas always change direction. Part of the time they will go up and part of the time they will go down. The "a" of the ax^2 term decides the direction of the function and how wide or narrow it is. If ax^2 is positive, the parabola will turn up on the ends, like a smiley face [+, ☺]. If ax^2 is negative, the parabola will turn down on the ends, like a frowny face [–, ☹].

Maximum and Minimum

The maximum or minimum of any quadratic always occurs at the vertex. In section A17 of the previous chapter, we saw that to find the x value of a vertex we can use the formula:

$$x = \frac{-b}{2a}$$

This formula only gives you half of the vertex. To find the y value of the vertex, evaluate the quadratic at the x value given by the above formula. With this information you will be able to answer questions like the following:

Example 1

On which interval does the maximum value of $f(x) = -2x^2 + 16x - 14$ occur?

a) $(-\infty, -7)$
b) $(-7, -1)$
c) $(-1, 1)$
d) $(1, 7)$
e) $(7, \infty)$

First identify a and b. Remember the equation for a quadratic function: $f(x) = ax^2 + bx + c$. In this example, $a = -2$ and $b = 16$. Now use the vertex formula to identify the x value of the maximum point of the parabola.

$$x = \frac{-b}{2a} = \frac{-16}{2(-2)} = \frac{16}{4} = 4$$

The value $x = 4$ falls in the interval $(1, 7)$, so the answer is *d*.

Width

The smaller the value of a, the wider the parabola. As the absolute value of a increases, the parabola becomes more narrow.

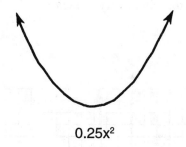
0.25x²

1x²

4x²

Y–Intercept

The y–intercept occurs when x = 0. In other words, the y–intercept is located at (0, c).

Roots or Zeros

The x–intercepts, or roots, occur when the value of the polynomial is zero. A second degree polynomial can have none, one, or at most two real roots. If F(3) = 0, then 3 is a root of the polynomial.

We already have two methods of finding the zeros of a quadratic equation.

- Factoring (section A4)
- The quadratic formula (section A14)

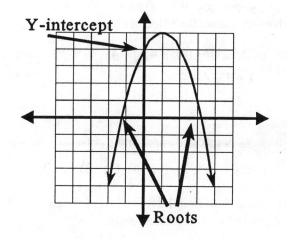

CUBIC FUNCTIONS

$$F(x) = ax^3 + bx^2 + cx + d$$

A cubic equation is a third degree polynomial. If a is positive, the graph will start low and end high (from left to right). If a is negative, then the graph will start high and end low.

$+ax^3$

$-ax^3$

The y–intercept is located at (0, d). To find the zeros try to factor the equation.

CUBIC FUNCTIONS, continued

Example 1

Graph H(x) = x³ + x² − 4x − 4

First, find the zeros. Next, set the polynomial equal to zero. Finally, try to factor.

$0 = x^3 + x^2 - 4x - 4$

$0 = (x^3 + x^2) + (-4x - 4)$

$0 = x^2(x + 1) + (-4)(x + 1)$

$0 = (x + 1)(x^2 - 4)$

$0 = (x + 1)(x + 2)(x - 2)$

$x = \{-1, -2, 2\}$

Therefore, the roots are:

(−1, 0), (−2, 0) and (2, 0)

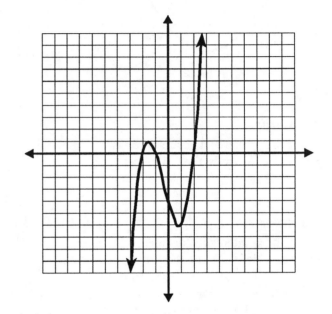

The y–intercept is (0, d) or (0, −4).
Now calculate the value of F(1):

$F(1) = (1)^3 + (1)^2 - 4(1) - 4$

$= 1 + 1 - 4 - 4$

$= -6$

Plot the points and connect the dots.

(−2, 0), (−1, 0), (0, −4), (1, −6), (2, 0)

If you cannot find the roots, just make an x–y chart, plug in several values, plot the points on a graph, and then connect the points.

DOMAIN

Domain, as we saw earlier, is the input, or the source, for the function. In polynomial functions the input can be any real number. There is never any danger with what you input into polynomial functions. In other words, x can be anything. Mathematically, this type of domain can be written:

$$\{x | x \in \mathbb{R}\}$$

Read this as "x such that x is an element of the real numbers." This is another way of saying x can be anything.

Often questions on the test will begin with a phrase, "For all x ≠..." This phrase indicates you are working with a problem that has a restriction on the domain. The problem probably contains a rational expression. For the most part, you can ignore the phrase and just concentrate on the subject and verb of the question.

RATIONAL FUNCTIONS

The word "rational" is usually associated with fractions in mathematics. The name "rational function" implies a function that involves fractions. **Rational functions** can be defined as the quotient of two polynomial functions. In other words, one polynomial divided by another. This means that a variable will be located in the denominator. Before we allow variables into a denominator we must be aware of a very important fact: having a zero in the denominator is the *worst* thing that can happen in your entire life!

The point is that by allowing variables into the denominator we might sometimes, just by accident, allow a zero to slip into the denominator. That would be so bad that we must constantly guard against this occurrence. When someone, or some situation, tries to place a zero in your denominator, you must not hesitate, identify the offending element, the one that would force a zero in the denominator, and declare, "This element is not in the domain of this function!" For example, consider the function K(x):

$$K(x) = \frac{2x + 5}{x + 3}$$

If x = –3 the numerator would evaluate to be –1. But the denominator would be 0. This must *never* be allowed to happen. So we say x ≠ –3. Or, more formally, we can say:

$$\{x | x \in \mathbb{R}, x \neq -3\}$$

Read this as "x such that x is a member of the real numbers, x cannot equal negative three." The value of K(–3) is undefined.

OPERATIONS ON POLYNOMIALS +, –, x, ÷

We can add, subtract, multiply, and divide polynomials in a straightforward manner.

Example 1   Let F(x) = 2x + 5 and G(x) = 3x – 6.
Find F(x) + G(x). Find F(x) – G(x). Find F(x)G(x). Find F(x)/G(x).

F(x) + G(x) = (2x + 5) + (3x – 6) = 2x + 5 + 3x – 6 = 5x – 1

F(x) – G(x) = (2x + 5) – (3x – 6) = 2x + 5 – 3x + 6 = –x + 11

F(x)G(x) = (2x + 5)(3x – 6) = 6x² – 12x + 15x – 30 = 6x² + 3x – 30

$$F(x) \div G(x) = \frac{(2x + 5)}{(3x - 6)}$$

Also note that we can write the sum, difference, product and quotient of functions in two different ways:

F(x) + G(x) = (F + G)(x)
F(x) – G(x) = (F – G)(x)
F(x)G(x) = FG(x)
F(x)/G(x) = (F/G)(x)

When we found F(x)/G(x) we placed a variable in the denominator so we must place a restriction on the domain. To find the restriction set G(x) equal to 0.

$$G(x) = 3x - 6 = 0$$
$$3x = 6$$
$$x = 2$$

So the domain of F(x)/G(x) is $\{x | x \in \mathbb{R}, x \neq 2\}$.

COMPOSITE FUNCTIONS

Another way of combining functions is to put one inside the other. In other words, one function becomes the variable for the other function.

Let $f(x) = 4x - 5$ and $g(x) = x^2 + 2$.

Now let's put $g(x)$ inside of $f(x)$:

$$f(g(x)) = 4(g(x)) - 5 = 4(x^2 + 2) - 5 = 4x^2 + 8 - 5 = 4x^2 + 3$$

The composition of functions can be written two different ways.

$$f(g(x)) = f \circ g\ (x)$$
$$g(f(x)) = g \circ f\ (x)$$

Note: $f \circ g\ (x) \neq g \circ f\ (x)$

$$f \circ g\ (x) = 4(g(x)) - 5 = 4(x^2 + 2) - 5 = 4x^2 + 8 - 5 = 4x^2 + 3$$
$$g \circ f\ (x) = (4x - 5)^2 + 2 = (16x^2 - 40x + 25) + 2 = 16x^2 - 40x + 27$$

Application

Given a Fahrenheit temperature, this function will produce an equivalent Celsius:

$$C(F) = \frac{5}{9}\ (F - 32)$$

Given a Celsius temperature, this function will produce an equivalent Kelvin:

$$K(C) = C + 273$$

Find a function $H(F)$ that will produce a Kelvin reading given a Fahrenheit temperature.

Example 1 $H(F) = K \circ C(F) = K\left(\dfrac{5}{9}\ (F - 32)\right) = \dfrac{5}{9}(f - 32) + 273$

INVERSE OF A FUNCTION

An **inverse** of a function swaps inputs and outputs. For example, if the function G is defined to be $G = \{(a, 1), (b, 2), (c, 3)\}$, then the inverse must be $G^{-1} = \{(1, a), (2. b), (3, c)\}$. Notice the notation for the inverse, $G^{-1}(x)$ looks like G raised to the negative one power. It actually reads as "the inverse of G of x."

To find the inverse function of a function (if it exists) follow this four-step procedure.

Step 1.   Replace $f(x)$ with y.

Step 2.   Swap x and y.

Step 3.   Solve for y.

Step 4.   Replace y with $f^{-1}(x)$.

Example1   Find the inverse of f(x) = 2x + 3.

$$f(x) = 2x + 3$$
$$y = 2x + 3$$

1. Replace f(x) with y.

$$x = 2y + 3$$

2. Swap x and y.

$$x - 3 = 2y$$
$$\frac{x - 3}{2} = \frac{2y}{2}$$

3. Solve for y.

$$\frac{x - 3}{2} = y$$
$$f^{-1} = \frac{x - 3}{2}$$

4. Replace y with f⁻¹(x).

These two charts show a few values for the function and its inverse. From the chart, notice that when x = 0, then f(x) = 3. Also notice that if x = 3, then f⁻¹(x) = 0. The inverse of a function will return the original input.

x	f(x)
0	3
1	5
2	7

x	f⁻¹(x)
3	0
5	1
7	2

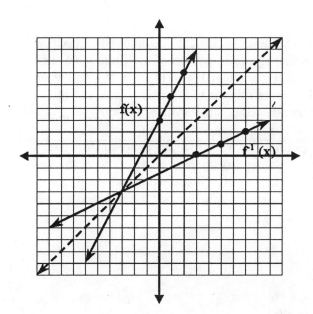

Graphs of inverses are reflections across the line y = x. If a function intersects its inverse the intersection must be on the line y = x.

The inverses of some functions are not functions themselves. These relations that are not functions will fail the vertical line test. For the inverse of a function to produce another function it must be what is called a one–to–one function. A function is one–to–one if for every input there is a different output. The easiest way to tell if a function is one–to–one is with the horizontal line test.

To the right is a graph of the equation g(x) = x² + 6x + 5 and its inverse correspondence; notice that g(x) fails the horizontal line test, therefore, the inverse of g(x) does not pass the vertical line test. This inverse correspondence is not a function.

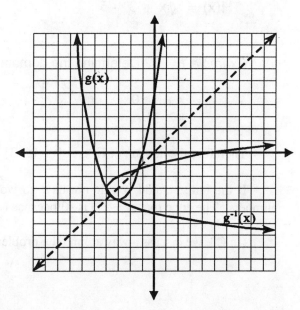

RADICAL FUNCTIONS

Radical functions are functions that have variables inside radicals. For example:

$$F(x) = \sqrt{x}$$

x	F(x)
0	0
1	1
4	2
9	3

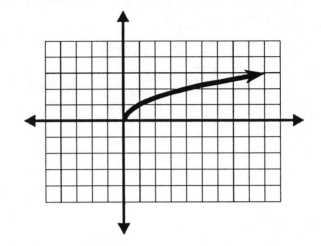

Notice that there is only one arrow on the drawing of the function. This is because the graph only extends in one direction.

DOMAIN OF A RADICAL FUNCTION

What is the square root of –25? It cannot be 5 because 5 • 5 = 25. It cannot be –5 because (–5) • (–5) = 25. It has to be a number that, when you square it, you get –25. There is no such number in the real number system, because when a positive is squared $(+)^2 = (+)(+) = (+)$. And when a negative is squared $(-)^2 = (-)(-) = (+)$. Since there is no solution to negatives inside radicals in the real number system, we say that negatives are not allowed in the domain of radicals.

If the very *worst* thing that can happen in your life is have a zero in the denominator, then a very distant second is to have a negative radicand. So anytime there is a radical with an even number index we must guard against the radicand becoming negative, just as we would guard against zeros in the denominator. To determine the domain of a radical function, set the radicand greater than or equal to zero, and then solve.

$$H(x) = \sqrt{x + 3} - 5$$

Example 1   Determine the domain of H(x).

$$x + 3 \geq 0$$
$$x \geq -3$$

Therefore the domain of H(x) is $\{x | x \geq -3\}$.

If the index is odd you do not have to worry about negatives, since the domain is all real numbers. The cube root of (–27) is –3 because (–3)(–3)(–3) = –27.

(In C3, we discuss a way around the problem of negative radicands.)

Example 2   Graph $g(x) = \sqrt{x+4} - 3$.

The domain is $\{x|x \geq -4\}$, so start computing values at $x = -4$.

x	g(x)
-4	-3
-3	-2
0	-1
5	0
12	1

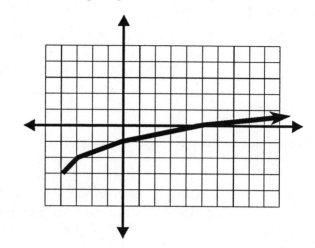

C1 Practice.

1.   On which interval does the maximum value of $h(x) = -x^2 + 8x + 15$ occur?   a. $(-5, -3)$ b. $(-3, -1)$ c. $(3, 5)$ d. $(5, 7)$ e. $(1, 3)$

2.   Let $f(x) = x^2 + 4x + 4$ and $g(x) = 2x - 7$. Find the following:

   a) $(f + g)(x)$

   b) $(f - g)(x)$

   c) $(f)(g)(x)$

   d) $(f/g)(x)$

   e) $f \circ g(x)$

   f) $g \circ f(x)$

3.   If $y = 10x - 20$ and $z = 3y - 8$, find an expression for z in terms of x.

4.   If $H(x)$ contains the point $(3, 7)$ then $H^{-1}(x)$ must contain the point _____.

5.   What is the domain of each of these functions?

   a) $f(x) = \dfrac{7}{2x + 6}$

   b) $g(x) = \sqrt{x + 8} - 7$

(*Answers* to all practices in Chapter Four are found on p. 86.)

C2 EXPONENTS *(see also A8)*

RATIONAL EXPONENTS

A rational exponent is a fraction used as an exponent. Rational exponents give us a different notation for writing radical expressions.

$$\sqrt{a} = a^{\frac{1}{2}} \qquad \sqrt[3]{b^2} = b^{\frac{2}{3}} \qquad \sqrt[y]{c^x} = c^{\frac{x}{y}}$$

The index of the radical becomes the denominator of the rational exponent. The regular exponent is the numerator.

The basics of exponents have been discussed in A8 and A12. The same rules apply for rational exponents. Below you will see a review of the rules with integer exponents followed by an example with rational exponents.

PRODUCT RULE OF EXPONENTS

Example 1

$$a^4 \bullet a^3 = a^{4+3} = a^7$$

When **multiplying** like bases, **add** the exponents.
(Multiplication becomes addition)

Example 2

$$a^{\frac{2}{3}} \bullet a^{\frac{1}{2}} = a^{\left(\frac{2}{3} + \frac{1}{2}\right)} = a^{\left(\frac{4}{6} + \frac{3}{6}\right)} = a^{\frac{7}{6}}$$

Recall that when adding fractions you must find a common denominator.

QUOTIENT RULE OF EXPONENTS

Example 1

When **dividing** like bases, **subtract** exponents. (Division becomes subtraction)

$$\frac{b^8}{b^5} = b^{8-5} = b^3$$

Example 2

Requires a common denominator.

$$\frac{b^{\frac{3}{4}}}{b^{\frac{1}{5}}} = b^{\left(\frac{3}{4} - \frac{1}{5}\right)} = b^{\left(\frac{15}{20} - \frac{4}{20}\right)} = b^{\frac{11}{20}}$$

ZERO EXPONENT RULE

$$C^0 = 1 \qquad \text{Anything (except zero) raised to the zero power is 1.}$$

Example 1

$$\frac{c^{\frac{2}{5}}}{c^{\frac{2}{5}}} = c^{\left(\frac{2}{5} - \frac{2}{5}\right)} = c^{\left(\frac{0}{5}\right)} = c^0 = 1$$

THE POWER RULE OF EXPONENTS

Example 1 $\qquad (D^4)^3 = D^{4 \cdot 3} = D^{12}$

When taking a power to a power, multiply the exponents.
(Power to a Power—exponents become multiplication)

$$\left(d^{\frac{2}{3}}\right)^{\frac{1}{2}} = d^{\left(\frac{2}{3} \cdot \frac{1}{2}\right)} = d^{\left(\frac{1}{3}\right)} \qquad \text{No need for a common denominator.}$$

Example 2

Translating radical expressions into rational exponential expressions gives us a familiar set of rules (adding fractions) to apply when multiplying unlike radicals.

$$\sqrt{a} \cdot \sqrt[3]{a} = a^{\frac{1}{2}} \cdot a^{\frac{1}{3}} = a^{\left(\frac{1}{2} + \frac{1}{3}\right)} = a^{\left(\frac{3}{6} + \frac{2}{6}\right)} = a^{\frac{5}{6}} = \sqrt[6]{a^5}$$

Example 3

Once you find a common denominator you can go back to radical notation.

$$\sqrt[3]{a} \cdot \sqrt[4]{b} = a^{\frac{1}{3}} \cdot b^{\frac{1}{4}} = a^{\frac{4}{12}} \cdot b^{\frac{3}{12}} = \sqrt[12]{a^4 b^3}$$

EXPONENTIAL FUNCTIONS

Exponential functions are functions that have a variable in the exponent.

Consider $F(x) = 2^x$. When graphing exponential functions, try using 3, 2, 1, 0, –1, –2, –3 as the domain to get you started.

x	F(x)
3	8
2	4
1	2
0	1
–1	$^1/_2$
–2	$^1/_4$
–3	$^1/_8$

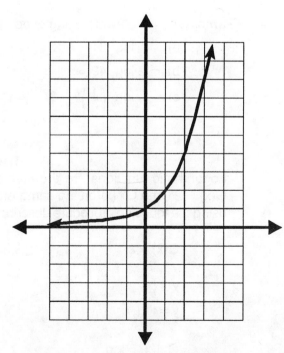

Notice that F(–1) is the reciprocal of F(1), and F(2) is the reciprocal of F(–2), and so forth. When graphing exponential functions by just inputting values into the function, it is important to use enough points to see the true character of the line.

LOGARITHMIC FUNCTIONS

$$\log_5 25 = 2$$

Read this as, "log base 5 of 25 is 2." One way to think about it is, "What exponent do I use on 5 to get 25? 2." The logarithm on the left side is equal to the exponent on the right. That makes a logarithm an exponent.

THREE COOL FACTS ABOUT LOGARITHMIC FUNCTIONS

Logarithmic functions can be intimidating, but just remember these three facts:

Fact #1 $a^b = c$ is the same as $\log_a c = b$

Fact #2   logarithmic functions are the inverses of exponential functions.

Fact #3   A logarithm is an exponent and follows the same rules.

Fact #1

The fact that $a^b = c$ is the same as $\log_a c = b$ is just a definition. You *must* commit it to memory; then you can apply it to different situations. This will allow you to rewrite exponential form to logarithmic form and vice versa.

Example 1   Rewrite using logarithmic notation.

    a) $6^2 = 36$ $\log_6 36 = 2$

    b) $x^3 = 64$ $\log_x 64 = 3$

    c) $1.5^4 = 5.0625$ $\log_{1.5} 5.0625 = 4$

Notice that each time you convert to logarithms, the base becomes the small number beside the word "log." The exponent goes off by itself to the other side of the equation. The answer to the exponential becomes the argument of the logarithmic.

Example 2   Rewrite using exponential notation.

    a) $\log_3 81 = 4$ $3^4 = 81$

    b) $\log_7 49 = 2$ $7^2 = 49$

    c) $\log_2 \left(\dfrac{1}{8} \right) = -3$ $2^{-3} = \dfrac{1}{8}$

Fact #2

Logarithmic functions are the inverse of exponential functions. Consider $G(x) = 2^x$ and $G^{-1}(x)$ on the same graph. First, let's find the inverse of $G(x)$ using the four step procedure described at the end of C1 for finding an inverse.

$G(x) = 2^x$		
$y = 2^x$	**Step 1.**	Replace $G(x)$ with y.
$x = 2^y$	**Step 2.**	Swap x and y.
$y = \log_2 x$	**Step 3.**	Solve for y by converting to a logarithm.
$G^{-1}(x) = \log_2 x$	**Step 4.**	Replace y with $G^{-1}(x)$.

x	G(x)
3	8
2	4
1	2
0	1
−1	$1/2$
−2	$1/4$
−3	$1/8$

x	G⁻¹(x)
8	3
4	2
2	1
1	0
$1/2$	−1
$1/4$	−2
$1/8$	−3

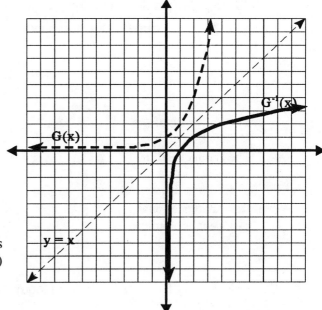

Notice that the inputs and the outputs have swapped, and that the graph of $G^{-1}(x)$ is a reflection of G(x) in the line y = x.

Fact #3

A logarithm is an exponent and therefore follows the same rules as exponents. This leads to the properties of logarithms that are associated with the rules about exponents.

PROPERTY 1: **The Product Rule** $\boxed{\log_a (M \bullet N) = \log_a M + \log_a N}$

Example 3 $\log_2 (4 \bullet 8) = \log_2 4 + \log_2 8 = 2 + 3 = 5$
$\log_2 (4 \bullet 8) = \log_2 32 = 5$

PROPERTY 2: **The Power Rule** $\boxed{\log_a M^p = p \bullet \log_a M}$

Example 4 $\log_2 4^3 = 3 \bullet \log_2 4 = 3 \bullet 2 = 6$
$\log_2 4^3 = \log_2 64 = 6$

PROPERTY 3: **The Quotient Rule** $\boxed{\log_a \left(\dfrac{M}{N}\right) = \log_a M - \log_a N}$

Example 5 $\log_2 \left(\dfrac{32}{8}\right) = \log_2 32 - \log_2 8 = 5 - 3 = 2$

$$\log_2 \left(\dfrac{32}{8}\right) = \log_2 4 = 2$$

PROPERTY 4: $\boxed{\log_a a^x = x}$

Example 6 $\log_2 2^x = ?$

Apply the Power Rule:

$\log_2 2^x = x \bullet \log_2 2$

Again, using the Power Rule ($\log_a M^p = p \bullet \log_a M$), we know that $\log_2 2 = 1$. If we plug that into $x \bullet \log_2 2$, we get:

$x \bullet (1) = x$ So, $\log_2 2^x = x$.

Using these properties, logarithmic expressions can be written in a variety of ways.

Example 7   Express as a single logarithm.

$$\frac{2}{3} \log_a X + 4 \log_a Y - 3 \log_a Z =$$

1. The Power Rule.

$$\log_a X^{\frac{2}{3}} + \log_a Y^4 - \log_a Z^3 =$$

2. The Product and the Quotient Rule.

$$\log_a \frac{X^{\frac{2}{3}} Y^4}{Z^3} =$$

3. Rewrite the rational exponent as a radical.

$$\log_a \frac{Y^4 \sqrt[3]{X^2}}{Z^3}$$

Example 8   Express in terms of logarithms.

1. Rewrite radicals as rational exponents and simplify.

$$\log_a \sqrt[4]{\frac{x^8}{y^4 z^3}} = \log_a \frac{x^{\frac{8}{4}}}{y^{\frac{4}{4}} z^{\frac{3}{4}}} = \log_a \frac{x^2}{y \, z^{\frac{3}{4}}} =$$

2. Quotient Rule.

$$\log_a x^2 - \log_a y - \log_a z^{\frac{3}{4}} =$$

3. Power Rule.

$$2\log_a x - \log_a y - \frac{3}{4} \log_a z$$

C2   Practice.

1. Simplify.

$$a^{\frac{2}{5}} \cdot a^{\frac{1}{6}}$$

2. Simplify.

$$\frac{b^{\frac{3}{5}}}{b^{\frac{2}{3}}}$$

3. Simplify.

$$\left(c^{\frac{2}{5}}\right)^{\frac{3}{4}}$$

4. Simplify.

$$\sqrt[4]{a^3} \cdot \sqrt[3]{a}$$

5. Simplify.

$$\sqrt[3]{b^2} \cdot \sqrt[5]{2}$$

6. Express as a single logarithm.

$$\frac{1}{4} \log_a x - \frac{3}{4} \log_a y$$

7. Express in terms of logarithms.

$$\log_a \sqrt[3]{\frac{x^{12} y^6}{z}}$$

C3 COMPLEX NUMBERS

IMAGINARY NUMBERS

$$\sqrt{-1} = i$$

$$(\sqrt{-1})^2 = -1$$

$$i^2 = -1$$

Before we can have **complex numbers** we need **imaginary numbers**. The number i is defined to be the square root of negative 1.

The square root of -1 squared is -1.

Therefore, i squared is -1.

AUTOMATICS INVOLVING i

   • Whenever you have a negative inside a radical, the next turn you will have an i outside the radical and no more negative inside.

   • Whenever you have an i^2, the next turn you will have a -1 and no i.

POWERS OF i

   Memorize the first four: 1, i, -1, - i

Powers of i
$i^0 = 1$
$i^1 = i$
$i^2 = -1$
$i^3 = (i)^2(i) = -i$

more powers of i

$i^4 = (i)^2(i)^2 = (-1)(-1) = 1$

$i^5 = i^4 i = i$

$i^6 = i^4 i^2 = i^2 = -1$

$i^7 = i^4 \cdot i^3 = -i$

   Because the powers of i repeat every fourth time, finding values like i^{66} (i to the 66th power) is easy. To find the value of i raised to some power, divide the power by 4. The remainder is the new exponent. So if the exponent were 66, you would divide by 4, the remainder would be 2 and the new exponent would be 2. Then refer to the powers of i chart. i^2 is -1. Therefore $i^{66} = i^2 = -1$.

   Example 1   What is i^{27} ?

   Divide 27 by 4 and you get 6 with a remainder of 3.
   So, the answer should be i³, which equals - i.
   $(i^4)^6(i^3) = (1)^6(-i) = -i$

COMPLEX NUMBERS

   A complex number is any number that can be written in "a + bi" form. The first part "a" is the real part. The second part "bi" is called the imaginary part.

ADDITION AND SUBTRACTION

When adding or subtracting complex numbers, just drop the parentheses and combine like terms. Write your final answer in "a + bi" form.

Example 2   Add.

$(3 + 2i) + (4 - 8i) = 3 + 2i + 4 - 8i = 7 - 6i$

Example 3   Subtract.

$(5 + 6i) - (7 - 8i) = 5 + 6i - 7 + 8i = -2 + 14i$

Be careful to distribute the negative sign.

MULTIPLICATION

Multiplication is straightforward except you must substitute a (-1) for any i^2. Write your final answer in "a + bi" form.

Example 4   Multiply.

a) $4i \bullet 5 = 20i = 0 + 20i$

b) $3i \bullet 8i = 24i^2 = -24 = -24 + 0i$

c) $3i(5 + 6i) = 15i + 18i^2 = 15i - 18 = -18 + 15i$

d) $(3 + 2i)(4 - 5i) = 12 - 15i + 8i - 10i^2 = 12 - 7i + 10 = 22 - 7i$

DIVISION

Division of complex numbers is accomplished with a particular type of multiplication by the number one. Look at the denominator. If it is a monomial with an i, multiply the top and bottom by i. If the denominator is in "a + bi" form, multiply the top and the bottom by "a – bi". What should happen in both cases is that there will be no "i" value in the denominator when you are done.

Example 5   Divide.

a) $\dfrac{3}{2i} = \dfrac{3}{2i} \bullet \dfrac{i}{i} = \dfrac{3i}{2i^2} = \dfrac{3i}{-2} = 0 - \dfrac{3}{2}i$

b) $\dfrac{5}{4 - 3i} = \dfrac{5}{4 - 3i} \bullet \dfrac{4 + 3i}{4 + 3i} = \dfrac{5(4 + 3i)}{16 + 12i - 12i - 9i^2}$

$= \dfrac{5(4 + 3i)}{16 + 9} = \dfrac{5(4 + 3i)}{25} = \dfrac{4 + 3i}{5} = \dfrac{4}{5} + \dfrac{3}{5}i$

i AND THE QUADRATIC FORMULA

Because *i* allows us to have negatives inside the radical, we can now solve any quadratic equation.

Example 6   Solve $x^2 + 2x + 5 = 0$

$$a = 1 \quad b = 2 \quad c = 5$$

$$x = \frac{-b \pm \sqrt{b^2 - 4ac}}{2a}$$

$$x = \frac{-(2) \pm \sqrt{(2)^2 - 4(1)(5)}}{2(1)}$$

$$x = \frac{-(2) \pm \sqrt{4 - 20}}{2}$$

$$x = \frac{-(2) \pm \sqrt{-16}}{2}$$

$$x = \frac{-(2) \pm 4i}{2}$$

$$x = -\frac{2}{2} \pm \frac{4i}{2}$$

$$x = 1 \pm 2i$$

C3 Practice.
Leave all of your answers in a + bi form.

1. Add
   $(7 + 2i) + (8 - 5i)$

2. Subtract
   $(4 - 3i) - (8 - 5i)$

3. Multiply
   $(2 + 3i)(7 + 2i)$

4. Divide
   $$\frac{2 + 3i}{2 - 3i}$$

5. Solve
   $2x^2 + 2x = -5$

6. Solve
   $x^2 + 8 = 3x$

ANSWERS TO PRACTICES

C1 Answers

1. The maximum value occurs at the vertex 4. Therefore C is the answer because 4 is between 3 and 5
2.
   a) $x^2 + 6x - 3$
   b) $x^2 + 2x + 11$
   c) $2x^3 + x^2 - 20x - 28$
   d) $\dfrac{(x^2 + 4x + 4)}{(2x - 7)}$
   e) $4x^2 - 20x + 25$
   f) $2x^2 + 8x + 1$
3. $z = 3(10x - 20) - 8 = 30x - 60 - 8 = 30x - 68$
4. $(7, 3)$
5.
   a) $\{x | x \in \mathbb{R}, x \neq -3\}$
   b) $\{x | x \in \mathbb{R}, x \geq -8\}$

C2 Answers

1. $a^{\frac{17}{30}}$ 　　 2. $\dfrac{1}{b^{\frac{1}{15}}}$ 　　 3. $c^{\frac{3}{10}}$ 　　 4. $a^{\frac{13}{12}}$ 　　 5. $\sqrt[15]{8b^{10}}$

6. $\log_a \sqrt[4]{\dfrac{x}{y^3}}$ 　　　　 7. $4\log_a x + 2\log_a y - \dfrac{1}{3}\log_a z$

C3 Answers

1. $15 - 3i$
2. $-4 + 2i$
3. $8 + 25i$
4. $-\dfrac{5}{13} + \dfrac{12}{13}i$
5. $-\dfrac{1}{2} \pm \dfrac{3}{2}i$
6. $\dfrac{3}{2} \pm \dfrac{\sqrt{23}}{2}i$

CHAPTER FIVE

GEOMETRY

About 85% of the Geometry portion of the **COMPASS** exam is concerned with triangles, circles, and angles. The remaining 15% covers a wide variety of topics including: rectangles, trapezoids, parallelograms, and composite shapes. Consequently, this chapter is divided into four sections corresponding to the weight **COMPASS** places on them.

G1	**Angles**	**Supplementary, complementary, adjacent, vertical**
G2	**Triangles**	**Perimeter, area, Pythagorean Theorem, Triangle Angle Sum, exterior angle, similar triangles**
G3	**Circles**	**Perimeter, area, arcs**
G4	**Other**	**Rectangles, parallelograms, trapezoids, composites**

G1 ANGLES

Much of geometry relies on definition, so to get us started, here are some definitions.

▶ **Point** - A thing so small, it has no shape or size, only location. Points are labeled with capital letters.

▶ **Line** - A collection of points in a straight path that has no end and no beginning. Since it is made out of points it has no height, no width, only infinite length. Lines are named by using any two points on the line. The order of the points is not important. Lines can also be named with just one lowercase letter.

▶ **Ray** - A half line. A ray has a beginning point called an endpoint. A ray extends forever away from the endpoint. Rays are named by the endpoint and any other point on the ray. The order of the points is important, Ray AB is different than Ray BA.

▶ **Line segment** - A part of a line, it is a collection of points between two endpoints. A line segment is named by using the two endpoints. The order of the points is not important.

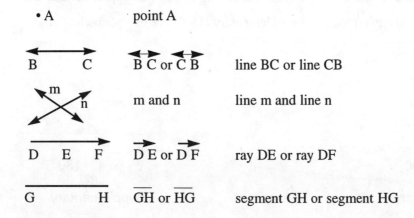

•A	point A	
B——C	$\overleftrightarrow{B C}$ or $\overleftrightarrow{C B}$	line BC or line CB
m and n	m and n	line m and line n
D——E——F	$\overrightarrow{D E}$ or $\overrightarrow{D F}$	ray DE or ray DF
G——H	$\overline{GH}$ or $\overline{HG}$	segment GH or segment HG

▶ **Angle** - An angle is formed when two rays share the same endpoint. The shared endpoint is called the vertex of the angle.

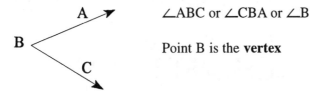

∠ABC or ∠CBA or ∠B

Point B is the **vertex**

▶ **Right angle** - A right angle is any angle that measures 90°. Four right angles are formed when two lines meet in a 90° angle.

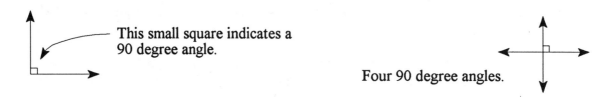

This small square indicates a 90 degree angle.

Four 90 degree angles.

The four 90° right angles add up to 360°. Halfway around would be two right angles or 180°. This is sometimes called a straight angle.

▶ **Straight angle** - A straight angle is an angle that measures 180°.

▶ **Acute angle** - An acute angle is an angle that measures less than 90°.

▶ **Obtuse angle** - An obtuse angle is an angle that measures more than 90° but less than 180°.

Perhaps it will help you remember which one is which if you notice that just as 90 comes before 180, acute comes before obtuse in the alphabet.

Straight

Acute

Obtuse

▶ **Complementary angles** - Two angles that add up to 90° are complementary angles.

▶ **Supplementary angles** - Two angles that add up to 180° are supplementary angles.

Notice that complementary (90°) and supplementary (180°) are in alphabetical order.

∠1 +∠2 = 90

Complementary

∠3 +∠4 = 180

Supplementary

► **Vertical angles** - are formed whenever two lines intersect. ∠1 and ∠3 are a vertical angle pair. ∠2 and ∠4 are also vertical angles.

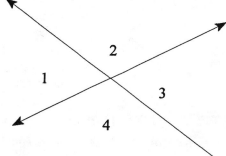

∠1 + ∠2 = 180°   Supplemental
∠1 = 180° − ∠2
∠3 + ∠2 = 180°   Supplemental
∠3 = 180° − ∠2
∠1 = ∠3

This is always the case with vertical angles. Vertical angles are always equal.

∠1 = ∠3 and ∠2 = ∠4

G1   Practice. Find the missing angles.

1. ∠1 = 42°

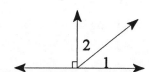

2. ∠3 = 34°

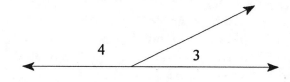

3. ∠5 = 40°

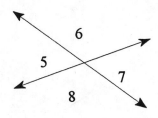

4. ∠a = 30°, angles d and c are complementary.

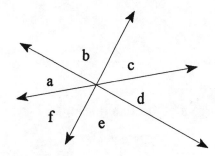

5. Which of the angles in problems 1 through 4 are acute? obtuse? right?

(Answers to all practices in Chapter Five are found on p.100.)

G2 TRIANGLES

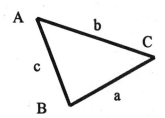

A triangle literally means three angles. A triangle is a three sided figure made up of three line segments. The shared endpoints of the segments are **vertices.** Vertices are denoted by capital letters. The sides opposite the vertices are denoted by lowercase letters that match the letters of the angle. In other words side "a" is opposite ∠ A (angle A). Triangles can be classified according to either the measures of the angles or the lengths of the sides.

CLASSIFICATION BY SIDES

Equilateral - All three sides are equal.

Isosceles - At *least* two sides are equal.

Scalene - No sides are equal.

If a triangle is equilateral, then it is equiangular. **Equiangular** means all angles are equal. Every equilateral triangle is isosceles, but every isosceles is not equilateral. The base angles of an isosceles triangle are equal.

CLASSIFICATION BY ANGLES

Acute - All angles are acute.

Right - One angle is a right angle.

Obtuse - One angle is obtuse.

THREE COOL FACTS ABOUT TRIANGLES

Triangle Angle Sum - The angles of any triangle will always add up to 180°.

Triangle Inequality Law - No side of a triangle can be larger than the sum of the other two sides.

$$a < b + c \qquad b < a + c \qquad c < a + b$$

Exterior Angles - An exterior angle is equal to the sum of the two remote interior angles. In the drawing below ∠1 and ∠2 are remote to ∠4.

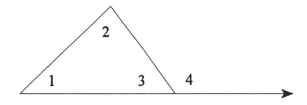

Proof of the Exterior Angle Theorem:

	Statement	Justification
1.	∠1 + ∠2 + ∠3 = 180°	Triangle angle sum
2.	∠1 + ∠2 = 180° − ∠3	Subtraction
3.	∠4 + ∠3 = 180°	Supplemental angles
4.	∠4 = 180° − ∠3	Subtraction
5.	∴ ∠1 + ∠2 = ∠ 4	Substitution

The symbol ∴ means "therefore." ∴ is very useful when you are taking notes for just about any class.

AREA $A = \dfrac{1}{2} bh$

Memorize this formula. It says that the area of a triangle is equal to the product of the base and the height divided by 2. The height, h, is the perpendicular distance of a vertex from a side called b, the base.

Example 1
What is the area of this triangle?
Ignore the 17m and 25m.

$A = \dfrac{1}{2}$ (30)(15) = (15)(15) = 225m^2

What is the perimeter?

17 + 25 + 30 = 72m

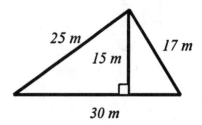

Notice that perimeter is a one dimensional measurement, so the unit of measure is m^1. Area is a two dimensional measurement, so the unit of measure is m^2. If we were looking for a volume measurement the unit of measure would be m^3. The exponent used in the unit of measure indicates the number of dimensions.

PYTHAGOREAN THEOREM

One of the oldest and perhaps the most famous of theorems is the Pythagorean Theorem.

In any right triangle, the square of the hypotenuse is equal to the sum of the squares of the other two sides.

$a^2 + b^2 = c^2$

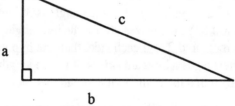

The side opposite the right angle is called the hypotenuse. It is always the longest side of a right triangle. The two shorter sides are called legs.

Example 2
Find the missing side in a right triangle. a = 12 and c = 13

$a^2 + b^2 = c^2$
$12^2 + b^2 = 13^2$
$144 + b^2 = 169$
$b^2 = 169 - 144$
$b^2 = 25$
$\sqrt{b^2} = \sqrt{25}$
$b = 5$

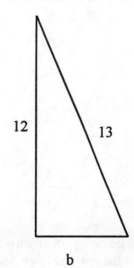

91

SPECIAL RIGHT TRIANGLES

45° – 45° – 90° Triangle

The diagonal of a square divides the square into two right isosceles triangles. The measures of the angles in these triangles is 45°–45°–90°. The hypotenuse of this triangle is always the product of the side and the square root of $\sqrt{2}$.

$a^2 + b^2 = c^2$

$s^2 + s^2 = c^2$

$\sqrt{2(s)^2} = \sqrt{c^2}$

$s\sqrt{2} = c$

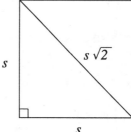

This means rather than using the Pythagorem Theorem next time you work with the diagonal of a square all you have to do is multiply a side by $\sqrt{2}$

30° – 60° – 90° Triangle

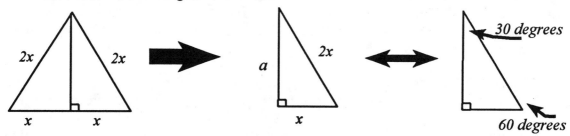

Take an equiangular triangle, where all the angles are equal to 60°, and bisect one of the angles. The bisected angle is 30° and the untouched angle is still 60°. That leaves 90° for the new angle. If the equilateral triangle measured 2x on each side, then the hypotenuse is still 2x. The shortest leg is a bisected side so it is x in length. The remaining leg can be found using the Pythagorean theorem.

$a^2 + b^2 = c^2$

$a^2 + x^2 = (2x)^2$

$a^2 + x^2 = 4x^2$

$a^2 = 4x^2 - x^2$

$a^2 = 3x^2$

$\sqrt{a^2} = \sqrt{3x^2}$

$a = x\sqrt{3}$

∴ The short leg of a 30°–60°–90° triangle is always half of the hypotenuse. The longest leg is the product of the shortest leg and the square root of three.

Example 3

Find the perimeter and the area of a 30°–60°–90° triangle with a hypotenuse of 10ft.

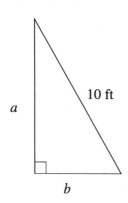

c = 10

b = 5

$a = 5\sqrt{3}$

Perimeter = a + b + c

$= 5\sqrt{3} + 5 + 10$

$= (15 + 5\sqrt{3})$ ft.

Area = $\frac{1}{2}$ bh

$= (5)(5\sqrt{3})$

$= \dfrac{25\sqrt{3}}{2}$ ft.²

Notice that since the legs of a right triangle meet in a 90° angle we can use them as the base and height for area computations.

A few words about the sides of triangles:

The longest side of a triangle is always opposite the largest angle. The smallest side is always is always opposite the smallest angle. So if side a is the shortest, $\angle A$ is the smallest. If $\angle B$ is the largest, side b is the longest.

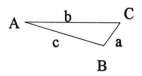

Equilateral triangles have all sides equal. Because all the sides are equal, all of the angles are equal as well. If all three angles are equal and they sum to 180°, then each must be equal to 60°. The "tick" marks indicate equal lengths.

Isosceles triangles have at least two sides equal. These two equal sides are opposite equal angles. The point that joins the two equal sides is called the vertex angle of the isosceles triangle. The other two equal angles are called base angles. The vertex angle has this relationship with the base angles: (vertex) = 180° − 2(1 base angle). So if you know one angle of an isosceles triangle you can figure out the other two.

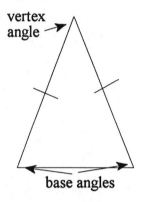

Example 4
What is the vertex angle of an isosceles triangle that has a base angle of 40°?

Because the two base angles are equal to 40°:
$\angle A + 40° + 40° = 180°$
$\angle A + 80° = 180°$
$\angle A = 180° − 80°$
$\angle A = 100°$

Or, using the formula:
(vertex) = 180° − 2(1 Base angle)
$\angle A = 180° − 2(40)°$
$\angle A = 180° − 80° = 100°$

SIMILAR TRIANGLES

Similar triangles are triangles that may or may not be different sizes, but have exactly the same angles. Similar triangles are proportional. This means that if we know that a pair of triangles are similar, then we can set up ratios and proportion statements about the triangles.

$$\Delta ABC \sim \Delta A`B`C`$$

Read as "triangle ABC is similar to triangle A prime, B prime, C prime."

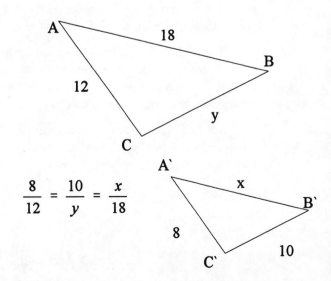

$$\frac{8}{12} = \frac{10}{y} = \frac{x}{18}$$

G2 Practice.

1. If the legs of a right triangle are both equal to 4m, what are the measurements of the angles? What is the perimeter? What is the area?

2. If one leg of a right triangle is 8 feet and the hypotenuse is 10 feet, then what is the area? What is the perimeter?

3. If the short leg of a 30°-60°-90° is 5 cm., what is the perimeter? What is the area?

4. $\angle 1 = 130°$ $\angle 4 = 35°$. Find the missing angles.

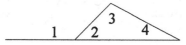

5. $\angle A = \angle BDE$
   AB = 6, DB = 4, DE = 8, BE = 6
   What is the perimeter of $\triangle ABC$?

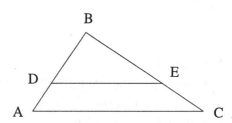

G3 CIRCLES

A circle is a collection of all points in a plane equidistant from the center. This distance, r, is called the radius. A segment that has endpoints on a circle and passes through the center is d, the diameter. d = 2r

The perimeter of a circle is called C, the circumference. π, pi, is a Greek letter that represents an irrational number that is about 3.14159. π is defined to be the ratio of the circumference to the diameter.

So, to find the circumference of a circle, multiply the diameter by π. If you know the value of C, r, or d, you know the value of the others.

$$\frac{C}{d} = \pi$$

$$d\left(\frac{C}{d}\right) = (\pi)$$

$$C = d\pi = 2r\pi$$

To find the area of a circle: $\mathbf{A = \pi r^2}$

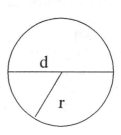

$\mathbf{d = 2r}$

$\mathbf{C = 2\pi\, r}$

$\mathbf{A = \pi r^2}$

Example 1
    What is the circumference and the area of a circle with a diameter of 10 feet?

Circumference:

   C = dπ = 10π

   C = 10π feet

Area:

   A = πr²

   2r = d = 10

   r = 5

   A = π(5)² = 25π

   A = 25π square feet

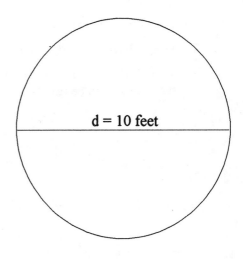

ARC

    An arc is a portion of a circle. There are 360° of arc in a circle. 180° of arc is half of a circle, or a semi-circle.

   arc $\overset{\frown}{AC}$ = 120°   arc $\overset{\frown}{AXC}$ = 240°

   arc $\overset{\frown}{AC}$ + arc $\overset{\frown}{AXC}$ = 360°

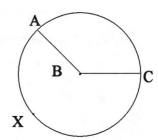

CENTRAL ANGLE

    A central angle is defined by three points, two on the circle and the vertex at the center. The measure of an arc is equal to the central angle of that arc. Each side of the central angle passes through the endpoints of the arc. ∠ABC is the central angle for arc $\overset{\frown}{AC}$.

   ∠ABC = 86°   arc $\overset{\frown}{AC}$ = 86°

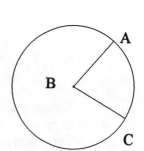

INSCRIBED ANGLES

    An inscribed angle is defined by three points on a circle. The vertex of an inscribed angle is on the circle. The measure of an inscribed angle is half the measure of the central angle of the same arc. For a given arc there is one central angle but many different inscribed angles.

   Arc $\overset{\frown}{AC}$ = 86°   ∠AXC = ∠AYC = ∠AZC = 43°

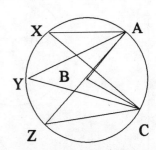

LINES AND CIRCLES

A line and a circle always fall into one of three possible cases.

1. They do not intersect.

2. They intersect exactly twice.

3. They intersect exactly once. In this case, they are said to be **tangent.**

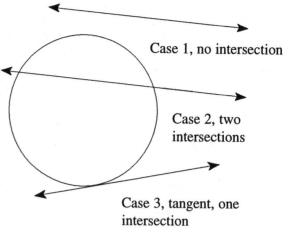

Case 1, no intersection

Case 2, two intersections

Case 3, tangent, one intersection

G3   Practice.

1. If the radius of a circle is 5 ft., what is the area? What is the circumference?

2. If the circumference of a circle is 12π meters, what is the area?

3. A circle with center B has a radius of 5". A, C and D are on the circle. Arc AC is 60°. What is the measure of line segment $\overline{AC}$? What is $\angle ADC$?

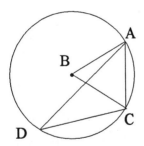

4. Circle A with center A has a diameter of 12. A second circle B with center B has a diameter of 6. Point A is on circle B. Point C is on both circles. If you subtract the area of the smaller circle from the area of the larger circle, how much area is left?

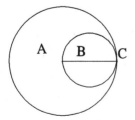

96

G4 OTHER GEOMETRIC FIGURES

QUADRILATERAL

A quadrilateral is a four-sided polygon. The interior angle sum (add up all of the angles inside) is 360°.

TRAPEZOID

A trapezoid is a quadrilateral with only one pair of sides parallel. It is like a triangle with the top cut off. Consecutive angles along a non-parallel side are supplemental.

$A = \dfrac{1}{2} (b_1 + b_2)h$

$\angle ABC + \angle BAD = 180°$

$\angle BCD + \angle ADC = 180°$

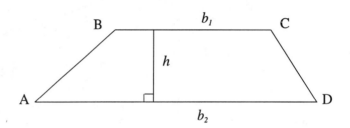

PARALLELOGRAM

A parallelogram is a quadrilateral with two pairs of parallel sides. Opposite sides are equal. Opposite angles are equal. Any consecutive angles are supplemental. The base (b) and the length (l) are the same.

$A = b \cdot h$
$P = 2l + 2w$

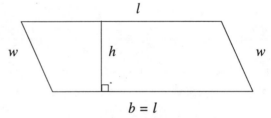

RECTANGLES

A rectangle is parallelogram with all angles equal. Every angle is 90°. Opposite sides are equal in length and parallel.

$A = l \cdot w$
$P = 2l + 2w$

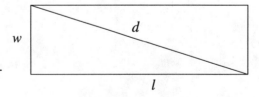

The **diagonal** is the hypotenuse of a right triangle. $d^2 = l^2 + w^2$

RHOMBUS

A rhombus is an equilateral parallelogram.

$A = b \cdot h$
$P = 4s$

97

SQUARE

A square is an equilateral, equiangular quadrilateral. A square is a regular quadrilateral. A square is a rhombus. A square is a rectangle.

$A = s^2$
$P = 4s$

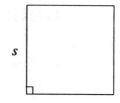

HIERARCHY CHART OF THE QUADRILATERAL FAMILY

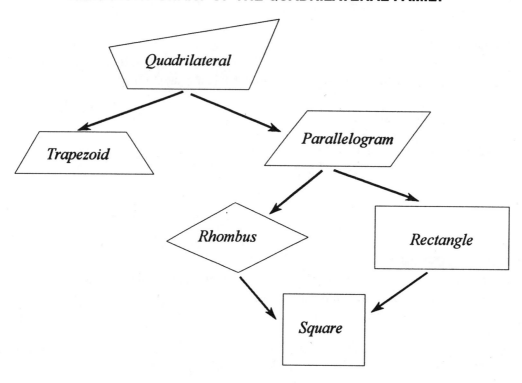

In this hierarchy chart, each quadrilateral has the characteristics of the quadrilaterals above it. For example, a square is always a rectangle, but a rectangle is not always a square.

COMPOSITE STRUCTURES

Composite Structures are two or more simple objects put together to make a more complex object.

Example 1   The figure below is constructed entirely with right angles. Find the area.

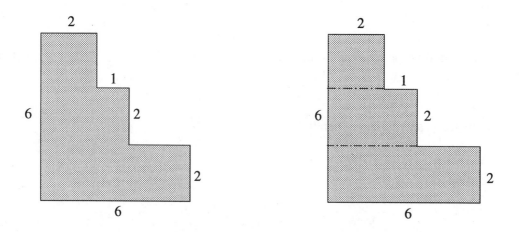

Try to find the simpler figures in the complex figure, and then add up the parts.

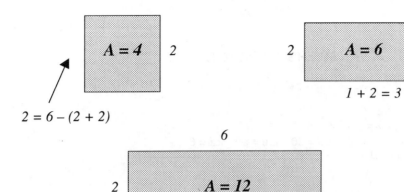

$2 = 6 - (2 + 2)$

$1 + 2 = 3$

$4 + 6 + 12 = 22$

So, the area is 22 units.

G4   Practice.

1. The diagonals of a rhombus meet in right angles. What is the perimeter of a rhombus with one diagonal that measures 6 inches and the longer diagonal measures 8 inches?

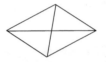

2. The trapezoid ABCD has an area of 66cm².
Line AB is parallel to line CD ∠C = 90˚.
Segment AB = 10 cm.
Segment BC = 6 cm.
What is the measure of segment CD?
What is the measure of ∠B? What is the measure of ∠A + ∠D?

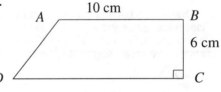

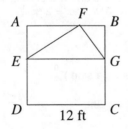

3. Square ABCD has sides that measure 12 feet each.
E is the midpoint of segment AD
Point F is collinear with points A and B
G is the midpoint of segment BC
What is the area of the square ABCD less the triangle EFG?

4. ABCD is a square.
F is collinear with points C and D
Point E is the midpoint of AD and is the center of circle E
Segment AB is 8 inches in length
Segment DF is 12 inches in length
Point A and point D are on Circle E
Find the area of the figure.

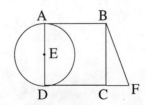

ANSWERS TO PRACTICES

G1 Answers
1. $\angle 2 = 48°$
2. $\angle 4 = 146°$
3. $\angle 6 = 140°$ $\angle 7 = 40°$ $\angle 8 = 140°$
4. $\angle a = 30°$ $\angle b = 90°$ $\angle c = 60°$ $\angle d = 30°$ $\angle e = 90°$ $\angle f = 60°$
5. Acute 1, 2, 3, 5, 7, a, c, d, f,
   Obtuse 4, 6, 8
   Right b, e

G2 Answers
1. 45°-45°-90°, $P = (8 + 4\sqrt{2})$m, $A = 8$m²
2. $A = 24$ ft.², $P = 24$ ft.
3. $P = (15 + 5\sqrt{3})$cm $A = \dfrac{25\sqrt{3}}{2}$ cm²
4. $\angle 2 = 50°$ $\angle 3 = 95°$
5. 27

G3 Answers
1. $A = 25\pi$ ft² $C = 10\pi$ft
2. $A = 36\pi$ m²
3. Segment $\overline{AC}$ measures 5"

Segments $\overline{BA}$ and $\overline{BC}$ are both radii of the same circle, so they are equal so triangle ABC is isosceles. Since arc AC = 60°, then $\angle B = 60°$. The base angles of an isosceles triangle are equal. $\angle BAC = \angle BCA = 60°$. That means triangle ABC is an equilateral triangle with all sides equal. Therefore, segment $\overline{AC} = 5"$.

$\angle ADC = 30°$

$\angle ADC$ is an inscribed angle. Therefore it is half of arc AC which is 60°.

4. 27π

The large circle has a radius of 6, therefore the large circle has an area of 36π. The smaller circle has a raduis of 3, therefore the small circle has an area of 9π. $35\pi - 9\pi = 27\pi$.

G4 Answers
1. 20 inches (Each right triangle measures 3, 4 and 5 inches on a side.)
2. Segment $\overline{CD} = 12$ cm. $\angle B = 90°$ $\angle A + \angle D = 180°$
3. Square ABCD area = 144 Triangle EFG = 36 $144 - 36 = 108$ft.²
4. Semi-circle = 8π
   Square = 64
   Triangle = 16
   $8\pi + 64 + 16 = (80 + 8\pi)$ inches²

CHAPTER SIX

MATHEMATICS PRACTICE TESTS

This chapter contains a practice test for Pre–algebra, Algebra, College Algebra, and Geometry—four tests in all. Each test consists of twenty questions in no particular order. Make sure you know which tests to study for. Many people will not have to take the geometry test at all, so may not want to spend any time practicing for it.

When you prepare for COMPASS using these tests on the following pages, work on them one question at a time. As soon as you select an answer, turn to the solution section at the end of each test and see how you did. Make sure you understand how to get the correct answer before you move on to another problem.

The tests in this book are longer than the one you will take for COMPASS, unless you take multiple mathematics test in your test session. Most COMPASS test sessions will be seventeen problems or less. Do not try to guess your score by the number of problems you take.

Look over the hints in the mathematics introduction at the beginning of Chapter 2, but always keep in mind the most important thing: TIME DOES NOT MATTER. Take as long as you want on any problem.

TEST ONE PRE–ALGEBRA

Select the best answer.

1. Simplify. $23 + (-8) + 22 - (-12) + 8$
   - A. 17
   - B. 33
   - C. 49
   - D. 57
   - E. 45

2. Compute. $\dfrac{3}{8} + \dfrac{4}{5}$
   - A. $\dfrac{7}{13}$
   - B. $\dfrac{3}{10}$
   - C. $\dfrac{7}{40}$
   - D. $\dfrac{11}{20}$
   - E. $\dfrac{47}{40}$

3. Divide. $\dfrac{5}{9} \div \dfrac{7}{18}$

○ A. $\dfrac{35}{162}$

○ B. $\dfrac{4}{9}$

○ C. $\dfrac{7}{10}$

○ D. $1\dfrac{3}{7}$

○ E. $2\dfrac{1}{7}$

4. Simplify. $\dfrac{4}{5} + \dfrac{5}{9} \cdot \dfrac{-4}{7} - \dfrac{4}{5}$

○ A. $1\dfrac{13}{35}$

○ B. $-\dfrac{20}{63}$

○ C. $\dfrac{8}{27}$

○ D. 0

○ E. $1\dfrac{16}{45}$

5. Jack is making pencil holders for a yard sale. Each pencil holder costs $1.20 to make. If he sells the pencil holders for $2.00 each, how many will he have to sell to make a profit of exactly $20.00?

○ A. 10
○ B. 15
○ C. 20
○ D. 25
○ E. 30

6. What is the average (arithmetic mean) of 10, 9, 5, 7, 7, 4, and 4?

○ A. $4\dfrac{6}{7}$

○ B. $5\dfrac{3}{4}$

○ C. $6\dfrac{4}{7}$

○ D. 6.5

○ E. $7\dfrac{2}{3}$

7.   Simplify. $30 - 3 \times 4 + 6$

    ○ A.   0
    ○ B.   24
    ○ C.   52
    ○ D.   86
    ○ E.   270

8.   Simplify. $\dfrac{14 - 9}{4^2 - 2^3}$

    ○ A. $\dfrac{5}{12}$

    ○ B. $\dfrac{1}{4}$

    ○ C. $\dfrac{5}{8}$

    ○ D. $\dfrac{23}{24}$

    ○ E. $2\dfrac{1}{2}$

9.   16 is 25% of what number?

    ○ A.   4
    ○ B.   40
    ○ C.   400
    ○ D.   32
    ○ E.   64

10.   A shirt has been marked down 20% and now sells for $12.60. What was the original selling price?

    ○ A. $10.08
    ○ B. $11.80
    ○ C. $13.40
    ○ D. $15.12
    ○ E. $15.75

11.   Pat charged $300 worth of goods on her credit card. On her first bill, she was not charged any interest, and she made a payment of $80. She then charged another $50 worth of goods. On her second bill, a month later, she was charged 3% interest on her entire unpaid balance. How much interest was Pat charged on her second bill?

    ○ A. $7.70
    ○ B. $8.10
    ○ C. $9.00
    ○ D. $9.70
    ○ E.   12.90

12. If four pounds of bananas cost $1.60, what is the cost of 10 pounds?

- ○ A. $0.40
- ○ B. $2.40
- ○ C. $3.20
- ○ D. $3.60
- ○ E. $4.00

13. The largest prime factor of 90 is

- ○ A. 2
- ○ B. 3
- ○ C. 5
- ○ D. 6
- ○ E. 11

14. What is the least common multiple of 6, 8, and 12?

- ○ A. 12
- ○ B. 18
- ○ C. 24
- ○ D. 48
- ○ E. 72

15. How many yards of material remain from a 24-yard length after two pieces, each 2 1/2 yards long, and four pieces, each 3 1/4 yards long, are removed?

- ○ A. $5\frac{3}{4}$
- ○ B. 6
- ○ C. $6\frac{1}{4}$
- ○ D. 18
- ○ E. $18\frac{1}{4}$

16. What is the average (arithmetic mean) of 8, 12, 18, 13, 11, 14?

- ○ A. 7
- ○ B. 11
- ○ C. $11\frac{1}{3}$
- ○ D. 12
- ○ E. $12\frac{2}{3}$

17. What is the meaning of 3^5?

   ○ A. $3 \cdot 3 \cdot 3 \cdot 3 \cdot 3$

   ○ B. 15

   ○ C. $3 \cdot 5$

   ○ D. $5 \cdot 5 \cdot 5$

   ○ E. $\dfrac{3}{5}$

18. Multiply 1.2 x 8.5

   ○ A. .92

   ○ B. 9.2

   ○ C. .102

   ○ D. 1.02

   ○ E. 10.2

19. What is 40% of 70?

   ○ A. 18

   ○ B. 20

   ○ C. 24

   ○ D. 28

   ○ E. 35

20. Six pieces of wire are cut from a length of wire that is 50 feet long. Two of the pieces are each 12 $\frac{1}{3}$ feet long. Two of the pieces are 3 1/4 feet long each. Two of the pieces are 8 1/2 feet long each. How many feet of wire is left from the original length?

   ○ A. $1 \dfrac{5}{6}$

   ○ B. $1 \dfrac{1}{12}$

   ○ C. $25 \dfrac{11}{12}$

   ○ D. $24 \dfrac{1}{12}$

   ○ E. 4

Answers and solutions on next page

ANSWERS FOR TEST 1

1. D
2. E
3. D
4. B
5. D
6. C
7. B
8. C
9. E
10. E
11. B
12. E
13. C
14. C
15. B
16. E
17. A
18. E
19. D
20. A

SOLUTIONS FOR TEST 1

1.   **Simplify. 23 + (−8) + 22 − (−12) + 8**

Answer D

$$23 + (−8) + 22 − (−12) + 8$$
$$15 + 22 − (−12) + 8$$
$$15 + 22 + 12 + 8$$
$$37 + 12 + 8$$
$$49 + 8$$
$$57$$

►   NOTE: The answers are in ascending order.

►   Distractors, the incorrect answers, are computed with the same numbers with the wrong signs. This problem is about signed numbers. The only way to get it wrong is by adding wrong. Therefore, take your time. And do the problem several times before you select your answer.

2.   **Compute.** $\dfrac{3}{8} + \dfrac{4}{5}$

Answer E

$$\frac{3}{8} + \frac{4}{5} = \frac{3}{8}\left(\frac{5}{5}\right) + \frac{4}{5}\left(\frac{8}{8}\right) = \frac{15}{40} + \frac{32}{40} = \frac{47}{40}$$

►   Note that some of the distractors do not even have the common denominator.

►   Some of the distractors have been reduced.

106

3.   **Divide.** $\dfrac{5}{9} \div \dfrac{7}{18}$

Answer D

$$\frac{5}{9} \div \frac{7}{18} = \frac{5}{9} \cdot \frac{18}{7} = \frac{5}{1} \cdot \frac{2}{7} = \frac{10}{7} = 1\frac{3}{7}$$

▶ Don't ask why, just flip and multiply.

4.   **Simplify** $\dfrac{4}{5} + \dfrac{5}{9} \cdot \dfrac{-4}{7} - \dfrac{4}{5}$

Answer B

▶ First notice 4/5 and – 4/5 wash out.

$$\frac{5}{9} \cdot \frac{-4}{7} = -\frac{20}{63}$$

5.   **Jack is making pencil holders for a yard sale. Each pencil holder costs $1.20 to make. If he sells the pencil holders for $2.00 each, how many will he have to sell to make a profit of exactly $20.00.**

Answer D

Jack is making $0.80 profit per sale. Divide 20 by 0.8.

$$\frac{20}{0.8} = \frac{200}{8} = \frac{100}{4} = 25$$

▶ Profit is the difference in revenue and costs.

6.   **What is the average (arithmetic mean) of 10, 9, 5, 7, 7, 4, and 4?**

Answer C

$$\frac{10 + 9 + 5 + 7 + 7 + 4 + 4}{7} = \frac{46}{7} = 6\frac{4}{7}$$

▶ Memorize this method; it will give you confidence.

7.   **Simplify. 30 – 3 x 4 + 6**

Answer B

30 – 3 x 4 + 6
30 – 12 + 6
18 + 6
24

▶ Order of Operations

8.   **Simplify.** $\dfrac{14 - 9}{4^2 - 2^3}$

Answer C

$$\frac{14 - 9}{4^2 - 2^3} = \frac{14 - 9}{16 - 8} = \frac{5}{8}$$

▶   Exponents come first.

9.   **16 is 25% of what number?**

Answer E

$$16 = 25\% \text{ of } w?$$
$$16 = 0.25(w)$$
$$\frac{16}{0.25} = w$$
$$w = \frac{16}{0.25} \cdot \frac{100}{100} = \frac{16 \cdot 100}{25} = 16 \cdot 4 = 64$$

10.   **A shirt has been marked down 20% and now sells for $12.60. What was the original selling price?**

Answer E

If a shirt has been marked down 20%, that means the current selling price is 80% of the original. In other words, $12.60 is 80% of what?

$$\$12.60 = 80\% \text{ of } w?$$
$$12.6 = 0.8(w)$$
$$\frac{12.6}{0.8} = w$$
$$w = \frac{12.6}{0.8} \cdot \frac{10}{10} = \frac{126}{8} = \frac{63}{4} = \$15.75$$

11.   **Pat charged $300 worth of goods on her credit card. On her first bill, she was not charged any interest, and she made a payment of $80. She then charged another $50 worth of goods. On her second bill, a month later, she was charged 3% interest on her entire unpaid balance. How much interest was Pat charged on her second bill?**

Answer B

$300 - 80 = 220$	(1st month purchases) – (payment) = balance after first month
$220 + 50 = 270$	(balance brought forward) + (purchase) = unpaid balance
$270 \cdot 0.03 = 8.10$	(unpaid balance) • 3% = interest $8.10

▶   Take a problem like this one step at a time.

▶   Write down what things mean.

12. **If four pounds of bananas cost $1.60, what is the cost of 10 pounds?**

Answer E

$1.60 / 4 = $0.40. Each pound costs $0.40. Ten pounds would cost $4.00.

▶ Figure the cost per unit then multiply by the desired number of units.

▶ You could use a proportion to solve as well.

13. **The largest prime factor of 90 is**

Answer C

        A.   2
        B.   3
        C.   5
        D.   6
        E.   11

▶ Process of elimination. 11 will not divide into 90. 6 is not a prime.

▶ Numbers 13 and 14 are good examples of working backwards from the given answers.

14. **What is the least common multiple of 6, 8, and 12?**

Answer C

        A.   12
        B.   18
        C.   24
        D.   48
        E.   72

▶ Process of elimination. 8 will not divide into 12 or 18.

15. **How many yards of material remain from a 24-yard length after two pieces, each 2 1/2 yards long, and four pieces 3 1/4 yards long, are removed.**

Answer B

$24 - 2(2 \frac{1}{2}) - 4(3 \frac{1}{4}) = 24 - 5 - 13 = 19 - 13 = 6$

▶ Make sure you answer the question that is asked. Don't go for a distractor just because it is an answer in an intermediate step.

▶ Take your time, it is only a fraction.

16.   What is the average (arithmetic mean) of 8, 12, 18, 13, 11, 14?

Answer E

$$\frac{8 + 12 + 18 + 13 + 11 + 14}{6} = \frac{76}{6} = 12\frac{2}{3}$$

17.   What is the meaning of 3^5?

Answer A

$3 \cdot 3 \cdot 3 \cdot 3 \cdot 3$

► Repeat 3 five times as a factor.

18.   Multiply 1.2 x 8.5.

Answer E

► Count the number of decimals behind the point.

► If you multiply by a number bigger than 1, 1.2 in this case, you must get a number bigger than what you started with. B and E are the only possibilities.

19.   What is 40% of 70?

Answer D

$w = 40\% \cdot 70$
$w = 0.4 \cdot 70$
$w = 28$

► "of" means **x** (multiply), and "is" means = (equals)

20.   Six pieces of wire are cut from a length of wire that is 50 feet long. Two of the pieces are 12 1/3 feet long. Two of the pieces are 3 1/4 feet long. Two of the pieces are 8 1/2 feet long. How many feet of wire is left from the original length?

Answer A

$50 - 2(12\frac{1}{3}) - 2(3\frac{1}{4}) - 2(8\frac{1}{2}) = 1\frac{5}{6}$

TEST TWO ALGEBRA

Select the best answer.

1.   If x = –1 and y = 3, what is the value of the expression $3x^3 - 2xy$?

   ○ A. –9
   ○ B. –3
   ○ C. 3
   ○ D. 9
   ○ E. 21

2.   Which of the following expressions represents the product of three less than x and five more than twice x?

   ○ A. $2x^2 + 11x + 15$
   ○ B. $2x^2 - 11x + 15$
   ○ C. $2x^2 + x - 15$
   ○ D. $2x^2 - x - 15$
   ○ E. $2x^2 + 22x + 15$

3.   A student earned scores of 83, 78, and 77 on three of four tests. What must the student score on the fourth test to have an average (arithmetic mean) of exactly 80?

   ○ A. 80
   ○ B. 82
   ○ C. 84
   ○ D. 85
   ○ E. 86

4.   What is the equation of the line that contains the points (2, 3) and (14, –6)?

   ○ A. $y = -\dfrac{3}{4}x + 5$

   ○ B. $y = -\dfrac{3}{4}x + \dfrac{9}{2}$

   ○ C. $y = \dfrac{3}{4}x + 5$

   ○ D. $y = -\dfrac{4}{3}x + \dfrac{17}{3}$

   ○ E. $y = -\dfrac{1}{2}x + \dfrac{5}{2}$

5. For all $x \neq \pm 4$, $\dfrac{x^2 - x - 20}{x^2 - 16} = ?$

    ○ A. $\dfrac{x + 5}{x - 4}$

    ○ B. $\dfrac{x + 4}{x - 4}$

    ○ C. $\dfrac{x - 5}{x + 4}$

    ○ D. $\dfrac{x + 5}{x + 4}$

    ○ E. $\dfrac{x - 5}{x - 4}$

6. A rope 36 feet long is cut into three pieces. The second piece is four feet longer than the first, and the last piece is three times as long as the second. If x represents the length of the first piece, then which equation determines the length of the first piece?

    ○ A. $36 = 5x + 8$
    ○ B. $36 = x + (x + 4) + (3x)$
    ○ C. $36 = 3x + 12$
    ○ D. $36 = x + (x + 4) + 3(x + 4)$
    ○ E. $36 = 3x + 16$

7. The product $(x^2 + 3)(x - 1)$ is

    ○ A. $x^3 + 3x^2 - x - 3$
    ○ B. $x^2 + 2x - 3$
    ○ C. $3x - 3$
    ○ D. $x^3 - 3$
    ○ E. $x^3 - x^2 + 3x - 3$

8. If n is an integer, which expression must be an even integer?

    ○ A. $2n + 1$
    ○ B. $2n - 1$
    ○ C. $n + 1$
    ○ D. $2n^2$
    ○ E. n^2

9. If $x = -3$, what is the value of $2x^2 + 3x - 5$?

    ○ A. -22
    ○ B. -6
    ○ C. -5
    ○ D. 4
    ○ E. 22

10. Which of the following is the complete factorization of $2x^2 - 13x - 24$?

○ A. $(2x - 6)(x + 4)$
○ B. $(x - 6)(2x + 4)$
○ C. $(2x - 3)(x - 8)$
○ D. $(2x + 3)(x - 8)$
○ E. $2(x + 3)(x - 4)$

11. Which of these is the product of $(a + 2b)$ and $(c - d)$?

○ A. $ac + ad + bc - 2bd$
○ B. $ac - ad + bc - 2bd$
○ C. $ac - ad + bc - 2bd$
○ D. $ac - ad + 2bc + 2bd$
○ E. $ac - ad + 2bc - 2bd$

12. If $a = -2$ and $b = 3$, what is the value of the expression $3(a + b)(a - b)$?

○ A. -5
○ B. 5
○ C. 15
○ D. -15
○ E. 75

13. This is a graph of which equation?

○ A. $y = -\dfrac{3}{2}x + 6$

○ B. $y = \dfrac{3}{2}x + 6$

○ C. $y = \dfrac{2}{3}x + 6$

○ D. $y = -\dfrac{2}{3}x + 6$

○ E. $y = -\dfrac{2}{3}x - 6$

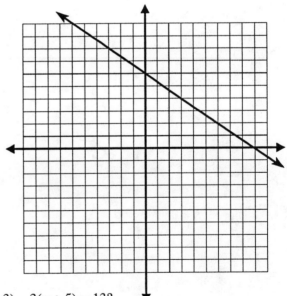

14. What is the solution to the equation $2(x + 3) - 3(x + 5) = 13$?

○ A. -22
○ B. -12
○ C. -4
○ D. 5
○ E. 15

15. Peggy gets paid a weekly salary of D dollars a week plus a commission of 8% on her total sales S. Which expression below best describes Peggy's weekly pay?

    ○ A. D + S

    ○ B. 8D + S

    ○ C. D + 8S

    ○ D. D + .08S

    ○ E. .08(D + S)

16. Which of these is the product of $(D^3 + 2D^2 - 2D + 3)$ and $(D - 5)$?

    ○ A. $D^4 + 2D^3 - 2D^2 + 3D$

    ○ B. $D^4 - 3D^3 - 8D^2 + 13D - 15$

    ○ C. $D^4 - 3D^2 - 12D^2 + 13D + 15$

    ○ D. $D^4 + 7D^3 + 12D^2 + 13D + 15$

    ○ E. $D^4 - 3D^3 - 12D^2 + 13D - 15$

17. What is the distance from point A to point B?

    ○ A. 13

    ○ B. 85

    ○ C. $\sqrt{5}$

    ○ D. $\sqrt{13}$

    ○ E. $\sqrt{85}$

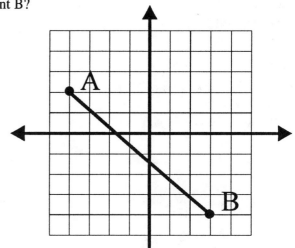

18. For all $a \neq 0$ and $b \neq 0$, $\dfrac{a^{-3}b^2}{a^5b^{-4}}$

    ○ A. $\dfrac{a^2}{b^2}$

    ○ B. $\dfrac{b^3}{a^4}$

    ○ C. $\dfrac{b^6}{a^2}$

    ○ D. $\dfrac{b^6}{a^8}$

    ○ E. $\dfrac{1}{a^2b^2}$

19. For all a, b, and c, $(a^3b^2c)^2$

   ○ A. $a^5b^4c^2$

   ○ B. $a^6b^4c^2$

   ○ C. $a^9b^4c^2$

   ○ D. $a^5b^4c^3$

   ○ E. $2a^3b^2c$

20. For all x, $3(2x + 5) - 4(x - 2) = 3(2x + 2) + 1$

   ○ A. $x = 9$

   ○ B. $x = -5$

   ○ C. $x = 4$

   ○ D. $x = 3$

   ○ E. $x = 0$

Answers and solutions on next page

ANSWERS FOR TEST 2

1. C
2. D
3. B
4. B
5. E
6. D
7. E
8. D
9. D
10. D
11. E
12. D
13. D
14. A
15. D
16. E
17. E
18. D
19. B
20. C

SOLUTIONS TO TEST 2

1.   If x = –1 and y = 3, what is the value of the expression $3x^3 – 2xy$?

Answer C

$$3(-1)^3 – 2(-1)(3) =$$
$$3(-1) – 2(-1)(3) =$$
$$-3 – (-6) =$$
$$-3 + 6 =$$
$$3$$

2.   Which of the following expressions represents the product of three less than x and five more than twice x?

Answer D

This question asks to multiply the binomials "3 less than x" $(x – 3)$ and "five more than twice x" $(2x + 5)$

$$(x – 3)(2x + 5) = 2x^2 + 5x – 6x – 15 = 2x^2 – x – 15$$

3.   A student earned scores of 83, 78, and 77 on three of four tests. What must the student score on the fourth test to have an average (arithmetic mean) of exactly 80?

Answer B

$$\frac{83 + 78 + 77 + x}{4} = 80$$

$$4 \cdot \frac{83 + 78 + 77 + x}{4} = 80 \cdot 4$$

$$83 + 78 + 77 + x = 320$$

$$238 + x = 320$$

$$x = 320 - 238$$

$$x = 82$$

4.   What is the equation of the line that contains the points (2, 3) and (14, –6)?

Answer B

▶ Note that all of the answers are presented in y = mx + b format. Find the slope first. This eliminates every answer except for A and B.

$$m = \frac{y_2 - y_1}{x_2 - x_1} = \frac{3 - (-6)}{2 - 14} = \frac{9}{-12} = -\frac{3}{4}$$

▶ Now we must find the value of b. We could plug either ordered pair into the equation. Let's choose (2, 3) since the numbers are smaller and we will not have to worry about negative signs.

$$y = mx + b$$

$$(3) = -\frac{3}{4}(2) + b$$

$$3 = -\frac{3}{2} + b$$

$$3 + \frac{3}{2} = b$$

$$\frac{6}{2} + \frac{3}{2} = b$$

$$\frac{9}{2} = b$$

▶ Therefore, the answer is B.

▶ Note that if you did not remember the slope formula and the slope intercept for the line, you could just plug in both points into all five choices until you eliminate four of them.

5.   For all $x \neq \pm 4$, $\dfrac{x^2 - x - 20}{x^2 - 16}$ = ?

Answer E

▶   This problem is both a rational expression problem and a factoring problem.

Factor the numerator: Factor the denominator:
$x^2 - x - 20 = (x - 5)(x + 4)$ $x^2 - 16 = (x + 4)(x - 4)$

▶   The $(x + 4)$ cancel and you are left with answer E.

▶   Pay close attention to the signs. Every possibility is covered in the distractors.

6.   **A rope 36 feet long is cut into three pieces. The second piece is four feet longer than the first, and the last piece is three times as long as the second. If x represents the length of the first piece, then which equation determines the length of the first piece?**

Answer D

▶   Let x represent the first length. Then $(x + 4)$ represents the second. The third length is 3 times the second (not 3 times the first): $3(x + 4)$. Therefore, the equation is D.

$x + (x + 4) + 3(x + 4) = 36$

▶   If you have some alternate way of finding that the length of the shortest rope is 4, you can plug it in until you find the equation that works.

7.   **The product $(x^2 + 3)(x - 1)$ is**

Answer E

▶   This is just a binomial times a binomial, which is a FOIL problem.

$(x^2 + 3)(x - 1) = x^3 - x^2 + 3x - 3$

8.   **If n is an integer, which expression must be an even integer?**

Answer D

Most people will do a problem like this by process of elimination.

▶   If you plug any number into A or B you always get an odd number so we can eliminate them as possible answers.

▶   If you plug 3 into C you get an even number, but if you plug 4 into C you get an odd number, so eliminate it.

▶   If you plug any odd number into E you get an odd number.

▶   Therefore, the only possible answer is D.

Some people will think about the definition of even (any integer divisible by 2) and see that since $2n^2$ is a product of some number (n^2) and 2 that it will always be even.

9. **If x = –3, what is the value of 2x² + 3x – 5?**

Answer D

$2(–3)^2 + 3(–3) – 5 =$
$2(9) + 3(–3) – 5 =$
$18 – 9 – 5 =$
4

10. **Which of the following is the complete factorization of 2x² – 13x –24?**

Answer D

▶ If you cannot factor, just FOIL out each of the distractors.

11. **Which of these is the product of (a + 2b) and (c – d)?**

Answer E

$FOIL(a + 2b)(c – d) = ac – ad + 2bc – 2bd$

▶ Watch out for signs when you select your answer.

12. **If a = –2 and b = 3, what is the value of the expression 3(a + b)(a – b)?**

Answer D

$3(a + b)(a – b)$
$3((–2) + (3))((–2) – (3)) =$
$3(1)(–5) =$
$3(–5) = – 15$

▶ Check your work carefully. Suppose you left the three off the beginning of the multiplication. Distractor A = –5 is there and would look very good to you. You could select that, think you had the correct answer, and never know it was wrong just because of that sneaky 3 in front of the FOIL.

13. **This is a graph of which equation?**

Answer D

▶ Do this problem by process of elimination.

▶ First, the slope is negative. That eliminates B and C. Second, the y intercept is +6, which eliminates E. So we must decide between A and D. Select any other point on the graph, (9, 0) for example, and plug it into both equations.

A. $0 = -\dfrac{3}{2}(9) + 6$

$0 = -\dfrac{27}{2} + \dfrac{12}{2}$

$0 = -\dfrac{15}{2}$ False

D. $0 = -\dfrac{2}{3}(9) + 6$

$0 = -\dfrac{18}{3} + 6$

$0 = -6 + 6$ True

119

14.   **What is the solution to the equation 2(x + 3) – 3(x + 5) = 13?**

Answer A

$$2(x + 3) - 3(x + 5) = 13$$
$$2x + 6 - 3x - 15 = 13$$
$$-x - 9 = 13$$
$$-x = 22$$
$$x = -22$$

► Make certain in a distribution problem like this, that you distribute to every term with the correct sign. Many people miss the –3(5) multiplication in the second binomial and solve incorrectly as follows:

$$2(x + 3) - 3(x + 5) = 13$$
$$2x + 6 - 3x - 5 = 13$$
$$-x + 1 = 13$$
$$-x = 12$$
$$x = -12 \quad \text{INCORRECT}$$

► This happens to be distractor B. The other distractors contain similar small errors. Take your time and don't commit the small fatal error.

15.   **Peggy gets paid a weekly salary of D dollars a week plus a commission of 8% on her total sales S. Which expression below best describes Peggy's weekly pay?**

   A. $D + S$
   B. $8D + S$
   C. $D + 8S$
   D. $D + .08S$
   E. $.08(D + S)$

Answer D

► This is another process of elimination problem.
   A.   Does not work because there is no 8% involved.
   B.   Does not work because the 8% is on the D salary. Also, the % conversion is wrong.
   C.   Does not work because the % conversion is wrong.
   E.   Does not work because the 8% is on the D salary.

   D.   Does work.

16. **Which of these is the product of $(D^3 + 2D^2 - 2D + 3)$ and $(D - 5)$?**

Answer E

► The word "product" indicates that you need to multiply the polynomial by the binomial. This means that there will be a total of eight multiplications before you are finished. Make sure each term of the binomial is multiplied by each term of the polynomial.

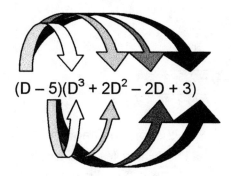

$$(D - 5)(D^3 + 2D^2 - 2D + 3)$$

► Sometimes it helps to rewrite this type of multiplication as a monomial times a polynomial plus a monomial times a polynomial:

$D(D^3 + 2D^2 - 2D + 3) = D^4 + 2D^2 + 3D$ (notice that each exponent went up by 1)

$\mathbf{+}$

$(-5)(D^3 + 2D^2 - 2D + 3) = -5D^3 - 10D^2 + 10D - 15$ (notice that each term changed signs because of the negative 5)

► And carefully and watch signs.

$$\begin{aligned} D^4 + 2D^3 - 2D^2 + 3D \\ \underline{+ - 5D^3 - 10D^2 + 10D - 15} \\ D^4 - 3D^3 - 12D^2 + 13D - 15 \end{aligned}$$

► Look carefully at the difference between the choices given. Choices B and E are almost identical:

B. $D^4 - 3D^3 - 8D^2 + 13D - 15$
E. $D^4 - 3D^3 - 12D^2 + 13D - 15$

► When selecting your answer, make sure you get the one that you want and not just the one that looks like the answer you want.

17. **What is the distance from point A to point B?**

Answer E

▶ There are two ways to do this problem: with the Distance Formula or the Pythagorean Theorem.

Distance Formula

▶ First you have to find out what the points are: A (–4, 2) and B (3, –4) then plug those points into the distance formula.

$$d = \sqrt{(x_2 - x_1)^2 + (y_2 - y_1)^2}$$
$$d = \sqrt{(3 - (-4))^2 + ((-4) - 2)^2}$$
$$d = \sqrt{(7)^2 + (-6)^2} \quad = \quad \sqrt{49 + 36} \quad = \quad \sqrt{85}$$

Pythagorean Theorem

▶ Notice that segment AB could be the hypotenuse of a right triangle with a vertex at (–4, –4). You can count the legs of this triangle as 6 and 7 units. Then plug this into the Pythagorean equation.

$$a^2 + b^2 = c^2$$
$$6^2 + 7^2 = c^2$$
$$36 + 49 = c^2$$
$$85 = c^2$$
$$\sqrt{85} = c$$

18. **For all $a \neq 0$ and $b \neq 0$,** $\dfrac{a^{-3}b^2}{a^5b^{-4}}$

Answer D

$$\frac{a^{-3}b^2}{a^5b^{-4}} \quad = \quad \frac{b^2b^4}{a^5a^3} \quad = \quad \frac{b^6}{a^8}$$

▶ First make all of the exponents positive, then add the exponents of like bases.

19. **For all a, b, and c, $(a^3b^2c)^2$**

Answer B

▶ When taking a power to a power, just multiply the exponents. Since we are raising the expression to the second power, each exponent gets doubled.

20. **For all x, $3(2x + 5) - 4(x - 2) = 3(2x + 2) + 1$**

Answer C

$$3(2x + 5) - 4(x - 2) = 3(2x + 2) + 1$$
$$6x + 15 - 4x + 8 = 6x + 6 + 1$$
$$2x + 23 = 6x + 7$$
$$23 - 7 = 6x - 2x$$
$$16 = 4x$$
$$4 = x$$

TEST THREE COLLEGE ALGEBRA

Select the best answer.

1. If F(x) = 2x² + 3x – 8, then F(–2) = ?

   ○ A. –22
   ○ B. –10
   ○ C. –6
   ○ D. –2
   ○ E. –4x² – 6x + 16

2. If g(3) = 9 and g(1) = 5, which of the following could represent g(x)?

   ○ A. x + 4
   ○ B. 2x + 3
   ○ C. 3x
   ○ D. 4x – 3
   ○ E. x² – 4x + 12

3. If $\dfrac{y^{\frac{3}{2}}}{y^{\frac{1}{3}}} = y^k$, then k =

   ○ A. 2
   ○ B. –2
   ○ C. $\dfrac{7}{6}$
   ○ D. $-\dfrac{7}{6}$
   ○ E. $\dfrac{1}{2}$

4. If a = 3b + 2 and b = 7 – 2c, express a in terms of c.

   ○ A. a = –6c + 23
   ○ B. a = 6c – 23
   ○ C. a = 21 – 6c
   ○ D. a = 2c – 21
   ○ E. a = 10b – c

5. For i = √–1, if 2i(4 – 3i) = x + 8i, then x = ?

   ○ A. 6
   ○ B. 8
   ○ C. 6i
   ○ D. –6i
   ○ E. –8i

6. Let $F(x) = 2x^2 + 3x - 5$ and $G(x) = x + 5$, then $F \circ G(x) =$

- ○ A. 36
- ○ B. $2x^2 + 3x$
- ○ C. $2x^2 + 4x$
- ○ D. $2x^2 + 23x + 60$
- ○ E. $2x^3 + 13x^2 + 10x - 25$

7. For all x such that $x^2 + 25 = 0$, $x = ?$

- ○ A. -25
- ○ B. 5
- ○ C. ± 5
- ○ D. $5i$
- ○ E. $\pm 5i$

8. For all x such that $\dfrac{18}{\sqrt{x^2 + 4}} = 6$, $x^2 = ?$

- ○ A. 9
- ○ B. 5
- ○ C. $\sqrt{5}$
- ○ D. $\dfrac{9}{4}$
- ○ E. -13

9. If $F(x) = 2x + 5$ then $F^{-1}(x) = ?$

- ○ A. $\dfrac{x + 5}{2}$
- ○ B. $-2x - 5$
- ○ C. $\dfrac{x - 2}{5}$
- ○ D. $\dfrac{x - 5}{2}$
- ○ E. $\dfrac{4x + 10}{2}$

10. For $a > 0$, $\quad \sqrt{a} \cdot \sqrt[3]{a^2} \quad ?$

- ○ A. $\sqrt[4]{a^3}$
- ○ B. $\sqrt[4]{a^2}$
- ○ C. $\sqrt[3]{a^3}$
- ○ D. $\sqrt[6]{a^3}$
- ○ E. $a\sqrt[6]{a}$

11. If $i = \sqrt{-1}$, then express $\sqrt{-72x^3}$ in terms of i and simplify.

    ○ A. $4x\sqrt{-18x}$

    ○ B. $4x\sqrt{18x^3}$

    ○ C. $6xi\sqrt{2x}$

    ○ D. $xi\sqrt{72x}$

    ○ E. $6x\sqrt{2xi}$

12. Simplify $9^{\frac{7}{10}} \cdot 9^{\frac{4}{5}}$

    ○ A. $9^{\frac{14}{25}}$

    ○ B. 3

    ○ C. 9

    ○ D. 27

    ○ E. 81

13. What are the roots, where the function equals zero, of the function $f(x) = x^3 - 3x^2 - 4x + 12$?

    ○ A. 4, 3

    ○ B. 4, –3

    ○ C. 2, 3

    ○ D. 2, –2, 3

    ○ E. 2, –2, –3

14. In which interval does the function $h(x) = -3x^2 + 12x - 9$ obtain its maximum value?

    ○ A. between –3.5 and –0.5

    ○ B. between –0.5 and 1.5

    ○ C. between 1.5 and 3.5

    ○ D. between 3.5 and 5.5

    ○ E. between 5.5 and 7.5

15. For $p \neq 0$, $\left(\dfrac{1}{P}\right)^{x^2} = P^{-4}$, for what values of x?

    ○ A. 4

    ○ B. ± 4

    ○ C. 0

    ○ D. 2

    ○ E. ± 2

16. If $i = \sqrt{-1}$, $i^2 + i^3 + i^4 + i^5 + i^6 =$

    ○ A. 0

    ○ B. 1

    ○ C. –1

    ○ D. i

    ○ E. –i

17. What is the sum of the solutions of $2x^2 = 7x + 15$?

    ○ A. $-\dfrac{7}{2}$

    ○ B. $-\dfrac{3}{2}$

    ○ C. $\dfrac{3}{2}$

    ○ D. $\dfrac{7}{2}$

    ○ E. $\dfrac{13}{2}$

18. If $\dfrac{2x^2 + kx - 15}{x - 5} = 2x + 3$, then k = ?

    ○ A. 7
    ○ B. −7
    ○ C. 0
    ○ D. 2
    ○ E. −2

19. The operation ★ is defined to be: $x \star y = 3x - 2y$. If $4 \star a = 8$, then a = ?

    ○ A. 4
    ○ B. −4
    ○ C. −1
    ○ D. 2
    ○ E. −2

20. For what values of x is the equation $\log_2 x + \log_2 (x - 2) = 3$ true?

    ○ A. 4
    ○ B. ± 4
    ○ C. 2
    ○ D. ± 2
    ○ E. 2, 4

Answers and solutions on next page

ANSWERS FOR TEST 3

1. C
2. B
3. C
4. A
5. A
6. D
7. E
8. B
9. D
10. E
11. C
12. D
13. D
14. C
15. E
16. C
17. D
18. B
19. D
20. A

SOLUTIONS FOR TEST 3

1.   If F(x) = 2x² + 3x – 8, then F(–2) = ?

Answer C

$$2(-2)^2 + 3(-2) - 8$$
$$= 2(4) + 3(-2) - 8$$
$$= 8 + (-6) - 8$$
$$= -6$$

2.   If g(3) = 9 and g(1) = 5, which of the following could represent g(x)?

Answer B

▶   Do this problem by process of elimination. Find the choice that will give you a 9 when you plug in a 3 and a 5 when you plug in a 1.

▶   When you plug in a 3, you get 9 for all choices except A. So eliminate choice A. When you plug 1 into the rest of the choices, B is the only one that will yield a 5. Therefore the answer is B.

3.   If $\dfrac{y^{\frac{3}{2}}}{y^{\frac{1}{3}}}$ = y^k, then k =

Answer C

▶ When dividing like bases, subtract exponents.

$$k = \frac{3}{2} - \frac{1}{3} = \frac{9}{6} - \frac{2}{6} = \frac{9-2}{6} = \frac{7}{6}$$

4.   If a = 3b + 2 and b = 7 – 2c, express a in terms of c.

Answer A

▶ Substitute b = 7 – 2c into a = 3b + 2

a = 3(7 – 2c) + 2
a = 21 – 6c + 2
a = 23 – 6c   which is the same as a = –6c + 23

5.   For $i = \sqrt{-1}$, if 2i(4 – 3i) = x + 8i, then x = ?

Answer A

2i(4 – 3i) = x + 8i
$8i - 6i^2$ = x + 8i
8i + 6 = x + 8i
6 = x

6.   Let $F(x) = 2x^2 + 3x - 5$ and G(x) = x + 5, then F ∘ G(x) =

Answer D

F ∘ G(x) = $2(x + 5)^2 + 3(x + 5) - 5$
          = $2(x^2 + 10x + 25) + 3(x + 5) - 5$
          = $2x^2 + 20x + 50 + 3x + 15 - 5$
          = $2x^2 + 23x + 60$

7.   For all x such that $x^2 + 25 = 0$, x = ?

Answer E

$x^2 + 25 = 0$
$x^2 = -25$
$\sqrt{x^2} = \pm \sqrt{-25}$
x = ±5i

8.   For all x such that $\dfrac{18}{\sqrt{x^2+4}} = 6$, $x^2 = ?$

Answer B

▶ Watch out! This problem does not want to know what x is. This problem is looking for the value of x^2.

$$\dfrac{18}{\sqrt{x^2+4}} = 6$$

$$\dfrac{18}{6} = \sqrt{x^2+4}$$

$$3 = \sqrt{x^2+4}$$

$$3^2 = \sqrt{x^2+4}^2$$

$$9 = x^2 + 4$$

$$5 = x^2$$

9.   If $F(x) = 2x + 5$ then $F^{-1}(x) = ?$

Answer D

$$F(x) = 2x + 5$$

1.	Replace F(x) with y	$y = 2x + 5$
2.	Swap x and y	$x = 2y + 5$
3.	Solve for y	$x - 5 = 2y$

$$\dfrac{x-5}{2} = \dfrac{2y}{2} = y$$

4.   Replace y with $F^{-1}(x)$ $F^{-1}(x) = \dfrac{x-5}{2}$

10.   For $a > 0$, $\sqrt{a}\ \sqrt[3]{a^2}$?

Answer E

$$\sqrt{a}\ \sqrt[3]{a^2} = a^{\frac{1}{2}} \cdot a^{\frac{2}{3}} = a^{\frac{1}{2}+\frac{2}{3}} = a^{\frac{3}{6}+\frac{4}{6}} = a^{\frac{7}{6}} = \sqrt[6]{a^7} = a\,\sqrt[6]{a}$$

11.   If $i = \sqrt{-1}$, then express $\sqrt{-72x^3}$ in terms of i and simplify.

Answer C

▶ The negative sign inside the radical tells you that the answer will have have an i in it. This eliminates choices A, B, and E.

▶ We know that $\sqrt{72} = \sqrt{36 \cdot 2} = 6\sqrt{2}$. This eliminates choice D; therefore, the answer is C.

129

12. Simplify $9^{\frac{7}{10}} \cdot 9^{\frac{4}{5}}$

Answer D

$$9^{\frac{7}{10}} \cdot 9^{\frac{4}{5}} = 9^{\frac{7}{10} + \frac{4}{5}} = 9^{\frac{7}{10} + \frac{8}{10}} = 9^{\frac{7+8}{10}} = 9^{\frac{15}{10}} = 9^{\frac{3}{2}} \quad (\sqrt{9})^3 = 3^3 = 27$$

13. What are the roots, where the function equals zero, of the function
$f(x) = x^3 - 3x^2 - 4x + 12$?

Answer D

$$f(x) = x^3 - 3x^2 - 4x + 12$$
$$0 = x^3 - 3x^2 - 4x + 12$$
$$0 = x^2(x - 3) - 4(x - 3)$$
$$0 = (x - 3)(x + 2)(x - 2)$$

$$x = \{3, -2, 2\}$$

14. In which interval does the function $h(x) = -3x^2 + 12x - 9$ obtain its maximum value?

Answer C

▶ Recall that the vertex of a parabola always has an x value of $-b/2a$.

$$\frac{-b}{2a} = \frac{-12}{2(-3)} = \frac{-12}{-6} = 2$$

▶ This value, 2, is on the interval between 1.5 and 3.5.

15. For $p \neq 0$, $\left(\dfrac{1}{P}\right)^{x^2} = P^{-4}$, for what values of x?

Answer E

▶ Notice that the bases $1/P$ and P are reciprocals of each other. To make the bases exactly the same and thus make the exponents equal, change the sign of the (-4).

$$\left(\frac{1}{P}\right)^{x^2} = P^{-4}$$

$$\left(\frac{1}{P}\right)^{x^2} = \left(\frac{1}{P}\right)^4$$

$$x^2 = 4$$
$$\sqrt{x^2} = \pm\sqrt{4}$$
$$x = \pm 2$$

16. If $i = \sqrt{-1}$, $i^2 + i^3 + i^4 + i^5 + i^6 =$

Answer C

$i^2 = -1 \qquad i^3 = -i \qquad i^4 = 1 \qquad i^5 = i \qquad i^6 = -1$
$i^2 + i^3 + i^4 + i^5 + i^6 = (-1) + (-i) + (1) + (i) + (-1) = -1$

17. **What is the sum of the solutions of $2x^2 = 7x + 15$?**

Answer D

$2x^2 = 7x + 15$
$2x^2 - 7x - 15 = 0$
$(2x + 3)(x - 5) = 0$

$x = \left\{ \dfrac{-3}{2}, 5 \right\}$

► Now add the solutions.

$5 + \dfrac{-3}{2} = \dfrac{10}{2} + \dfrac{-3}{2} = \dfrac{7}{2}$

18. **If $\dfrac{2x^2 + kx - 15}{x - 5} = 2x + 3$, then k = ?**

Answer B

► This rational equation is just an unusual way to ask you to FOIL the binomials.

$\dfrac{2x^2 + kx - 15}{x - 5} = 2x + 3$
$2x^2 + kx - 15 = (x - 5)(2x + 3)$
$2x^2 + kx - 15 = 2x^2 + 3x - 10x - 15$
$2x^2 + kx - 15 = 2x^2 - 7x - 15$
$kx = -7x$
$k = -7$

► Watch out for the sign! It would be a shame to do all that work and select A. +7, just because you were being careless.

19. **The operation $\star$ is defined to be: $x \star y = 3x - 2y$. If $4 \star a = 8$, then a = ?**

Answer D

► Plug in the values of 4 and a into $3x - 2y$. 8 is a result, not an argument.

$3x - 2y =$
$3(4) - 2a = 8$
$12 - 2a = 8$
$12 - 8 = 2a$
$4 = 2a$
$2 = a$

20. **For what values of x is the equation $\log_2 x + \log_2 (x - 2) = 3$ true?**

Answer A

$\log_2 x + \log_2 (x - 2) = 3$
$\log_2 (x^2 - 2x) = 3$
$x^2 - 2x = 2^3$
$x^2 - 2x = 8$
$x^2 - 2x - 8 = 0$
$(x - 4)(x + 2) = 0$

$x = \{4, -2\}$

▶ The negative 2 must be rejected since it is not in the domain of $\log_2 x$. Therefore, $x = 4$.

TEST FOUR GEOMETRY

Select the best answer.

1. In the figure below, $\overline{AB}$ and $\overline{CD}$ are perpendicular. If the measure of ∠EDB is 33°, what is the measure of ∠EDC?

    ○ A. 33°
    ○ B. 57°
    ○ C. 66°
    ○ D. 123°
    ○ E. 147°

    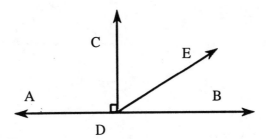

2. Line segments $\overline{AB}$ and $\overline{CD}$ intersect at point E. If ∠AEC is 142°, what is ∠AED?

    ○ A. 18°
    ○ B. 28°
    ○ C. 38°
    ○ D. 48°
    ○ E. 58°

    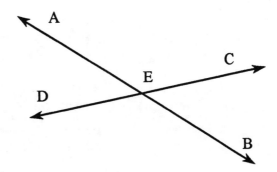

3. Lines $\overleftrightarrow{AB}$, $\overleftrightarrow{CD}$, and $\overleftrightarrow{EF}$ all intersect at the point G. $\overleftrightarrow{AB}$ is perpendicular to $\overleftrightarrow{CD}$. If ∠AGF is 27°, what is ∠CGE?

    ○ A. 33°
    ○ B. 43°
    ○ C. 53°
    ○ D. 63°
    ○ E. 153°

    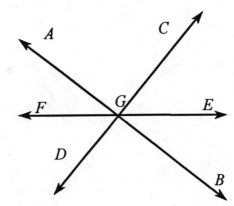

4. In the drawing point B is colinear with point A and point D. If $\angle ACB$ is 100° and $\angle CBD$ is 130°, what is $\angle CAB$?

○ A.   30°
○ B.   40°
○ C.   80°
○ D.   100°
○ E.   130°

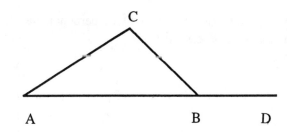

5. Square ABCD has an area of 64 ft². Point E is collinear with points C and D. Segment $\overline{DE}$ is 2 feet long. What is the perimeter of triangle BCE?

○ A.   5 feet
○ B.   10 feet
○ C.   14 feet
○ D.   24 feet
○ E.   48 feet

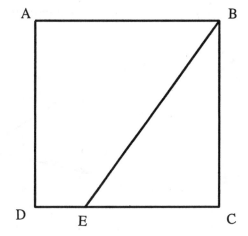

6. In the figure below $\angle BAC = \angle BDE$. If $\dfrac{\overline{BE}}{\overline{EC}} = \dfrac{4}{1}$, then $\dfrac{\overline{BD}}{\overline{BA}} = ?$

○ A.   1
○ B. $\dfrac{1}{4}$
○ C. $\dfrac{4}{1}$
○ D. $\dfrac{4}{5}$
○ E. $\dfrac{5}{4}$

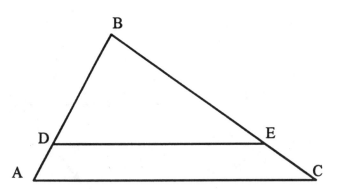

7. If both legs of a right triangle are 1 meter in length, what is the perimeter of the triangle?

○ A. $\sqrt{2}$ meters
○ B. 2 meters
○ C. 3 meters
○ D. $(2 + \sqrt{2})$ meters
○ E. 4 meters

8. A ladder 13 feet long is placed 5 feet away from the base of a wall and then leaned against the wall. How high up does the ladder reach?

○ A. 8 feet
○ B. 9 feet
○ C. 12 feet
○ D. 15 feet
○ E. 18 feet

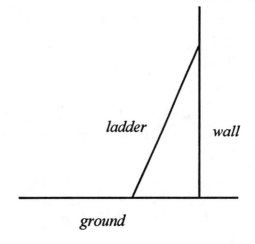

ground

9. A rectangular hallway that measures 6 feet by 18 feet is to be tiled using square tiles that measure 9 inches on a side. What is the minimum number of tiles that can be used to cover this entire area?

○ A. 108
○ B. 136
○ C. 164
○ D. 192
○ E. 220

10. In the drawing below, lines $\overleftrightarrow{AB}$ and $\overleftrightarrow{CD}$ are parallel. Line $\overleftrightarrow{EH}$ intersects line $\overleftrightarrow{AB}$ at F. Line $\overleftrightarrow{EH}$ intersects line $\overleftrightarrow{CD}$ at G. If ∠HGD is 125°, what is ∠AFE?

○ A. 25°
○ B. 55°
○ C. 90°
○ D. 125°
○ E. 180°

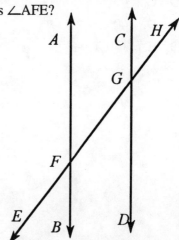

11. The vertex angle of an isosceles triangle is 120°. How much is one base angle?

○ A. 15°

○ B. 30°

○ C. 55°

○ D. 60°

○ E. 120°

12. If the diameter of a circle is 12 meters, how many square meters is the area?

○ A. 6π

○ B. 12π

○ C. 24π

○ D. 36π

○ E. 144π

13. In an isosceles triangle, one of the angles measures 70°. What other angles are possible in this triangle?

      I.   55° and 55°

      II.   110°

      III.   40° and 70°

○ A. I

○ B. II

○ C. I, II

○ D. I, III

○ E. I, II, III

14. Points A, B, and C are on the circle with center O. Segment $\overline{AB}$ is a diameter. If ∠BOC is 40°, what is ∠ACO?

○ A. 10°

○ B. 20°

○ C. 40°

○ D. 60°

○ E. 140°

15. In the drawing below, segment $\overline{AB}$ is a radius of the large circle and a diameter of the small circle. If $\overline{AB}$ = 10 meters, how much area is left when the area of the small circle is subtracted from the area of the large circle?

   ○ A.   25π square meters
   ○ B.   50π square meters
   ○ C.   75π square meters
   ○ D.   100π square meters
   ○ E.   125π square meters

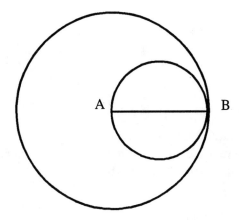

16. In the drawing below, the circle with center S is inscribed inside the square ABCD. The diameter of the circle is 8, the same length as the side of the square. If the area of the circle is subtracted from the area of the square, how much area is left?

   ○ A.   4
   ○ B.   8π
   ○ C.   8 – 4π
   ○ D.   64 – 16π
   ○ E.   64

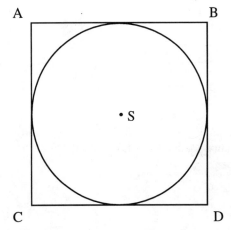

17. In the drawing below ∠A = ∠D and ∠E = ∠B. If $\overline{AB}$ is 24 feet long, $\overline{BC}$ is 18 feet long, and $\overline{DE}$ is 8 feet long, how long is $\overline{EF}$?

   ○ A.   6 feet
   ○ B.   9 feet
   ○ C.   12 feet
   ○ D.   15 feet
   ○ E.   18 feet

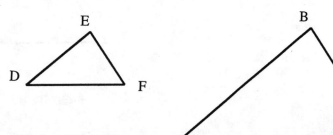

137

18. $\overline{AC}$ is the diagonal of rectangle ABCD. $\overline{AC}$ measures 15 units. $\overline{BC}$ measures 9 units. How many square units is the area of rectangle ABCD?

   ○ A. 54
   ○ B. 90
   ○ C. 108
   ○ D. 135
   ○ E. 180

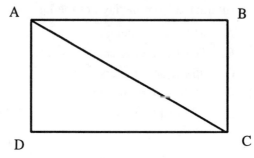

19. Square ABCD measures 8 units on a side. Point E is collinear with points C and D. Segment $\overline{ED}$ measures 4 units. $\overline{AB}$ is a diameter of the semicircle. How many square units is the area of the entire figure?

   ○ A. 88π
   ○ B. $80 + 8\pi$
   ○ C. $80 - 16\pi$
   ○ D. $96 + 8\pi$
   ○ E. $96 + 16\pi$

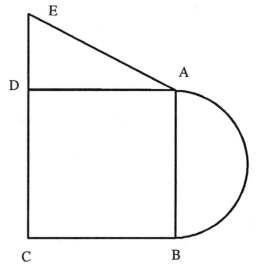

20. Triangle ABC is isosceles, $\overline{AB} = \overline{BC} = 8$ units. $\overline{BD}$ is perpendicular to $\overline{AC}$. $\overline{AD} = 4$ units. How many square units make up the area of triangle ABC?

   ○ A. $16 \sqrt{3}$
   ○ B. $16 \sqrt{5}$
   ○ C. $32 \sqrt{3}$
   ○ D. $32 \sqrt{5}$
   ○ E. 64

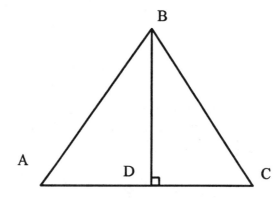

Answers and solutions on next page

ANSWERS FOR TEST 4

1.	B
2.	C
3.	D
4.	A
5.	D
6.	D
7.	D
8.	C
9.	D
10.	D
11.	B
12.	D
13.	D
14.	B
15.	C
16.	D
17.	A
18.	C
19.	B
20.	A

SOLUTIONS FOR TEST 4

1. In the figure below, $\overline{AB}$ and $\overline{CD}$ are perpendicular. If the measure of $\angle EDB$ is 33°, what is the measure of $\angle EDC$?

Answer B

   $\angle EDB$ and $\angle EDC$ are complimentary.
   $\angle EDB + \angle EDC = 90°$
   $33° + \angle EDC = 90°$
   $\angle EDC = 90° - 33° = 57°$

2. Line segments $\overline{AB}$ and $\overline{CD}$ intersect at point E. If $\angle AEC$ is 142°, what is $\angle AED$?

Answer C

   $\angle AEC$ and $\angle AED$ are supplementary.
   $\angle AEC + \angle AED = 180°$
   $142° + \angle AED = 180°$
   $\angle AED = 180° - 142° = 38°$

3. Lines $\overleftrightarrow{AB}$, $\overleftrightarrow{CD}$, and $\overleftrightarrow{EF}$ all intersect at the point G. $\overleftrightarrow{AB}$ is perpendicular to $\overleftrightarrow{CD}$. If $\angle AGF$ is 27°, what is $\angle CGE$?

Answer D

   $\angle AGF + \angle AGC + \angle CGE = 180°$
   $27° + 90° + \angle CGE = 180°$
   $117° + \angle CGE = 180°$
   $\angle CGE = 180° - 117° = 63°$

4. In the drawing point B is colinear with point A and point D. If ∠ACD is 100° and ∠CBD is 130°, what is ∠CAB?

Answer A

$\angle A + \angle C = \angle CBD$ Exterior angle theorem
$\angle A + 100° = 130°$
$\angle A = 130° - 100° = 30°$

5. Square ABCD has an area of 64 ft². Point E is collinear with points C and D. Segment $\overline{DE}$ is 2 feet long. What is the perimeter of triangle BCE?

Answer D

▶ First use the Pythagorean theorem to find the length of $\overline{BE}$. Then add the three sides
$\overline{EC} = 8 - 2 = 6$

$\overline{BC}^2 + \overline{EC}^2 = \overline{BE}^2$
$8^2 + 6^2 = \overline{BE}^2$
$64 + 36 = \overline{BE}^2$
$100 = \overline{BE}^2$
$10 = \overline{BE}$

Perimeter $8 + 6 + 10 = 24$

6. In the figure below ∠BAC = ∠BDE.   If $\dfrac{\overline{BE}}{\overline{EC}} = \dfrac{4}{1}$, then $\dfrac{\overline{BD}}{\overline{BA}} = ?$

Answer D

▶ As soon as we know two pairs of angles are equal we know these are similar triangles. This means you can set up ratios and proportions about the sides.

Take $\overline{BD}$ to be 4 and $\overline{BA}$ to be $(4 + 1) = 5$

7. If both legs of a right triangle are 1 meter in length, what is the perimeter of the triangle?

Answer D

▶ Find the hypotenuse and then add up all three sides.

$a^2 + b^2 = c^2$
$1^2 + 1^2 = c^2$
$1 + 1 = c^2$
$2 = c^2$
$\sqrt{2} = c$

Perimeter
$1 + 1 + \sqrt{2} = 2 + \sqrt{2}$

8. **A ladder 13 feet long is placed 5 feet away from the base of a wall and then leaned against the wall. How high up does the ladder reach?**

Answer C

► This problem is 100% Pythagorean.

$a^2 + b^2 = c^2$
$5^2 + b^2 = 13^2$
$25 + b^2 = 169$
$b^2 = 169 - 25$
$b^2 = 144$
$\sqrt{b^2} = \sqrt{144}$
$b = 12$

9. **A rectangular hallway that measures 6 feet by 18 feet is to be tiled using square tiles that measure 9 inches on a side. What is the minimum number of tiles that can be used to cover this entire area?**

Answer D

► First, convert feet to inches.
  $6 \times 12 = 72$ $18 \times 12 = 216$

► Now divide each dimension by 9 to find out how many tiles will fit on a side.
  $72 \div 9 = 8$ $216 \div 9 = 24$

► Now multiply the length by the width to get the number of tiles needed
  $8 \times 24 = 192$

10. **In the drawing below, lines $\overleftrightarrow{AB}$ and $\overleftrightarrow{CD}$ are parallel. Line $\overleftrightarrow{EH}$ intersects line $\overleftrightarrow{AB}$ at F. Line $\overleftrightarrow{EH}$ intersects line $\overleftrightarrow{CD}$ at G. If $\angle HGD$ is 125°, what is $\angle AFE$?**

Answer D

$\angle HGD$ and $\angle AFE$ are alternate exterior angles.

11.   **The vertex angle of an isosceles triangle is 120°. How much is one base angle?**

Answer B

▶   Two base angles plus the vertex angle = 180°

$2B + V = 180°$

$2B + 120° = 180°$

$2B = 180° - 120°$

$2B = 60°$

$B = 30°$

12.   **If the diameter of a circle is 12 meters, how many square meters is the area?**

Answer D

▶   Divide the diameter by 2 to get the radius. Then plug into the formula $A = \pi r^2$.

$d = 12$

$r = 6$

$A = \pi(6)^2 = 36\pi$

13.   **In an isosceles triangle, one of the angles measures 70°. What other angles are possible in this triangle?**

I.   55° and 55°

II.   110°

III.   40° and 70°

Answer D

▶   Whenever you see a multiple case problem like this, try process of elimination.

Case I: $55° + 55° + 70° = 180°$ True

Case II: $110° + 70° = 180°$ But what about the third angle? False

Case III: $40° + 70° + 70° = 180°$ True

▶   Therefore the answer is I and III, choice D.

14. **Points A, B, and C are on the circle with center O. Segment $\overline{AB}$ is a diameter. If $\angle BOC$ is 40°, what is $\angle ACO$?**

Answer B

▶ $\angle BOC = 40°$ means that $\angle AOC = 140°$

▶ Because triangle $\angle AOC$ is isosceles, $\angle ACO = \angle OAC$. Since $\angle AOC$ takes up 140° of the triangle, $\angle ACO = \angle OAC = 20°$.

▶ Or since $\angle BAC$ is inscribed on a 40° arc, it measures 20°. Since $\angle ACO$ is the other base angle of an isosceles triangle, it too must be 20°.

15. **In the drawing below, segment $\overline{AB}$ is a radius of the large circle and a diameter of the small circle. If $\overline{AB}$ = 10 meters, how much area is left when the area of the small circle is subtracted from the area of the large circle?**

Answer C

Large Circle
$$A = \pi r^2 = \pi(10)^2 = 100\pi$$

Small Circle
$$D = 2r = 10$$
$$r = 5$$
$$A = \pi r^2 = \pi(5)^2 = 25\pi$$

Area remaining
$$100\pi - 25\pi = 75\pi$$

16. **In the drawing below, the circle with center S is inscribed inside the square ABCD. The diameter of the circle is 8, the same length as the side of the square. If the area of the circle is subtracted from the area of the square, how much area is left?**

Answer D

Square
$$A = s^2 = 8^2 = 64$$

Circle
$$A = \pi r^2 = \pi(4)^2 = 16\pi$$

Area remaining
$$64 - 16\pi$$

17. In the drawing below ∠A = ∠D and ∠E = ∠B. If $\overline{AB}$ is 24 feet long, $\overline{BC}$ is 18 feet long, and $\overline{DE}$ is 8 feet long, how long is $\overline{EF}$?

Answer A

▶ Similar triangles mean you can set up ratios and proportions. Reduce the ratio for ease in computation.

$$\frac{small\ triangle}{large\ triangle} = \frac{8}{24} = \frac{1}{3}$$

$$\frac{1}{3} = \frac{x}{18}$$

$$18 = 3x$$

$$\frac{18}{3} = \frac{3x}{3}$$

$$6 = x = EF$$

18. $\overline{AC}$ is the diagonal of rectangle ABCD. $\overline{AC}$ measures 15 units. $\overline{BC}$ measures 9 units. How many square units is the area of rectangle ABCD?

Answer C

▶ First use the Pythagorean Theorem to find the length of $\overline{AB}$.

$$\overline{AB}^2 + \overline{BC}^2 = \overline{AC}^2$$

$$\overline{AB}^2 + 9^2 = 15^2$$

$$\overline{AB}^2 + 81 = 225$$

$$\overline{AB}^2 = 225 - 81 = 144$$

$$AB = 12$$

▶ Find the area

$$12 \times 9 = 108$$

19. Square ABCD measures 8 units on a side. Point E is collinear with points C and D. Segment $\overline{CD}$ measures 4 units. $\overline{AB}$ is a diameter of the semicircle. How many square units is the area of the entire figure?

Answer B

Area of square
$$A = s^2 = 8^2 = 64$$
Area of triangle
$$A = (1/2)bh = (1/2)(8)(4) = 16$$
Area of semicircle
$$A = (1/2)\pi r^2 = (1/2)\pi(4)^2 = (1/2)\pi(16) = 8\pi$$
Sum the three areas for a grand total.
$$64 + 16 + 8\pi = 80 + 8\pi$$

20. Triangle ABC is isosceles, $\overline{AB} = \overline{BC} = 8$ units. $\overline{BD}$ is perpendicular to $\overline{AC}$. $\overline{AD} = 4$ units. How many square units make up the area of triangle ABC?

Answer A

▶ First use the Pythagorean theorem to find the length of $\overline{BD}$, it is the altitude of the triangle.

$a^2 + b^2 = c^2$
$4^2 + b^2 = 8^2$
$16 + b^2 = 64$
$b^2 = 64 - 16$
$b^2 = 48$
$b = \sqrt{48} = 4\sqrt{3}$

▶ If $\overline{AD} = 4$, then $\overline{AC} = 8$.

- Because triangle ABC is isosceles, $\angle A = \angle C$.
- Because $\overline{BD}$ is perpendicular to $\overline{AC}$, $\angle BDA = \angle BDC$.
- Therefore triangle BDA is similar to triangle BDC.
- Since $\overline{BD} = \overline{BD}$ in both triangles, then $\overline{AD} = \overline{AC}$.
  $\overline{AC} = 8$

$A = \dfrac{1}{2}$ (b)(h) $= \dfrac{1}{2}$ (8)(4$\sqrt{3}$) $= 16\sqrt{3}$

COMPOSITION

The COMPASS Writing Skills Test is used by schools to help decide whether your writing and editing skills are advanced enough to place you in regular studies courses or if you would benefit from remedial work. The test consists of several essays of about two hundred words each. Your task is to revise each essay to its most correct form. The essays are divided into segments, or parts. There may be errors of usage, mechanics, or rhetorical skills in the essay. You are asked to use the mouse or the keyboard's arrow keys to move a pointer on the screen and select a segment. You then will be presented with options for making changes to the selected segment. Your task is to choose the best correction from among those given. If the segment is correct as written, no change is needed. Choice "A" is always the same as the uncorrected text. You also may be asked to determine where a sentence would logically fit or to change the order of the sentences. Additionally, there may be one or two other multiple choice items to answer once you finish revising the essay. After you make your revisions, ALWAYS read the essay again with the changes you have made. This is very important because once you confirm your choices, you will not be able to go back and change your answers.

THE CRAFT OF WRITING

Essays usually are not completed in one draft. All writing can be improved with careful proof-reading and editing. Writing is a process, and revisions are common and necessary. The COMPASS Writing Test assesses your ability to proofread and revise writing. This includes the following skills: recognizing and correcting errors in grammar, punctuation, usage and style.

Assume you have been asked to proofread and revise the essay that follows. Cross through the errors and make corrections directly on the page. Use the checklist provided after the essay to help you identify errors.

Its time for me to plan my life. The decision of what to do after high school is an important one. The pressure is on. Everyone is asking me what I'm going to do next. Graduation is almost here, and it feels like constant pressure. You see, I am undecide about my career choice. I know I need further schooling. High school are just not enough anymore. But where do I go?

Undecided, technical schools seem to be a good choice. Some are even called technical colleges now. It's not quite the same as college, some people say. A college degree would give me a real education, they think, and a technical school will give me a practical education. From a technical school I would go write to work earning a good salary at a job I'd like. That would be perfect if I knew what I'd like, auto mechanics or computers or nursing or something.

And, if I went to college I'd be educated, but what would I do? If I major in education I might find I hate teaching. A lot of major's require you to go to graduate schools or professional schools for more education. I don't think I could stand more than four more years of school for four more years. Well, there you go; that's something I know. Maybe I should stop missing those appointments with the career counselor and try to find out what's best for me. Maybe than the pressure will stop. My life will all be planned out. And someone else will be responsible for it. And, that's all I have to say about that.

ESSAY CHECKLIST

____ 1. The sentences seem to be in the right order.
____ 2. Transitional words are appropriate.
____ 3. There are enough supporting facts and details.
____ 4. There is an opening and a conclusion.
____ 5. There is no wordiness or redundancy.
____ 6. Tone and style remain consistent.
____ 7. The essay appears to be well organized.
____ 8. Sentences are varied and interesting.
____ 9. Spelling is correct.
____ 10. Capitalization is correct.
____ 11. The writer uses parallel structure.
____ 12. Modifiers are used correctly.
____ 13. There are no inappropriate shifts in tense.
____ 14. Pronouns are correctly used.
____ 15. Verb forms are correct.
____ 16. There is correct punctuation.

THE CRAFT OF WRITING AND COMPASS

The COMPASS Writing Skills Test will present you with an essay such as the one on the previous page. You will be asked to highlight segments you think have problems. Then you will be given options to correct the problems. The practice exercises in this book have numbered segments for you to consider just as you would consider parts of essays on the actual test.

The essay you have just edited is presented below with numbered segments. Each refers to an item with editing choices. Choose the option you believe is correct for each segment. Then, check your answers on page 195.

PRACTICE ESSAY

> **1/** Its time for me to plan my life. The decision of what to do after high school is an important one. **2/** The pressure is on. Everyone is asking me what I'm going to do next. Graduation is almost here and it feels like constant pressure. **3/** You see, I am undecide about my career choice. I know I need further schooling. **4/** High school are just not enough anymore. But where do I go?
>
> **5/** Undecided, technical schools seem to be a good choice. Some are even called technical colleges now. It's not quite the same as college some people say. **6/** A college degree would give me a real education, they think, and a technical school will give me a practical education. **7/** From a technical school I would go write to work earning a good salary at a job I'd like. **8/** That would be perfect if I knew what I'd like, auto mechanics or computers or nursing or something.
>
> **9/** And, if I went to college I'd be educated, but what would I do? If I major in education I might find I hate teaching. **10/** A lot of majors require you to go to graduate schools or professional schools for more education. **11/** I don't think I could stand more than four more years of school for four more years. **12/** Well, there you go; that's something I know. **13/** Maybe I should stop missing those appointments with the career counselor and try to find out what's best for me. **14/** Maybe than the pressure will stop. My life will all be planned out. And someone else will be responsible for it. **15/** And, that's all I have to say about that.

1/

- ○ A. Its time for me
- ○ B. Its' time for me
- ○ C. It's time for you
- ○ D. It's time for me
- ○ E. Its' time for you

2/

- ○ A. The pressure is on.
- ○ B. The pressure was on.
- ○ C. The pressure is being on.
- ○ D. The pressure be on.
- ○ E. The pressures on.

3/

    ⭘ A. You see, I am undecide about my career choice.

    ⭘ B. You see, I was undecide about my career choice.

    ⭘ C. You see I will be undecide about my career choice.

    ⭘ D. You see, I am undecided about my career choice.

    ⭘ E. You see, I am being undecided about my career choice.

4/

    ⭘ A. High school are just not enough anymore.

    ⭘ B. High school just are not enough anymore,

    ⭘ C. High school diplomas are just not enough anymore.

    ⭘ D. High school just not enough anymore.

    ⭘ E. High school just were not enough anymore.

5/

    ⭘ A. Undecided, technical schools seem to be a good choice.

    ⭘ B. Undecided, a good choice seems to be technical schools.

    ⭘ C. Technical schools, while undecided, seem to be a good choice.

    ⭘ D. Although I am still undecided, technical schools seem a good choice to be.

    ⭘ E. Although I am still undecided, technical schools seem to be a good choice.

6/

    ⭘ A. A college degree would give me a real education, they think, and a technical school will give me a practical education.

    ⭘ B. A college degree would give me a real education, they think, and a technical school would give me a practical education.

    ⭘ C. A college degree will give me a real education, they will think, and a technical school would give me a practical education.

    ⭘ D. A college degree would grant me a real education, they think, and a technical school will give me a practical education.

    ⭘ E. A college degree would have given me a real education, they think, and a technical school was giving me a practical education.

7/

    ⭘ A. From a technical school I would go write to work earning a good salary at a job I'd like.

    ⭘ B. From a technical school I would go right to work earning a good salary at a job I'd like.

    ⭘ C. From a technical school I would write to work earning a good salary at a job I'd like.

    ⭘ D. From a technical school writing to work earning a good salary at a job I'd like.

    ⭘ E. From a technical school right to work earning a good salary at a job I'd like.

8/

- ○ A. what I'd like, auto mechanics, or computers, or nursing or something.
- ○ B. what I'd like is auto mechanics, or computers, or nursing or something.
- ○ C. what I'd like: auto mechanics, or computers, or nursing or something.
- ○ D. what I'd like, "auto mechanics, or computers, or nursing or something.
- ○ E. what I'd like auto mechanics, or computers, or nursing or something.

9/

- ○ A. And, if I went to college I'd be educated, but what would I do?
- ○ B. Nevertheless, if I went to college I'd be educated, but what would I do?
- ○ C. Additionally, if I went to college I'd be educated, but what would I do?
- ○ D. On the other hand, if I went to college I'd be educated, but what would I do?
- ○ E. In conclusions, if I went to college I'd be educated, but what would I do?

10/

- ○ A. A lot of major's require you to go to graduate school...
- ○ B. A lot of majors' require you to go to graduate school...
- ○ C. A lot of majors require you to go to graduate school...
- ○ D. A lots of majors requires you to go to graduate school...
- ○ E. A lot of majors required you to go to graduate school...

11/

- ○ A. I don't think I could stand four more years of school for four more years.
- ○ B. I don't think I could stand more than four more years of school for four more years.
- ○ C. I don't think I could stand for four more years of school.
- ○ D. I don't think four more years of school I could stand.
- ○ E. I don't think I could stand four more years of school.

12/

- ○ A. Well, there you go; that's something I know.
- ○ B. Well, there you go; thats something I know.
- ○ C. Well there you go; that's something I know.
- ○ D. Well there you go that's something I know.
- ○ E. Well, there you go that's something I know.

13/

- ○ A. Maybe I should stop missing those appointments with the career counselor and try to find out what's best for me.

- ○ B. Maybe I should stop missing those appointments with the career counselor or try to find out what's best for me.

- ○ C. Maybe I should stop missing those appointments with the career counselor also finding out what's best for me.

- ○ D. Maybe I should stop missing those appointments with the career counselor while she finds out what's best for me.

- ○ E. Maybe those appointments with the career counselor can find out what's best for me.

14/

- ○ A. Maybe than the pressure will stop.

- ○ B. Maybe then the pressure will stop.

- ○ C. Maybe, however, the pressure will stop.

- ○ D. Maybe also the pressure will stop.

- ○ E. Maybe therefore the pressure will stop.

15/

- ○ A. And, that's all I have to say about that.

- ○ B. And, that's all I have to say about that. The end.

- ○ C. And, for my ending, that's all I have to say about that.

- ○ D. This sentence would be more logical at the end of the first paragraph.

- ○ E. This sentence should be left out.

CHAPTER SEVEN

MECHANICS AND USAGE

The COMPASS Writing Test assesses your ability to write in what is called Standard English. This is English that follows certain rules. These rules are in categories referred to as **MECHANICS** and **USAGE.**

Mechanics refers to the ability to format your writing and use correct spelling, capitalization, and punctuation. Your ability to understand parts of sentences and create interesting and varied essays depends on your knowledge of mechanics. The COMPASS Writing Test assesses your ability to determine how to use mechanics to clearly express your ideas.

Usage refers to the ability to use correct grammar in constructing sentences. Topics in this area include subject-verb agreement, pronoun-antecedent, noun forms, verb forms, adjectives, adverbs, articles, and so on. The COMPASS Writing Test assesses your ability to recognize errors in usage and correct them.

Mechanics and usage help make sense of the written word. You would not be able to understand pages of words without punctuation. Tenses and cases help you understand the who, what, when, where, and how of writing. Proper use of pronouns, verbs, adjectives, adverbs, and prepositions is essential. You must be able to find and correct errors in your writing to make it understandable. COMPASS items in this category make up approximately 70% of the writing skills test. Read the following review of usage and mechanics and complete the exercises.

MECHANICS

SPELLING

The ability to spell correctly is important in writing and in proofreading. You may think that because you use a word processing program with the ability to check your spelling you do not have to worry about spelling. However, a word processing program will not correct an incorrect word choice such as a homonym that is spelled correctly. Spelling is more than simply knowledge of phonics. Read the following rules for spelling and be especially careful of spelling demons.

---

1. **I** before **E** except after **C** or when sounding like **A**: **achieve, receive, sleigh.**

2. Words ending in **Y** change it to **I** before adding endings: **happy/happiness.**

3. Some words referring to a particular person or persons are hyphenated: **mother-in-law/sisters-in-law.**

4. Numbers from **twenty-one** to **ninety-nine** are hyphenated.

5. If a word ends with a vowel then consonant, and its suffix begins with a vowel, sometimes the consonant is doubled: **commit/committed.**

6. Words ending in silent **E** drop the **E** before adding an ending unless the suffix begins with a consonant. Consider **concentrate/concentration** and **taste/tasteless.**

7. Some words need to be learned by their meanings and construction. These are sometimes called "**spelling demons.**"

COMMON SPELLING DEMONS

exercise	psychology	it's/its
prejudice	tragedy	wait/weight
magic	across	occur
write/right	discipline	to/two/too

Exercise 1

Find ten spelling errors in the following paragraph.

My first day in colege it became immediatly aparent that I was going to succeed. We were asked to right an essay on the topic My Most Embarassing Moment. A Commitee read the essays and gave us feedback at the end of the day. The coments on mine read, "good job," "a little to brief, but interesting," "you're write on topic," and "I can't weight to have you in class."

(*Answers* to all exercises in Chapter Seven are found on pp.195-198.)

CAPITALIZATION

Always capitalize the following:

1. Days: weekdays, months, Holy Days and holidays
2. Places: streets, towns, cities, states, countries, mountains, rivers, parks, planets
3. Names: people, pets, relatives when they are used as names, I (first person singular)
4. Titles of people, books, movies, songs, stories, poems
5. Academic courses
6. Events
7. Organizations
8. Companies, buildings, corporations, institutions
9. Races and religions
10. Brand names

Exercise 2

Correct any capitalization errors in the following paragraph by crossing out the incorrect letter and replacing it.

My summer vacation officially starts on the fourth of july. The last day of june we head for the beach and our cottage in martha's vineyard. That is in massachusetts, and it is a beautiful spot for relaxing, swimming, and fishing. We prepare for vacation kickoff for nearly a week. Mother and father go to cheri's bakery and order a special cake. Dad prepares the steak marinade and checks the stash of fireworks. We purchase all our groceries for the vacation month. My brother, nate, has to decide whether the vacation cereal this year will be cheerios or kix. Once vacation starts we don't venture beyond the beach at the end of hiawatha road unless we have to.

PUNCTUATION

Writers use punctuation to indicate breaks in thought and relationships of words, phrases, clauses, and sentences. Use of correct punctuation is essential in order to make the writer's material clear. Items in this category of COMPASS test your ability to identify punctuation that is omitted, unnecessary, or in the wrong place. Knowing the basics of correct punctuation will help you identify what you should change.

COMMAS

There are many uses for the comma: to separate items in a series, introductory elements, interrupters, independent clauses (which can stand on their own) joined by a coordinating or subordinating conjunction, quotations, correspondence, numbers, parenthetical expressions, nonessential clauses, coordinate adjectives, sharply contrasting coordinate elements, appositives, and direct address. They are also used to prevent misreading of a sentence. Here is a quick review of comma usage:

▶ **Series**   The artist limited her landscapes to rivers, lakes, and seashores.

▶ **Introductory element**   After removing his coat, my father would whistle for our two border collies.

▶ **Interrupter**   It is snowing. The sun, however, is shining.

▶ **Independent clauses**   Kate is currently performing in a play, so she must budget her time wisely.

▶ **Quotations**   "Heather," he said, "perhaps you should consult the map before heading to Columbus."

▶ **Correspondence**   Dear Susan, *or* 101 West Peachtree Road, Atlanta, Georgia

▶ **Numbers**   10,000

▶ **Parenthetical expression/nonessential clause**   Mrs. LaTulippe, who was always my favorite, baked delicious birthday cakes.

▶ **Coordinate adjectives**   The abandoned children became starved, violent savages.

▶ **Sharply contrasting coordinate adjectives**   The old sports car was rusty, yet charming in that way old things can be.

▶ **Appositive**   Our boat, a leaky old tub, was no match for the shiny new runabout.

▶ **Direct address**   Help me with the groceries, David, and I'll get dinner started.

▶ **Preventing misreading**   As Hamlet, David would cry out for his father's ghost.

Hint: Most people have trouble with commas because they use them too frequently. Make sure you are following a comma rule whenever you place one.

COLONS

Colons are used after a clause introducing a list, after a statement introducing an explanation or amplification, after a statement introducing a long quotation, in the salutation of a formal letter, to separate hour and minute, in Bible verses, and to separate title and subtitle.

▶ **A list**   This course will cover the following topics: first aid, CPR, nutrition, exercise, and stress management.

▶ **Explanation or amplification** (you could also use a dash)   There was one explanation for his success: luck.

▶ **Long quotation**   Benjamin Franklin once wrote:

▶ **Formal correspondence**   Dear Sir:

▶ **Bible reference**   John 3:16

▶ **Time**   10:45 p.m.

▶ **Title/Subtitle**   *Why Some Stay and Some Don't: An Analysis of First–Year College Students*

SEMICOLONS

A semicolon is used to separate independent clauses when there is no conjunction or to separate those that have a conjunction but also have heavy internal punctuation.

▶ **Independent clauses with no conjunction**   We went to see a movie; then we had lunch and did some shopping in the mall.

▶ **Heavy internal punctuation with coordinate elements**   The tour group visited museums in Vienna, Austria; Paris, France; Florence, Italy; Madrid, Spain; and London, England.

APOSTROPHES

The apostrophe (') is used for two purposes: to show possession and to form contractions. Writers use an apostrophe (') or an apostrophe s ('s) added to nouns or some adjectives to indicate possession. In deciding whether an apostrophe is correctly placed or not, ask yourself whether the noun or adjective is singular or plural.

Add apostrophe s ('s) to singular nouns and some possessive adjectives to indicate possession in this way:

the King**'s** horses   Joe**'s** new car   a day**'s** work   the cat**'s** claw

Add only the apostrophe (') to the end of a plural noun ending in s. If the plural noun does not end in s, however, add the apostrophe s ('s) just as you would for a single noun. Add apostrophe s to singular nouns ending in s (especially proper nouns) unless it would be too difficult to read (such as Athens's citizens).

the cats**'** toys   the women**'s** offices   Charles**'s** home   two months**'** vacation

MORE ON APOSTROPHES

Contractions are combinations of words. They are appropriate only in informal writing and conversation. Apostrophes are used to indicate what letters are left out when contractions are formed. Place them **only** where the letters are missing and **not** between the two words (wasn't **not** was'nt).

you are   you're   we are   we're   we will   we'll   they are   they're

Finally, use apostrophes with letters, numbers, and symbols that are plural and used as words:

Your **1's** look like **6's,** so I made the check out incorrectly.

PERIODS

Periods are used at the end of a declarative sentence, an imperative sentence, or an indirect question.

▶ **Declarative**   John hosted a dinner party for twelve after his daughter's dance recital.

▶ **Imperative**   Move to the middle of the transit car.

▶ **Indirect question**   Quintilla asked whether she could borrow the lawn mower.

QUESTION MARKS

Question marks are used only after directly stated questions. They are not used with politely stated requests or indirect questions.

▶ **Directly stated question**   What time does her flight arrive from Hong Kong?

▶ **Indirect**   He asked if the attorney had prepared her witnesses.

▶ **Business (politely stated request)**   Would you please review my resume.

EXCLAMATION POINTS

An exclamation mark is ending punctuation used after a statement of strong feeling.

▶ I have never been so angry!

DASHES

Dashes are used for emphasis when the writer wants the reader to pause a length of time somewhere between a comma and a period. Like parentheses, dashes should be used infrequently.

▶ My sister – may she be covered in freckles and peeling skin – was invited to the beach for our spring vacation.

PARENTHESES

Information that is extra or incidental to the sentence is set off by parentheses. A common use of parentheses is to indicate dates. Parentheses should not be used often.

▶ Susan (my oldest sibling) is writing a biography of our family.

▶ Tinto (1993) discusses the reasons why students leave college.

Exercise 3

Complete the following exercise by inserting the correct punctuation.

1. I like <u>Runaway Jury</u> the best of all the books John Grisham has written

2. Have you read, <u>The Client</u>, his book about a female attorney

3. "Do you want to go Joseph asked "or would you prefer to stay a little longer"

4. I just cannot do mathematics

5. Hey, don't drink out of my water glass!

6. Kate's birthday is July 4, 1979.

7. Because we ran out of money, we went home early.

8. We were seventeen, attractive, and foolish the year we rented the house at the beach.

9. The Jungle, a book by Upton Sinclair, exposed the evils of the Chicago stockyards.

10. Tiramisu, on the other hand, is a dessert worth wasting the calories.

11. Atlanta, Georgia has been the site of many conferences, the Superbowl, and the Olympics.

12. Frank, I thought I asked you to pick up my registration booklet?

13. My favorite all–time movies are the following: *Diner, Pulp Fiction,* and *The Holy Grail.*

14. I finish classes at 4:00 p.m. consequently, I cannot attend a 3:45 p.m. meeting.

15. New Jersey and Delaware are mid–Atlantic states; Maryland is as well.

SENTENCE CONSTRUCTION

Sentence construction may take several forms. Clauses may stand alone or be connected in many different configurations. The rule is, however, that a sentence must express a complete thought and have the elements of subject and verb to stand alone. Be careful of fragments and fused sentences, comma–splices, or run–ons.

Fragments are pieces of sentences. They have a capital letter at the beginning and a period at the end but cannot stand alone. Fragments are constructed in four main ways: dependent clauses made to look like sentences, –ing ending verbs that stand alone, sentences that are split by capitalization and punctuation, and modifiers that are set up as sentences although they have no subject. Study these examples:

▶ **Dependent clause** When I learned to drive at the age of fifteen.

▶ **–ing form** The mayor standing up on the platform.

▶ **Split sentence** Jimmy Carter, who lost the 1980 Presidential election. Is probably best known for his humanitarian work.

▶ **Modifying phrase set up like a sentence** Because he is the most famous living President. Ronald Reagan attracts attention wherever he goes.

Comma–splices, run–ons, or fused sentences occur when two complete thoughts that could be two separate sentences are incorrectly combined. Here are several such sentences:

▶ When she was first diagnosed with breast cancer, she tried to hide it she had never been so frightened in her life.

▶ **When she was first diagnosed with breast cancer, she tried to hide it because she had never been so frightened in her life.**

▶ He lied she believed him.

▶ **He lied, and she believed him.**

▶ The Olympic Games in Georgia will be dangerous for athletes they will be subjected to very high temperatures and soaring humidity.

▶ **The Olympic Games in Georgia will be dangerous for athletes; they will be subjected to very high temperatures and soaring humidity.**

Hint: You could correct the last three examples easily by making each into two separate sentences. Beginning writers should do that. Mature writers (college level) should learn to correct them in other ways, by rewriting the sentences or with punctuation.

USAGE

AGREEMENT

VERBS AND THEIR SUBJECTS

A verb must agree in number with its subject. A singular subject requires a singular verb. A plural subject requires a plural verb. It's not quite as simple as it sounds, however. The first step in determining subject and verb agreement is identifying the subject and verb. Try not to be concerned with other words in the sentence as they may confuse you.

▶ The Tooth Fairy always paid well for the pearly white nuggets under the pillow. **(Tooth Fairy/paid)**

▶ The characters make the play come to life. **(characters/make)**

Be careful of plural words that come between subject and verb.

▶ Our concern for the young, the elderly, and the ill causes us to volunteer frequently. **(concern/causes)**

Sometimes verbs come before subjects. Watch for this when the following words precede the subject: there, here, which, who, what, where.

▶ Across the window ledge stretches the cat to her fullest length. **(stretches/cat)**

▶ There are your slippers. **(slippers/are)**

Sometimes the subject is compound. Nouns, noun phrases, or pronouns connected by **and** are compound subjects that usually take a plural verb.

▶ Tammy, Mandy, and I are all wearing blue to the winter formal. **(Tammy, Mandy, and I/are)**

Subjects that are combined using "either...or," "neither...nor," or "not only...but also" require the verb that agrees with the subject closest to the verb.

▶ Either a ring or bangle bracelets are what I want for my birthday. **(bracelets/are)**

Sometimes the subject is a collective noun. A collective noun takes a singular verb when the members are treated as a unit and a plural verb when they are treated as individuals.

▶ The class is attending the play tomorrow. **(acting as a unit)**

▶ The class are writing their autobiographies. **(acting as individuals)**

ADJECTIVES AND ADVERBS

Adjectives are used for comparison. They have three forms: absolute or positive, comparative, and superlative. The comparative form can be made by adding –er or the adverb "more," and the superlative can be made by adding –est or "most." Comparative form is used when comparing one thing to another. Superlative is used when comparing to three or more persons or things. Additionally, some adjectives (usually with two or more syllables) must use "more" and "most" to form the comparative and superlative forms. Also, some adjectives are absolute. For example, you cannot have degrees of **final, complete, empty, dead, full,** or **perfect.** Finally, look at the close relationship between adjectives and adverbs as represented by **good/well** and **bad/badly.** These pairs have the same comparative and superlative forms.

POSITIVE	COMPARATIVE	SUPERLATIVE
fine	finer	finest
short	shorter	shortest
dumb	dumber	dumbest
happy	happier	happiest
foolish	more foolish	most foolish
nervous	more nervous	most nervous
good	better	best
well	better	best
bad	worse	worst
badly	worse	worst

► Stan is **tall**. He is **taller** than his twin brother. He is the **tallest** player on the team.

Adjectives modify only nouns and pronouns and adverbs modify verbs, adjectives, and adverbs. A common mistake people make is using an adjective instead of an adverb after a verb.

Note the following examples:

► He rode the horse **easy**. (should be **easily**)
► The moose ran **aggressive** toward the boat. (should be **aggressively**)

Hint: Do not confuse the use of **well (an adverb)** and **good (an adjective.) Some words may be adjectives or adverbs. Their use is determined by the word they modify.**

Exercise 4

Complete the following exercise by underlining the correct choice, changing incorrect words, or rewriting sentences.

1. The dolphins (was, were) swimming along with the boat.

2. Neither the captain nor his first mate (seem, seems) concerned that we are taking on water.

3. One of the Senatorial contenders was our (most best, best) friend.

4. The subject of the course (is, are) the political process in the United States.

5. Is he the man (who, whom) is running for office?

6. (Who, whom) did you see at the tennis match?

7. It was (he, him) who stole the money and ran.

8. (We, us) girls appreciate a night out once in awhile.

9. This demonstration, with signs, people shouting, and police barricades, (remind, reminds) me of the 60's.

10. At the age of six, Mozart's father gave him a harpsichord.

11. Kate read the play about overcoming hardships while riding the exercise bicycle.

12. While fixing dinner, the hamburger burned.

13. It was a present from her grandmother, the antique.

14. When Bill and Tom came in, I told him about the case.

15. The seagulls were diving at the shellfish which scared the children.

PRONOUNS

Pronouns usually substitute for nouns and, as such, may be subjects, objects, or possessives. You must check the pronoun/antecedent relationship and watch for singular plural status. Consider:

Personal Pronouns: *I, you, he, she, it, we, you,* and *they* are used as subjects. *Me, you, him, her, it, us,* and *them* are used as objects. *My, mine, your, yours, his, her, hers, its, our, ours, their,* and *theirs* are used to show possession.

Reflexive Pronouns: *Myself, yourself, himself, herself, ourselves, yourselves, themselves,* and *itself* are all reflexive pronouns used to reflect the sentence action back to the subject. They are frequently misused, so it is a good idea to avoid them.

Relative Pronouns: *Who, whom, which, that, whatever,* and *whomever* are relative pronouns used to join subordinate clauses to sentences. Clauses containing relative pronouns are not complete sentences. Students often confuse *who* with *whom* and *that* with *which.* Use *who* as a subject form and *whom* as an object form. Use *that* when the clause is essential and *which* if the clause could be left out without changing the meaning of the sentence.

Demonstrative Pronouns: *That, this, these,* and *those* are demonstrative pronouns and are used to clarify what you are talking about.

Interrogative Pronouns: *Which, who, whom,* and *what* can all be used as interrogatives asking a question.

Indefinite Pronouns: *Everything, everybody, many, more, much, plenty, several, some, enough, someone, any, anybody, anything, both, either, each, one, none, nothing, few, less,* and *neither* may all be indefinite pronouns. Understanding whether they are used as singular or plural is important to be able to match them to the appropriate verb. Requiring the plural verb are: *all, many, plenty, few, both,* and *several.* Singular verbs are required by: *anything, anybody, everybody, everything, nothing, either, neither, much, one, someone, somebody, something, each,* and *every.* The following are singular if treated as a group and plural otherwise: *none, some, and most.*

> **Hint:** Commonly confused possessive pronouns: it's, its; your, you're; who's, whose; their, they're.

Here is a brief word about gender usage and pronouns. Writing that requires consistent use of "he or she" or "him/her" or "(s)he" can be strengthened by using gender neutral words. Could the word "students," "people," or "workers" substitute for male- or female-specific words in your paper? Instead of fireman, policeman, businessman, or chairman, how about firefighter, police officer, business professional, or chair? As an added bonus such substitutions may help you avoid pronoun problems.

AGREEMENT: PRONOUNS AND ANTECEDENTS

A pronoun must agree in number with the word it replaces. The word replaced is called the **antecedent.** Pronouns include: I, you (singular and plural), he, she, it, they, and their declensions.

► Herman could not understand why he didn't make the team. (**Herman/he**)

Pronouns must clearly refer and relate to what they modify.

► Jane's husband works **downtown**, but she isn't interested in **it**. (**unclear**)

► Jane's husband works **downtown**, but she isn't interested in working **there**. (**clear**)

One mistake students frequently make in pronoun usage is shifting point of view. Pronouns must not present a shift in view.

► I love acting and being able to interpret characters on stage. It's more to **you** than just a job. (**shifts from I to you**)

► I love acting and being able to interpret characters on stage. It's more to **me** than just a job. (**no shift**)

► I hate the parts of school such as tests, quizzes, and writing assignments that stress you out. (**shifts from I to you**)

► I hate the parts of school such as tests, quizzes, and writing assignments that stress me out. (**no shift**)

Hint: Keep modifiers as close to the word they modify as possible.

Exercise 5

Match the following pronoun uses to a description:

1. **We** asked Sherry to prepare the holiday meal.

2. Sherry sent **us** an email asking for menu suggestions.

3. I sent her **my** list of favorites.

4. I **myself** volunteered to bring the wine.

5. Dan said that we needed to prepare for fifty, **whatever** the actual responses were.

6. Gloria said, "**That** is a winner apple pie!"

7. "**Who** is bringing the stuffing?"

8. The cranberry sauce, **which** is my personal favorite, was left behind in Melba's fridge.

9. The one thing **that** we all forgot was rolls.

10. I had one helping of mashed potatoes. Jake and **several** others had more.

Hint: Try leaving out parts of the sentence when deciding what pronoun form to use.

FORMING VERBS

We use different tenses of verbs to indicate time. Verb tenses are based on three parts of the verb: present, past and past participle. From these it is easy to form the past, present, and future tenses, along with the past, present, and future perfect tenses. Regular verbs are those that form the past and past participle by adding –d or –ed to their endings. These are usually not difficult to use. Here are some common verbs in the six tenses:

present	wash	eat	put	complete
present perfect	has washed	has eaten	has put	has completed
past	washed	ate	put	completed
past perfect	had washed	had eaten	had put	had completed
future	will wash	will eat	will put	will complete
future perfect	will have washed	will have eaten	will have put	will have completed

> **Present** describes something happening right now.
>
> **Present perfect** indicates something has started and is continuing.
>
> **Past** indicates something happened and is completed.
>
> **Past perfect** indicates something happened before the past tense.
>
> **Future** is for those things that have not happened yet.
>
> **Future perfect** is for something from the past and the future that has happened and will go on and end at a certain point.

IRREGULAR VERBS

Some verbs are irregular and form tenses differently. Study the following:

present	swim	dive	hang (painting)	hang (execute)
past	swam	dived	hung	hung
past participle	swum	dived	hanged	hanged

Notice the verb TO BE:

present	**past**	**past participle**
am, is, are	was, were	been
I am	I was	I have been
we are	we were	we have been
you are	you were	you have been
he, she, it is	they were	they have been

> **Hint:** Remember, the past participle form takes the helping word (has, have, had) and the past form does not.

SENTENCE STRUCTURE

RELATING CLAUSES

When writing sentences, it is important to structure the parts of a sentence to show equality or inequality of ideas. We show equality with what we call **parallelism** or **coordinate construction.** To do this, balance nouns with nouns, adjective clauses with adjective clauses, and prepositional phrases with prepositional phrases. When using the following conjunctions in parallel construction, always use them in pairs: **either/or; neither/nor; both/and; not only/ but also.**

- ▶ **Correct parallelism**   During summer vacation I am going to swim, to sail, and to sleep late every day.

- ▶ **Incorrect parallelism**   During summer vacation I am going to swim, sailing, and to sleep late every day.

- ▶ **Correct parallelism**   **Both** Jeff **and** Choi are tied in their checkers match.

- ▶ **Incorrect parallelism** (needs **"but also"** to make parallel)   I am **not only** the best all around athlete.

- ▶ **Correct parallelism**   **Neither** the player **nor** the coach would give interviews.

- ▶ **Incorrect parallelism** (needs **"neither/nor"**)   **Neither** the postmaster **or** the mail carrier could tell me where my package went.

When you are using ideas that are not equal you must use what is called **subordination.** In this type of sentence construction, the main idea is an independent clause (it can stand alone). The lesser or subordinate ideas are dependent clauses (cannot stand alone). Subordination is useful to keep short sentences from sounding choppy. The writer identifies the main idea and subordinates other ideas. Punctuate with a comma if the sentence is introduced by the dependent (cannot stand alone) clause. If the dependent clause is not introductory, then no comma is needed.

- ▶ If I score highly enough on the exam, I can exempt a college course. (**comma needed**)

- ▶ I can exempt a college course if I score highly enough on the exam. (**no comma needed**)

USING MODIFIERS

It is important that modifiers be placed correctly in a sentence to avoid ambiguity and to keep from splitting infinitives.

- ▶ At the end of the book, the characters begin to deliriously laugh.
  (**misplaced modifier splitting an infinitive**)

- ▶ At the end of the book, the characters begin to laugh deliriously.
  (**correctly placed modifier**)

AVOIDING SHIFTS

Good writing is consistent in **voice and tense.** Voice indicates whether the subject is acting or being acted upon. Active voice is the stronger and preferred use of the two. Avoid passive voice as much as possible.

▶ **Passive voice**   Data **were collected** by members of the research team.

▶ **Active voice**   The research team **collected** data.

▶ **Passive voice**   The computer **was used** by the criminals to identify potential victims.

▶ **Active voice**   The criminals **used** the computer to identify potential victims.

Tense of verbs must be a logical indication of time.

▶ **Tense shift**   Harry **was wondering** if he should make a sandwich or not when the doorbell **rang** and his best friend **walks** in.

▶ **Consistent tense**   Harry **was wondering** if he should make a sandwich or not when the doorbell **rang** and his best friend **walked** in.

▶ **Tense shift**   College students need to **manage** their time wisely so they **didn't** have an unrealistic amount of work at the end of the semester.

▶ **Consistent tense**   College students need to **manage** their time wisely so they **don't** have an unrealistic amount of work at the end of the semester.

STANDARD IDIOMS

Idioms are figurative language that are used most often in speaking. They are a type of slang found in speech patterns of people of certain age, place, and culture. While they may be used in popular casual writing, they are inappropriate for formal academic writing. Consider the following:

▶ I remember my childhood and the family gatherings with great fondness because now I only see my relatives **once in a blue moon.**

▶ I remember my childhood and the family gatherings with great fondness because now I only see my relatives **occasionally.**

▶ I need to go home before we go to dinner and get rid of my **five-o'clock-shadow**.

▶ I need to go home and **shave** before we go to dinner.

Exercise 6

Edit the following sentences by making changes where necessary.

1. A person who likes fast food should watch their fat intake.

2. When the members of the team fell behind it lost the desire to win.

3. Yellow and dried Susan kept the corsage from the prom for months.

4. Hanging on the hook we forgot to grab our coats.

5. Eating leaves from the top branches we enjoyed photographing the giraffes.

6. Information about the terrorist threats was received by the news bureau chiefs.

7. She was neither the best.

8. Having my birthday cake.

9. Mini–blinds have been shown to cause a lead hazard to children. Which is why they will no longer be sold in the United States.

10. So I can get into a better college I am taking Advanced Placement courses.

11. We had walk ten miles before he said anything.

12. We had agreed to never argue about that issue again.

13. Some students do not realize that it is difficult to go to school and to be working.

14. The boat, quickly taking on water, sunk by the time help arrived.

15. All of us decided to consciously ignore the speaker who had insulted our intelligence.

RHETORICAL SKILLS

STRATEGY

APPROPRIATENESS FOR AUDIENCE AND PURPOSE

Whenever you write something, there are two things you must consider: **audience** and **purpose.** By **audience** we mean who will be reading what you write. If you are writing a letter to a friend, then you will use slang expressions and other informal usage. You might even use incomplete sentences. If, however, you are writing to a different audience, such as a prospective employer, you would want to use a formal style because that would make a good first impression. Compare the following two examples:

Hi,

    I am a high school student and I need to find a college. Could you please tell me what it's like at Yale? I guess I need to know how much it costs also. If you have some pictures could you send some?

Dr. Smith:

    I am a high school junior, and I am interested in learning more about Yale University. Your reputation for academics, opportunity for pre–law advisement, and resident college program are three areas that make me feel Yale may be the right choice for me.

The **purpose** for writing is an important consideration also. If you are writing directions for someone, you will want to describe steps in a chronological order. If you are describing the way something looks, you might want to use spatial order. If you are trying to persuade someone, you might want to make your points from most important to least important.

SUPPORTING FACTS AND DETAILS

Effective writing makes use of details to support a topic. Those details must be relevant to the subject and not stray from the topic. There should be enough detail to completely cover the topic for the intended audience. Someone who is very familiar with the subject of your writing will not need as many details as someone who is not. Consider the audience for the following paragraph. Note the irrelevant detail.

    My mother is a doctor. She is not just any doctor, though. She is the best. As she has her morning coffee, she looks over her patient list and tries to recall something about every person she is going to see that day. **She cooks a really good breakfast too. (This is not a relevant detail. It strays from the topic.)** Her patients always stay with her a long time because she cares so much about them.

OPENINGS, TRANSITIONS, AND CLOSINGS

These are all devices that help your writing to be cohesive, that is, flow smoothly from opening to closing with logical order and transitions. An opening is important because it is an opportunity to "hook" the reader and make the reader want to know more about your topic. In your attempt to find an interesting beginning, however, avoid such things as clichés, statements of what you are to write about, or apologies for any lack of knowledge. Notice the differences between these two openings.

"As God is my witness, I'll never be hungry again," said Scarlett O'Hara, and this is how I feel about my latest diet. I'm going to tell you how to achieve that skinny-minny Scarlett's eighteen inch waist. **(inappropriate reference, cliché, states what will follow)**

How can you lose weight and not endure hunger? My latest diet provides all the nutrients I need to feel satisfied, and yet I burn enough calories to lose two pounds per week. **(attention-getting and yet not chatty and cliché-ridden)**

Closings are also important for the same reason. You want to leave the reader with a good, strong ending. Generally, avoid the same problems as in your opening. Avoid clichés, statements about what you just said, and excuses. Never introduce material in a conclusion that you have not previously discussed. Consider the following:

So, I dare you to come see the new me. I'll be the skinny one in the teeny weeny bikini. I'll be thin as a rail, and I'll also have a new hairstyle. **(clichés, new material)**

So, if you're interested in a nutritionally balanced diet that allows you to eat good food and still lose weight, this is a plan you might want to try. **(concludes what was written about and makes a strong statement)**

ORGANIZATION

LOGICAL ORDER

The order in which you arrange ideas in your writing depends on the way you decide to develop your essays. You should always be sure your arrangement is logical. Consider the following paragraph:

1/ Planning a meeting can be a stressful experience if you've never done it before. **2/** The site needs to include enough meeting space. **3/** Good food can make even a poor meeting a pleasure. **4/** The committee must research the needs of members who have special needs. **5/** When considering the site, the meeting place is the most important consideration. **6/** You should discuss the purpose for the meeting before considering a site. **7/** Then there are several other considerations. **8/** Finally, the program planners should devise a varied and interesting series of activities for all the members of the organization.

What would be a better arrangement of these sentences? _____

(*Answers* to Logical Order and Chapter Eight exercises are found on p.198.)

STYLE

MANAGING SENTENCE ELEMENTS/SUBORDINATION AND COMBINATION

As we have seen before, coordinate and subordinate construction are used to combine sentences. It is a mark of mature writing to be able to combine short, choppy sentences into longer, more effective sentences. In subordinate construction you determine the less important part of the sentence and place a subordinate conjunction before it. Coordinate construction (and coordinating conjunctions) is used when sentence elements are equal in importance.

▶ Coordinate conjunctions include: **or, nor, for, so, and, but,** and **yet.**

▶ Subordinate words include: **since, because, although, even though, though, when, where, how, after, as,** and **before.**

AVOIDING WORDINESS AND REDUNDANCY

Wordiness is the use of too many words to express your thoughts. Don't use more words than you need. Immature writers often do the following: string too many ideas together with *and*'s; use euphemisms; use worn out words; use the incorrect form of a word; use passive voice; use unnecessary words; repeat words.

MAINTAINING STYLE AND TONE

Be sure you maintain the same style, tone, and diction throughout writing. Notice how the following piece shifts in style.

Dr. Smith:

I was pleased to receive your invitation to interview for the faculty position in Biochemistry. Friday the thirteenth of August at 3:00 p.m. is a convenient time for me. I will be driving to Atlanta so I would appreciate it if you would provide a parking space. Maybe after the interview we could get a beer and take in a Braves game. I look forward to meeting you in August.

Sincerely,

Hardly A. Chance, Ph.D.

Exercise 7

Each of the following pieces of writing contains an error discussed in this section. Choose the letter of the corresponding fault for each sentence.

A. appropriateness for audience   F. wordiness

B. poor opening   G. redundancy

C. poor closing   H. maintaining style and tone

D. logical order   I. subordination/coordination

E. supporting facts and details

1. The rain was just what we needed. For weeks we had suffered under an unbearable burden of heat. All of our gardens were parched. Television programming was terrible.

2. As you can see, John F. Kennedy was a real "hear no evil, see no evil" kind of guy. The end.

3. Mr. James: I would like you to give me a job for the summer. I'm a really hard worker and I like being downtown.

4. Dear Sammi, It has been one week since we left on our vacation, and I have never had so much fun. We have visited museums, an aquarium, and other sites of interest. We have played miniature golf. I don't think Deborah is the best choice of girlfriend for James, do you?

5. The horses went galloping across the field. Over the stream and toward the hills, they raced. Two men had run to the barn and saddled horses.

6. I am going to see the Olympics so I don't have tickets yet.

7. In my honest opinion, if you know what I mean, and I'm sure you do, Cathy was one of the troublemakers.

8. Half a century has gone by since that happened fifty years ago.

9. Ghandi was a real people person and that's what this paper will be about.

CHAPTER NINE

PRACTICE TESTS

TEST ONE

Read the following paragraph carefully. For each numbered section, look at the choices that follow. Decide whether the section would be better with one of the changes or if it should remain unchanged. The choice "A" is always "no change." When you take the actual COMPASS test on the computer, the sections will not be numbered. You will have to move the cursor to the section you wish to change and highlight it. Then you will choose the letter of the change you would like to make. The item will be changed, and you will have the opportunity to see the changed text before going on.

1/ Hanging on the top of Faneuil Hall, in the market district, we always get excited when we see the grasshopper. **2/** Symbol of Boston. **3/** It's aged copper body is beloved by children and adults alike as one of the most famous landmarks of the city. **4/** Distinctively large as the gigantic grasshopper weathervane may be, however, it is one of **5/** many such easy identifiable Boston icons. **6/** Some others included the Statue of Paul Revere, the Public Gardens, the Old North Church, and the band shell on the Charles River.

The statue of Paul Revere is a famous reminder of the silversmith **7/** patriot which rode through the villages and **8/** warn of the approach of the British during the Revolutionary War. **9/** Much stories and poems have been written about him. **10/** The Old North Church which is where the **11/** lantern was hanged in the window, is another place worth visiting. **12/** Its graveyard is that very same place where many famous people are buried. **13/** The Public Gardens, across the street from the Common, has beautiful flowers and the famous Swan paddle boats. **14/** If you readed the story *Make Way for Ducklings* you have seen pictures of the Gardens and the Common. **15/** The famous band shell on the Charles River; that is where fans of the Boston Pops Orchestra have enjoyed summer-time concerts for many years. It is located on an esplanade where you can see the crew teams of the many nearby colleges and **16/** sailboats bobbing for the river.

17/ Boston is such a historic city filled with such history. **18/** Everyone should plan to take his vacation there. **19/** Where else could you find such a mix of old and new.

1/

○ A. Hanging on the top of Faneuil Hall, in the market district, we always get excited

○ B. We always get excited when we see the grasshopper hanging on the top of Faneuil Hall

○ C. Hanging on the top of Faneuil Hall, the grasshopper always gets excited when we see

○ D. Hanging on the top of Faneuil Hall, we see the grasshopper and we always get excited

○ E. We always see the grasshopper hanging on the top of Faneuil Hall, very excited

2/

- ○ A. Symbol of Boston.
- ○ B. Symbols of Boston.
- ○ C. It is a symbol of Boston.
- ○ D. Symbolic of Boston.
- ○ E. Symbols in Boston.

3/

- ○ A. It's aged copper body is beloved
- ○ B. Its aged copper body is beloved
- ○ C. Its's aged copper body is beloved
- ○ D. It aged copper body is beloved
- ○ E. Its' aged coped body is beloved

4/

- ○ A. Distinctively large as the gigantic grasshopper weathervane may be, however,
- ○ B. Distinctively large as the gigantic weathervane may can be, however,
- ○ C. Distinctively large as the weathervane may be, however,
- ○ D. Distinctively as large as can be, however,
- ○ E. Distinctive large as can be, however,

5/

- ○ A. many such easy identifiable
- ○ B. many such easier identifiable
- ○ C. many such more easier identifiable
- ○ D. many such easily identifiable
- ○ E. many much easily identifiable

6/

- ○ A. Some others included the Statue of Paul Revere
- ○ B. Some others include; the Statue of Paul Revere
- ○ C. Some others includes the Statue of Paul Revere
- ○ D. Some others includes: the Statue of Paul Revere
- ○ E. Some others include: the Statue of Paul Revere

7/

- ○ A. patriot which rode through
- ○ B. patriot who rode through
- ○ C. patriot whose rode through
- ○ D. patriot that rode through
- ○ E. patriot who's rode through

8/

- ◯ A. warn of the approach of
- ◯ B. warned of the approach that
- ◯ C. warned of the approach for
- ◯ D. warned for the approach of
- ◯ E. warned of the approach of

9/

- ◯ A. Much stories and poems have
- ◯ B. Much stories and poem have
- ◯ C. Much story and poem have
- ◯ D. Many stories and poems have
- ◯ E. Many story and poem have

10/

- ◯ A. The Old North Church which is where
- ◯ B. The Old North Church, which is where
- ◯ C. The Old North Church; which is where
- ◯ D. The Old North Church: which is where
- ◯ E. The Old North Church, which is that where

11/

- ◯ A. lantern was hanged in the window
- ◯ B. lantern was hanged; in the window
- ◯ C. lantern was; hanged in the window
- ◯ D. lantern was hung in the window
- ◯ E. lantern which was hung in the window

12/

- ◯ A. Its graveyard is that
- ◯ B. It's graveyard is that
- ◯ C. Its' graveyard is that
- ◯ D. His graveyard is that
- ◯ E. His' graveyard is that

13/

- ◯ A. The Public Gardens, across the street from the Common, has beautiful flowers
- ◯ B. The Public Gardens, across the street from the Common, have beautiful flowers
- ◯ C. The Public Gardens, across the street from the Common, having beautiful flowers
- ◯ D. The Public Gardens, across the street from the Common, they have beautiful flowers
- ◯ E. The Public Gardens, across the street from the Common, are having beautiful

14/

- ◯ A. If you readed the story
- ◯ B. If you have read the story
- ◯ C. If you had readed the story
- ◯ D. If you read the story
- ◯ E. If you have reading the story

15/

   ○ A. The famous band shell on the Charles River; that is where
   ○ B. The famous band shell on the Charles River: that is where
   ○ C. The famous band shell on the Charles River was the place that
   ○ D. The famous band shell on the Charles River, that is where
   ○ E. The famous band shell on the Charles River is where

16/

   ○ A. sailboats bobbing for the river.
   ○ B. sailboats bobbing on the river.
   ○ C. sailboats bobbing in the river.
   ○ D. sailboats bobbing to the river.
   ○ E. sailboats bobbing over the river.

17/

   ○ A. Boston is such a historic city filled with such history.
   ○ B. Boston is such a historic city, filled with such history.
   ○ C. Boston is such a historic city.
   ○ D. Boston is such a filled with history city.
   ○ E. Boston is such a city filled with history.

18/

   ○ A. Everyone should plan to take his vacation here.
   ○ B. Everybody should plan to take his vacation here.
   ○ C. Everybody should plan to take one's vacation here.
   ○ D. Everyone should plan to take one's vacation here.
   ○ E. Everyone should plan to take a vacation here.

19/

   ○ A. Where else could you find such a mix of old and new.
   ○ B. Where else could you find such a mix of old and new?
   ○ C. Where else could you find such a mix of old and new!
   ○ D. Where? Else could you find such a mix of old and new.
   ○ E. Where! Else could you find such a mix of old and new?

20/

If the following sentence needs to be inserted, where should it logically go?

For more information about visiting Boston, call your travel agent.

   ○ A. after sentence 6
   ○ B. at the end
   ○ C. at the beginning
   ○ D. before sentence 17
   ○ E. before sentence 15

NAME _____ DATE_____

TEST TWO

> **1/** There have been a lot of research done on what makes students successful in college. **2/** The general belief is that if you work hard, study, and make good grades he will complete a degree. **3/** Studies show that; students most often leave college for reasons unrelated to grades. **4/** Girlfriends, boyfriends, homesickness, finances, lack of support, isolation. **5/** Would you like to know the most importantest thing you can do to increase your chances of remaining in college? **6/** No, its not study, although that is also essential. You need to bond with the institution. **7/** Thats the single most effective thing a student can do. **8/** What do we mean by bond, and how do you do it. **9/** We mean you need to really connect with a professor, **10/** make some friends, and attending some campus activities. **11/** Students who travel home each weekend to see their families and old friends do not make the important connections you need at college. **12/** Their not making the transition you make by connecting with a professor, **13/** you go to office hours, engage in conversation, and seek advice from professionals on campus. In this way you get in the groove. You also need to make some friends or at least acquaintances on campus. **14/** You will be much more satisfied with your choice of college and yet less likely to leave when things do not go smoothly. **15/** A good way to make friends is to immediately start a study group. **16/** We all think we captured all of the lecture notes and read all the important material also when we get together with others we find out everybody has information to contribute. **17/** Study groups help academically; and, can also lead to lasting friendships. **18/** Finally, get out of your dorm room and attend some campus events. **19/** Colleges and universities, take my word for it, provide many recreation opportunities from feature movies to sporting events to weekend camping trips. Relaxation is important to students; and, these activities could have provided some of the most worthwhile experiences of your college career.

1/

- A. There have been a lot of research done
- B. There have been many research done
- C. There has been a lot of research done
- D. There had been many researches done
- E. There are many researches done

2/

- A. if you work hard and study and make good grades he will complete
- B. if you work hard and study and make good grades he will have completed
- C. if you work hard and study and make good grades you complete
- D. if you work hard and study and make good grades you will complete
- E. if you work hard and study and make good grades you completed

3/

- A. Studies show that; students most often leave
- B. Studies show that students most often leave
- C. Studies show: that students most often leave
- D. Studies show that students: most often leave
- E. Studies show that students most oftenest leave

179

4/

    ○ A. grades. Girlfriends, boyfriends, homesickness, finances, lack of support, isolation.

    ○ B. grades; girlfriends, boyfriends, homesickness, financed, lack of support, isolation.

    ○ C. grades, girlfriends, boyfriends, homesickness, finances, lack of support, isolation.

    ○ D. grades: girlfriends, boyfriends, homesickness, finances, lack of support, and isolation.

    ○ E. grades. Girlfriends and boyfriends and homesickness and finances and lack of support and isolation.

5/

    ○ A. Would you like to know the most importantest

    ○ B. Would you like to know the more importantest

    ○ C. Would you like to know the most important

    ○ D. Would you like to know the much more importantest

    ○ E. Would you like to know the importanter

6/

    ○ A. No, its not study, although that is also essential.

    ○ B. No, it's not study, although that is also essential.

    ○ C. No, it not study, although that is also essential.

    ○ D. No, its' not a study, although that is also essential.

    ○ E. No, it's not a study, although that is also essential.

7/

    ○ A. Thats the single most effective

    ○ B. That the single most effective

    ○ C. That's the single most effective

    ○ D. That's the single mostest effective

    ○ E. Thats the single more effectiver

8/

    ○ A. What do we mean by bond, and how do you do it.

    ○ B. What do we mean by bond, and who do you do it.

    ○ C. What do we mean by bond, and how do you do it?

    ○ D. What do you mean by bond, and how does it do it?

    ○ E. What do you mean by bond, and how did it do it?

9/

- ○ A. We mean you need to really connect with a professor,
- ○ B. We mean you really need to connect with a professor,
- ○ C. We mean you need to connect really with a professor,
- ○ D. We mean really, you need to connect with a professor,
- ○ E. We mean you need to connect with a real professor,

10/

- ○ A. make some friends, and attending some campus activities
- ○ B. make some friends, and be attending some campus activities
- ○ C. make some friends, and attended some campus activities
- ○ D. make some friends, who attended some campus activities
- ○ E. make some friends, and attend some campus activities

11/

- ○ A. Students who travel home each weekend to see their families and old friends do not make
- ○ B. Students who travel home each weekend to see his families and old friends do not make
- ○ C. Students who travel to home each weekend and see their family and old friends do not make
- ○ D. Students who travels home each weekend to see their families and old friends do not make
- ○ E. Student who travel home each weekend to see their families and old friends do not make

12/

- ○ A. Their not making the transition you need to make
- ○ B. They not making the transition you need to make
- ○ C. They're not making the transition you need to make
- ○ D. Theyre not making the transition you need to make
- ○ E. There not making the transition you need to make

13/

- ○ A. you go to office hours, engage in conversation, and seek advice from professionals
- ○ B. going to office hours, engaging in conversation, and seeking advice from professionals
- ○ C. go to office hours, engage in conversations, and seek advice from professionals
- ○ D. you going to office hours, you engaging in conversation, and you seeking advice from professionals
- ○ E. went to office hours, engaged in conversation, and sought advice from professionals

14/

- ○ A. You will be much more satisfied with your choice of college and yet less likely to leave
- ○ B. You will be much more satisfied with your choice of college but less likely to leave
- ○ C. You will be much more satisfied with your choice of college; nevertheless less likely to leave
- ○ D. You will be much more satisfied with your choice of college but likely to leave
- ○ E. You will be much more satisfied with your choice of college and less likely to leave

15/

    ○ A. A good way to make friends is to immediately start a study group

    ○ B. A good way to make friends is immediately to start a study group.

    ○ C. A good way to make friends is to start immediately a study group.

    ○ D. A good way to make friends is to start a study group immediately.

    ○ E. A good way to make friends is to start an immediate study group.

16/

    ○ A. important material also when we get together with others

    ○ B. important material; however, when we get together with others,

    ○ C. important material however when we get together with others

    ○ D. important material and also when we get together with others

    ○ E. important material so when we get together with others

17/

    ○ A. academically; and, can also lead

    ○ B. academically, and, can also lead

    ○ C. academically and can also

    ○ D. academically. And can also

    ○ E. academically, and: can also lead

18/

    ○ A. Finally, get out of your dorm room

    ○ B. Finally get out of your dorm room

    ○ C. Finally: get out of your dorm room

    ○ D. Finally; get out of your dorm room

    ○ E. Finally, get out of your: dorm room

19/

    ○ A. Colleges and universities, take my word for it,

    ○ B. Colleges and universities, you can take my word for it

    ○ C. Colleges and universities, why not take my word for it

    ○ D. Colleges and universities provides

    ○ E. Colleges and universities provide

20/

    If you were asked to read about how to study in college, would this article fit that assignment?

    ○ A. Yes, because it talks about studying to make good grades.

    ○ B. Yes, because it focuses on studying in a group.

    ○ C. Yes, because anything you can read is helpful.

    ○ D. No, because it doesn't give you specific study techniques.

    ○ E. No, because it says study is not too important.

TEST THREE

1/ The period we know as the Industrial Revolution lasted approximately one hundred and fifty years from 1700 to 1850. 2/ Wow, that's a long time for a revolution! 3/ Inventions that changed lives forever and inspired future development. 4/ For example the steam engine led to mining improvements because water could be pumped out of coal mines. These coal mines were dark, and one never knew when one would step into an abyss. 5/ The steam engine yet powered the first steamship to cross the Atlantic, the kiln used to develop Wedgewood china, and the early locomotive. 6/ Communication was improved by the invention of the telegraph. Transportation by the macadam roadway. 7/ Early laws to protect workers including young children began to be developed.

8/ Although other countries made strides in technology and manufacturing, England is credited with leadership in the Industrial Revolution. 9/ There are several reasons for this: geography, capital, labor, management, and government. 10/ The government fostered, helped, and assisted the growth of the middle class through an expansion of the House of Commons. 11/ Thus, there was a middle class that was a part of the government and not in opposition to it. 12/ England had a financial stable government. 13/ It's banks could loan money and many citizens had investment capital. 14/ Feudal society was in decline. Workers could move about and establishes urban enclaves of factory workers. 15/ Agriculture could support an industrialize urban population. 16/ Additionally the educated middle class provided upwardly mobile management. 17/ Geographically England had ports useful for the shipping trade. 18/ Canals and the railroads provided transportation options throughout the country. 19/ Native raw materials, specifically, coal and iron meant that heavy industry and manufacturing did not have to depend on foreign assistance.

1/

○ A. The period we know as the Industrial Revolution lasted approximately one hundred and fifty years from 1700 to 1850.

○ B. The period we know as the Industrial Revolution lasted approximately one hundred and fifty years, from 1700 to 1850.

○ C. The period we know, as the Industrial Revolution, lasted approximately one hundred and fifty years, from 1700 to 1850.

○ D. The period we know as the Industrial Revolution; lasted approximately one hundred and fifty years from 1700 to 1850.

○ E. The period we know as the Industrial Revolution last approximately one hundred and fifty years, from 1700 to 1850.

2/

○ A. Wow, that's a long time for a revolution!

○ B. That's too long to be called a revolution.

○ C. In those years revolutions were long.

○ D. Wow! That's a long time for a revolution!

○ E. That is a long period of time for a revolution.

3/

○ A. Inventions that changed lives forever and inspired future development.

○ B. Inventions that changed lives forever inspired development.

○ C. Inventions that changed lives; forever, inspired future development.

○ D. Inventions came about that changed lives forever and inspired future development.

○ E. Inventions come about and changing lives forever inspired future development.

4/

○ A. For example

○ B. For: example

○ C. For example,

○ D. Four example

○ E. For examples

5/

○ A. yet powered . . .

○ B. also powered . . .

○ C. and also power . . .

○ D. and yet powers . . .

○ E. and has powered . . .

6/

○ A. invention of the telegraph. Transportation by the

○ B. invention of the telegraph; transportation by

○ C. invention of the telegraph, transportation by the

○ D. invention of the telegraph and transportation by the

○ E. invention of the telegraph, and transportation by the

7/

○ A. Early laws to protect workers including young children

○ B. Early laws to protect workers, including young children,

○ C. Early laws to protect workers including young children;

○ D. Early laws to protect workers including young children:

○ E. Early laws to protect, workers including young children

8/

○ A. technology and manufacturing, England is

○ B. technology and manufacturing. England is

○ C. technology and manufacturing; England is

○ D. technology and manufacturing, England was

○ E. technology and manufacturing. England was

9/

- ○ A. reasons for this: geography
- ○ B. reasons for this; geography
- ○ C. reasons for this. Geography
- ○ D. reasons for this, geography
- ○ E. reasons for this geography

10/

- ○ A. fostered, helped, and assisted the growth
- ○ B. fostered helped, and assisted the growth
- ○ C. fostered and assisted the growth
- ○ D. fostered the growth of the middle class and assisted in their growth
- ○ E. fosters and assists the growth

11/

- ○ A. Thus,
- ○ B. Thus'
- ○ C. Thus
- ○ D. Thus's
- ○ E. Thus:

12/

- ○ A. a financial stable
- ○ B. a financial, stable
- ○ C. a financially stable
- ○ D. a financially, stable
- ○ E. a financially, stabler

13/

- ○ A. It's banks
- ○ B. Its banks
- ○ C. Its' banks
- ○ D. Its's banks
- ○ E. It banks

14/

- ○ A. and establishes
- ○ B. and establish
- ○ C. and established
- ○ D. and establishing
- ○ E. and would establish

15/

- ○ A. an industrialize
- ○ B. and industrialize
- ○ C. an industrialized
- ○ D. and industrialized
- ○ E. and industrializing

16/

- ○ A. Additionally
- ○ B. Additionally:
- ○ C. Additionally,
- ○ D. Additional information is
- ○ E. Additionally and all,

17/

- ○ A. Geographically England
- ○ B. Geographically, England
- ○ C. Geographically: England
- ○ D. Geographical
- ○ E. Geographical,

18/

- ○ A. Canals and the railroads
- ○ B. Canals, railroads
- ○ C. Canals and railroads
- ○ D. Canals, also railroads
- ○ E. Canals also railroads

19/

- ○ A. raw materials, specifically, coal and iron
- ○ B. raw materials specifically coal and iron
- ○ C. raw materials specifically: coal and iron
- ○ D. raw materials, specifically: coal and iron
- ○ E. raw materials, specifically coal and iron,

20/

If you were asked to write an essay discussing the social effects of the Industrial Revolution would this essay fulfill that?

- ○ A. Yes, because sentence 7 mentions a social problem.
- ○ B. Yes, because it mentions people moving about.
- ○ C. No, because it focuses on the inventions and conditions in England.
- ○ D. No, because the English work very hard and are not very social.
- ○ E. No, because there were no social effects. It was industrial only.

TEST FOUR

> **1/** Multiple Sclerosis is a nervous system disorder. **2/** Sclerosis means plaque, and multiple means many; hence, plaque in many sites. **3/** MS affect mostly people aged fifteen to fifty. **4/** More women contract MS than men, and those who live in the northern parts of the United States, Europe, and Canada are most likely to be affected. **5/** Caucasians have a greater chance of developing MS than people of other races. **6/** The cause of MS is not known, but a combination of factors–heredity, a suppressed immune system, and a virus–are all suspected. **7/** Many people are diagnosed after been seen by a doctor for another symptom. **8/** Diagnosis of MS is difficult but MRI and CT scans sometimes show the plaque formations. **9/** These formations develop, as science clearly has demonstrated in other diseases that are difficult to diagnose, when the myelin lining of the nerve axons is destroyed and plaque is left behind.
>
> **10/** Patients may experience weakness, numbness, dizziness, and hearing loss. **11/** They should know what cause their condition to worsen: stress, infection, and changes in climate. **12/** Emotional stability is sometimes affected. **13/** There is no cure for MS treatment is aimed at relieving symptoms. **14/** These treatment may include drug therapy, electrical stimulus, or surgery. **15/** These attempt to keep the patient active and functionally. **16/** The life expectancy of patients with MS is usually twenty–five years after you are diagnosed. **17/** Death is usually caused by infection that kills you. **18/** MS may be steadily progressive, or a patient could have episodes of progression and remission. **19/** Even, if there are steady periods of remission, each period of progression advances the disease.

1/

- ○ A. Multiple Sclerosis is a nervous system disorder.
- ○ B. Multiple Sclerosis being a nervous system disorder.
- ○ C. Multiple Sclerosis is being a nervous system disorder.
- ○ D. Multiple Sclerosis is becoming a nervous system disorder.
- ○ E. Multiple Sclerosis, a nervous system disorder.

2/

- ○ A. many; hence,
- ○ B. many, hence,
- ○ C. many hence;
- ○ D. many hence:
- ○ E. many, hence

3/

- ○ A. Multiple Sclerosis affect
- ○ B. Multiple Sclerosis have affect
- ○ C. Multiple Sclerosis will be affecting
- ○ D. Multiple Sclerosis do affect
- ○ E. Multiple Sclerosis affects

4/

- ○ A. More women contract MS than men,
- ○ B. More women contracts MS than men,
- ○ C. More women than men contract MS,
- ○ D. More women, men contract MS,
- ○ E. More women contract men than MS,

5/

- ○ A. have a greater chance of developing MS than people of other races.
- ○ B. are having greater chances of developing MS.
- ○ C. have been having greater chances of developing MS than people of other races.
- ○ D. will be having greater chances
- ○ E. would have had a greater chance of developing MS.

6/

- ○ A. and a virus—are all suspected.
- ○ B. and a virus are all suspected.
- ○ C. and a virus, are all suspected.
- ○ D. and, a virus, are all suspected.
- ○ E. and: a virus are all suspected.

7/

- ○ A. after been seen by a doctor for another symptom.
- ○ B. after seeing a doctor for another symptom.
- ○ C. after seen a doctor for another symptom.
- ○ D. after being saw by a doctor for another symptom.
- ○ E. after being sawn by a doctor for another symptom.

8/

- ○ A. difficult but MRI
- ○ B. difficult, but MRI
- ○ C. difficult, but; MRI
- ○ D. difficult; but, MRI
- ○ E. difficult: but, MRI

9/

- ○ A. develop, as science has clearly demonstrated in other diseases that are difficult to diagnose, when
- ○ B. develop, as science has shown us in other cases where it was difficult to diagnose, when
- ○ C. develop when the myelin
- ○ D. develop in similar ways to those in which scientists have a hard time diagnosing when
- ○ E. develop, not that they aren't easy to spot if you are a scientist, when

10/

   ◯ A. Patients may experience weakness, numbness, dizziness, and hearing loss.

   ◯ B. Patients may experience weakness numbness dizziness, and hearing loss.

   ◯ C. Patients maybe experience weakness, numbness, dizziness, and hearing loss.

   ◯ D. Patients may experiencing weakness, numbness, dizziness, and hearing loss.

   ◯ E. Patients maybe are experiencing weakness, numbness, dizziness, and hearing loss.

11/

   ◯ A. what cause their condition to worsen:

   ◯ B. what causes their condition to worsen:

   ◯ C. what causes their condition to worsen whereby

   ◯ D. what causes their condition to worsen such as

   ◯ E. what cause your condition to worsen:

12/

The best order of sentences 10, 11, 12, and 13 would be

   ◯ A. 10, 11, 12, 13

   ◯ B. 10, 12, 11, 13

   ◯ C. 10, 13, 12, 11

   ◯ D. 11, 13, 12, 10

   ◯ E. 11, 12, 13, 10

13/

   ◯ A. no cure for MS treatment

   ◯ B. no cure for MS; treatment

   ◯ C. no cure for MS, treatment

   ◯ D. no cure for MS as treatment

   ◯ E. no cure for MS: treatment

14/

   ◯ A. These treatment

   ◯ B. Anyway, treatments

   ◯ C. Thus, treatments

   ◯ D. Because these treatments

   ◯ E. These treatments

15/

   ◯ A. These attempt to keep the patient active and functionally.

   ◯ B. These attempt to keep the patient actively and function.

   ◯ C. These attempt to keep the patient actively and functionally.

   ◯ D. These attempt to keep the patient activity and functional.

   ◯ E. These attempt to keep the patient active and functional.

16/

   ○ A. The life expectancy of patients with MS is usually twenty–five years after you are diagnosed.

   ○ B. The life expectancy of patients with MS is usually twenty–five years after diagnosis is made of you.

   ○ C. The life expectancy of patients with MS is usually twenty–five years after they can diagnose you.

   ○ D. The life expectancy of patients with MS is usually twenty–five years after diagnosis.

   ○ E. The life expectancy of patients with MS is usually twenty–five years after they diagnose.

17/

   ○ A. Death is usually caused by infection that kills you.

   ○ B. An infection usually causes death that kills you.

   ○ C. Death is usually caused by an infection.

   ○ D. An infection causing death usually kills you.

   ○ E. Death causes an infection that kills you.

18/

   ○ A. progressive, or a patient could have episodes of

   ○ B. progressive thus, a patient could have episodes of

   ○ C. progressive and so a patient could have episodes of

   ○ D. progressive and so a patient could have had episodes of

   ○ E. progressive and so a patient could have been episodes of

19/

   ○ A. Even, if there are steady periods of remission

   ○ B. Even if, as far as we know from patients we have studied, there are steady periods of remission

   ○ C. Even if, there are steady periods of remission,

   ○ D. Even if there are steady periods of remission,

   ○ E. Even though we have studied and there are steady patients with periods of remission

20/

If the author wants to insert the following sentence, where would it be best to place it?

Some MS patients become so frustrated by their disease that they commit suicide.

   ○ A. At the beginning to grasp the reader's attention

   ○ B. At the end as a summation

   ○ C. After sentence 12 because this is an example of emotional instability

   ○ D. After sentence 14 because it contrasts with attempts to keep people alive

   ○ E. After sentence 4 because Canadians have a higher rate of suicide

TEST FIVE

1/ Arthur Miller's *Death of a Salesman* was published in 1949 but the Loman family has all the elements of a contemporary dysfunctional family. 2/ Considered a modern tragedy, *Salesman* tells the story of Willy Loman, a salesman, who failed at life and paid the ultimate price. 3/ Female characters in Miller's play can be said to be used yet victimized. 4/ They are Willy's mistress, his wife, and the women son Happy is continually acquiring. 5/ The male characters exhibit the real tragedy in the play, however. 6/ Willy aspires to be success. 7/ In the process he accumulates debt, loses his job, and loses the respect of the son he favors. 8/ Biff is Willy's most favoritest son. 9/ Indeed, he ignores Happy who he pays no attention to. 10/ Biff, Willy's oldest son, and by all accounts the son with the brighter future, the high school football star. 11/ He has many university scholarship offers to play football in college in exchange for free tuition. 12/ However, he failed math and doesn't graduate from high school. 13/ Having an affair, Willy is seen by Biff when he travels to New England to seek his guidance. 14/ He leaves home, turns to compulsive stealing, and is fired from several jobs. 15/ Happy is the neglected Loman brother. 16/ He makes up for the inattention of his family by pursued women. 17/A major theme of *Salesman* is dreams unfulfill. 18/ Willy is a man of dreams while his reality is crumbling around him. 19/ He even dreams his funeral will be a successfully event.

1/

- ○ A. was published in 1949 but the Loman family
- ○ B. was published in 1949, but the Loman family
- ○ C. was published in 1949 but, the Loman family
- ○ D. was published in 1949; but, the Loman family
- ○ E. was published in 1949, and the Loman family

2/

- ○ A. Considered a modern tragedy, *Salesman* tells the story of Willy Loman,
- ○ B. Considered a modern tragedy; *Salesman* tells the story of Willy Loman,
- ○ C. Considered a modern tragedy. *Salesman* tells the story of Willy Loman,
- ○ D. Considering a modern tragedy, *Salesman* tells the story of Willy Loman,
- ○ E. Consider a modern tragedy. *Salesman* tells the story of Willy Loman,

3/

- ○ A. can be said to be used yet victimized.
- ○ B. can be said to be used but victimized.
- ○ C. can be said to be used and also to be victimized.
- ○ D. can be said to be used up and victimized.
- ○ E. can be said to be victimized.

4/

- ○ A. They are Willy's mistress, his wife, and the women son Happy is continually acquiring.
- ○ B. They are Willys' mistress, his wife, and the women son Happy is continually acquiring.
- ○ C. They are Willys's mistress, his wife, and the women son Happy is continually acquiring.
- ○ D. There are Willy's mistress, his wife, and the women son Happy is continually acquiring.
- ○ E. They are: Willy's mistress, his wife, and the women son Happy is continually acquiring.

5/

- ○ A. The male characters exhibit the real tragedy in the play, however.
- ○ B. The male character exhibit the real tragedy in the play, also.
- ○ C. The male characters exhibit the realest tragedy in the play, however.
- ○ D. The male characters exhibits the greatest tragedy in the play, however.
- ○ E. The male characters exhibit the greatest tragedy in the play however.

6/

- ○ A. Willy aspires to be success.
- ○ B. Willy aspires to be successful.
- ○ C. Willy aspires to achieve successful.
- ○ D. Willy aspires to be a successful.
- ○ E. Willy aspire to be successful.

7/

If you wanted to combine sentences 6 and 7 which of the following would be the best way?

- ○ A. to be successful, and in the process
- ○ B. to be successful, but in the process
- ○ C. to be successful so in the process
- ○ D. to be successful because in the process
- ○ E. to be successful; because, in the process

8/

- ○ A. Willy's most favoritest son.
- ○ B. Willy's son's most favorite.
- ○ C. Willy's favorite son.
- ○ D. Willy's son's favorite.
- ○ E. his most favoritest son.

9/

- ○ A. Indeed, he ignores Happy, who he pays no attention to.
- ○ B. Indeed, he ignores Happy, who he pays no attention with.
- ○ C. Indeed, he ignores Happy.
- ○ D. Indeed, he ignores Happy who he pays no attention to.
- ○ E. Indeed, he ignore Happy.

10/

- ○ A. son with the brighter future, the high school football star.
- ○ B. son with the brighter future, will be the high school football star.
- ○ C. son with the brighter future, the one who will be the high school football star.
- ○ D. son with the brighter future, the one who is being the high school football star.
- ○ E. son with the brighter future, is the high school football star.

11/

- ○ A. university scholarship offers to play football in college in exchange for free tuition.
- ○ B. university scholarship offers to play football.
- ○ C. university scholarship offers to play football in college.
- ○ D. university scholarship offers to play football in exchange for free.
- ○ E. university offers to play football for free.

12/

- ○ A. However, he failed math and doesn't graduate from high school.
- ○ B. However, he fails math and doesn't graduate from high school.
- ○ C. However he is failing math, he does graduate from high school.
- ○ D. However he fails math and doesn't graduate from high school.
- ○ E. However, he fail math and doesn't graduate from high school.

13/

- ○ A. Having an affair, Willy is seen by Biff when he travels to New England.
- ○ B. Having an affair, Biff sees Willy when he travels to New England to seek his guidance.
- ○ C. To seek his guidance, Biff travels to New England where Willy is having an affair.
- ○ D. Biff travels to New England to seek Willy's guidance, and he finds Willy is having an affair.
- ○ E. Biff travels to New England for guidance; Willy is having an affair.

14/

- ○ A. turns to compulsive stealing, and is
- ○ B. turns to compulsive stealing and be
- ○ C. turned to compulsive stealing and is
- ○ D. turns to compulsive stealing; and is
- ○ E. turned to compulsive stealing and was

15/

- ○ A. Happy is the neglected Loman brother.
- ○ B. The neglected Loman brother is happy.
- ○ C. Happy, the neglected Loman brother.
- ○ D. Happy, is the neglected Loman brother.
- ○ E. Neglected Happy is the Loman brother.

16/

    ⭕ A. He makes up for the inattention of his family by pursued women.

    ⭕ B. He makes up for the inattention of his family by pursuing women.

    ⭕ C. Pursued by women he makes up for the inattention of his family.

    ⭕ D. His family, pursued by women , make up for the inattention.

    ⭕ E. Women he pursued make up for his family's inattention.

17/

    ⭕ A. A major theme of *Salesman* is dreams unfulfill.

    ⭕ B. A major theme of *Salesman* is dreams unfilled.

    ⭕ C. A major theme of *Salesman* is dream unfulfill.

    ⭕ D. A major theme of *Salesman* is dreamers unfulfilled.

    ⭕ E. A major theme of *Salesman* is dreams unfulfilled.

18/

    ⭕ A. dreams while his reality is crumbling around him.

    ⭕ B. dreams and his reality is crumbling around him.

    ⭕ C. dreams, yet his reality is crumbling around him.

    ⭕ D. dreams so his reality is crumbling around him.

    ⭕ E. dreams also his reality is crumbling around him.

19/

    ⭕ A. a successfully event.

    ⭕ B. a success event.

    ⭕ C. a success of an event.

    ⭕ D. a successful event.

    ⭕ E. a success, for an event.

20/

    If the author wants to add the following sentence, where would it logically go?
    He dreams in superlatives of success for himself and his sons.

    ⭕ A. between 6 and 7

    ⭕ B. conclusion

    ⭕ C. opening

    ⭕ D. between 5 and 6

    ⭕ E. between 11 and 12

ANSWER KEY FOR THE WRITING SKILLS SECTION

Practice Essay

1. **D** 2. **A** 3. **D** 4. **C** 5. **E** 6. **B** 7. **B** 8. **C**

9. **D** 10. **C** 11. **E** 12. **A** 13. **A** 14. **B** 15. **E**

Exercise 1

1. college
2. immediately
3. apparent
4. write
5. Embarrassing
6. Committee
7. comments
8. too
9. right
10. wait

Exercise 2

1. Fourth of July
2. June
3. Martha's Vineyard
4. Massachussetts
5. Father
6. Cheri's Bakery
7. Nate
8. Cheerios
9. Kix
10. Hiawatha Road

Exercise 3

1. I like <u>Runaway Jury</u> the best of all the books John Grisham has written. **(period)**

2. Have you read <u>The Client</u>, his book about a female attorney? **(comma and question mark)**

3. "Do you want to go," Joseph asked, "or would you prefer to stay a little longer?" **(commas and quotation marks)**

4. I just cannot do mathematics! **(exclamation or period)**

5. Hey, don't drink out of my water glass! **(comma and exclamation)**

6. Kate's birthday is July 4, 1979. **(comma)**

7. Because we ran out of money, we went home early. **(comma)**

8. We were seventeen, attractive, and foolish the year we rented the house at the beach. **(commas)**

9. <u>The Jungle</u>, a book by Upton Sinclair, exposed the evils of the Chicago stockyards. **(commas)**

10. Tiramisu, on the other hand, is a dessert worth wasting the calories. **(commas)**

(continued on next page)

11. Atlanta, Georgia has been the site of many conferences, the Superbowl, and the Olympics. **(commas)**

12. Frank, I thought I asked you to pick up my registration booklet. **(comma)**

13. My favorite all–time movies are the following: *Diner, Pulp Fiction,* and *The Holy Grail.* **(colon and commas)**

14. I finish classes at 4:00 p.m.; consequently, I cannot attend a 3:45 p.m. meeting. **(semi–colon, comma, period)**

15. New Jersey and Delaware are mid–Atlantic states; Maryland is as well. **(semi–colon or period)**

Exercise 4

1. The dolphins (was, **were**) swimming along with the boat.

2. Neither the captain nor his first mate (seem, **seems**) concerned that we are taking on water.

3. One of the Senatorial contenders was our (most best, **best**) friend.

4. The subject of the course **(is**, are) the political process in the United States.

5. Is he the man **(who**, whom) is running for office?

6. (Who, **whom**) did you see at the tennis match?

7. It was **(he**, him) who stole the money and ran.

8. **(We**, us) girls appreciate a night out once in awhile.

9. This demonstration, with signs, people shouting, and police barricades, (remind, **reminds**) me of the 60's.

10. At the age of six, Mozart's father gave him a harpsichord.
   (answers may vary – be sure the reader can tell who was six)

11. Kate read the play about overcoming hardships while riding the exercise bicycle.
   (answers may vary – what does riding the exercise bicycle modify?)

12. While fixing dinner, the hamburger burned.
   (answers may vary – was the hamburger fixing dinner?)

13. It was a present from her grandmother, the antique.
   (answers may vary – was the present the antique or was the grandmother the antique?)

14. When Bill and Tom came in, I told him about the case.
   (change him to them – pronoun reference)

15. The seagulls were diving at the shellfish which scared the children
   (answers may vary – did the seagulls diving scare the children or did the seashells scare them?)

Exercise 5

1. PERSONAL PRONOUN as subject

2. PERSONAL PRONOUN as object

3. PERSONAL PRONOUN to show possession

4. REFLEXIVE PRONOUN

5. RELATIVE PRONOUN

6. DEMONSTRATIVE PRONOUN

7. INTERROGATIVE PRONOUN

8. RELATIVE PRONOUN

9. RELATIVE PRONOUN

10. INDEFINITE PRONOUN

Exercise 6

1. A person who likes fast food should watch their fat intake.
   (change "their" to "his" or "her" – or – say "people who...should,"– or –eliminate the pronoun entirely)

2. When the members of the team fell behind it lost the desire to win.
   (change "it" to "they")

3. Yellow and dried, Susan kept the corsage from the prom for months.
   (answers may vary – what was yellow and dried?)

4. Hanging on the hook, we forgot to grab our coats.
   (answers may vary – what was hanging on the hook?)

5. Eating leaves from the top branches, we enjoyed photographing the giraffes.
   (answers may vary – who was eating the leaves from the branches?)

6. Information about the terrorist threats was received by the news bureau chiefs.
   (passive voice – change to the news bureau chiefs received the information...)

7. She was neither the best.
   (fragment – answers may vary)

8. Having my birthday cake.
   (fragment – answers may vary)

(continued on next page)

(Exercise 6, continued)

9. Mini–blinds have been shown to cause a lead hazard to children which is why they will no longer be sold in the United States.
   (combine – subordinate independent first)

10. So I can get into a better college, I am taking Advanced Placement courses.
    (comma – subordinate construction)

11. We had walked ten miles before he said anything.
    (walked – verb form)

12. We had agreed to never argue about that issue again.
    (split infinitive – change to "never to argue")

13. Some students do not realize that it is difficult to go to school and to be working.
    (verb form not parallel; change to and to work)

14. The boat, quickly taking on water, sunk by the time help arrived.
    (verb form – sank)

15. All of us decided to consciously ignore the speaker.
    (split infinitive – to ignore the speaker consciously)

Answers to ORGANIZATION: Logical Order, p.172

1, 6, 5, 2, 7, 4, 3, 8

Exercise 7

1.	E	6.	I
2.	C	7.	F
3.	A	8.	G
4.	H	9.	B
5.	D		

ANSWERS FOR THE WRITING SKILLS
PRACTICE TESTS

Question #	Test 1	Test 2	Test 3	Test 4	Test 5
1.	B	C	B	A	B
2.	C	D	E	B	A
3.	B	B	D	E	D
4.	C	D	C	C	E
5.	D	C	B	A	A
6.	E	B	D	A	B
7.	B	C	B	B	B
8.	E	C	A	B	C
9.	D	B	A	C	C
10.	B	E	C	A	E
11.	D	A	A	D	B
12.	A	C	C	B	B
13.	B	B	B	B	D
14.	D	E	B	E	A
15.	E	D	C	E	A
16.	B	B	C	D	B
17.	C	C	B	C	E
18.	E	A	C	A	C
19.	B	E	E	D	D
20.	B	D	C	C	A

READING

PASSAGES

The Reading portion of **COMPASS** consists of passages similar to what you may have read on other traditional comprehension tests, such as the SAT. The average length of a passage is 215 words, and reading level of all passages is equal to that encountered in the first year of college. The material for the passages comes from textbooks, essays, journals, and magazines commonly used in entry-level college courses. There are five types of passages:

Practical Reading	These passages address everyday situations and experiences.
Prose Fiction	These passages focus on narration of events or telling a story and providing information about characters.
Humanities	These passages describe or analyze ideas or works of art.
Social Sciences	These passages present information gathered by research in areas such as Psychology, Sociology, and History.
Natural Sciences	These passages present a science topic along with an explanation of its significance.

Before each passage, you will see a screen that provides the following information about that passage:

   a)   a question that will help you focus your reading,

   b)   the source from which the reading text was excerpted, *and*

   c)   the author, copyright date, and publisher.

All of this information has been provided before each passage in the two practice tests located in Chapter 12.

QUESTIONS

COMPREHENSION ITEMS

There are five reading comprehension items that accompany each passage. Three of the five items are called **referring items**, and they pose questions about material directly stated in a passage. The reader can find the answer to the referring items in the information given in the passage. The remaining two items are **reasoning items,** which pose questions about material that is not directly stated in the passage. The reader must infer the answers to the reasoning items from the information given.

After you answer all the questions about a passage, you will be able to go back and change your answers. Since the test requires that you answer all of the questions about a passage before allowing you to go back and make changes, we recommend that you follow this same procedure when taking the practice tests in Chapter 12.

Your institution may elect to include a supplement to the reading comprehension items called **prior-knowledge items.** These six items measure what you already know about the subject matter of the passage. These items are easier than the referring and reasoning items, and they can be answered without reading the passage. In fact, reading the passage would not provide any information to help you answer the prior-knowledge items. The questions are presented after you have finished the test and when you can no longer refer back to the passage. These items do not contribute to your reading score.

ITEM FORMATS

There are two formats for items on COMPASS: multiple choice and text-highlighting. Multiple choice items require you to select the correct answer from five alternatives, and you need to read through the passage to determine which alternative is correct. Multiple choice items on COMPASS may be answered in one of two ways:

1) Press the up/down arrows to choose the bubble beside A, B, C, D, or E. Then press ENTER to select this answer.

2) Type the letter (A, B, C, D, or E) of the answer you think is correct. Then press ENTER to select this answer.

You may choose the method of anwering you like best. Remember, you can go back and see the passage by pressing the S key.

Text-highlighting items ask you to locate within the passage a specific segment of the text that answers a question. This is done by highlighting a section of the passage. Sometimes, only a single word must be highlighted. Other questions may ask you to highlight several words or a sentence. For example, a text-highlighting item for a passage about abstract art might read:

Highlight the sentence in which the author sums up her feelings about abstract art.

CHAPTER TEN

REFERRING ITEMS

As mentioned before, three of the five comprehension items following the passage will be referring items. Referring items test your skill level in identifying the stated main idea, recognizing the details, and understanding relationships presented in the passage. They also test your ability to think critically about the information in the passage. A definition for each of these subcategories of referring items, along with strategies for answering items correctly and exercises that allow you to practice these strategies, are presented below.

MAIN IDEA OF A PARAGRAPH

DEFINITION

The main idea is the central or most important thought in the paragraph. Every other sentence and idea in the paragraph is related to the main idea.

STRATEGY 1

One strategy for recognizing a main idea that is directly stated in a paragraph is to know the difference between the topic and the main idea. The topic is the one thing the paragraph is about and can usually be stated in one or two words. The topic may often be stated in the title. Establishing the topic will allow you to start locating the main idea efficiently. To determine the topic, try asking yourself simply, "Who or what is this paragraph about?" Students typically can identify the topic with little difficulty but struggle with verbalizing the main idea of what they read. The main idea is what the author is trying to communicate about the "who or what," or the key idea being expressed by the author. Once you have established the topic, you can identify the main idea by asking yourself, "What is the author communicating about the topic?" Then answer your question with a complete sentence! (This will help structure your thinking.)

Exercise 1

Read the paragraph below and answer the questions for identifying the main idea.

Psychology is relevant to our daily lives. We might get an argument from biologists, chemists, physicists, geologists, and even some astronomers, but I'm willing to make the claim that no other science has more practical, useful application in the real world than does the science of psychology. In everyday life, people can get by without thinking about physics or geology or biology, but they cannot get by without thinking psychologically. They must take into consideration a multitude of sensations, perceptions, memories, feelings, and consequences of their actions if they are going to survive, and certainly if they are going to prosper. [1]

1. Who or what is this paragraph about? _____

_____

2. What is the author trying to communicate to me about this who or what? _____

_____

_____

(Answers on next page)

These questions should have structured your thinking. The paragraph is about psychology and the author is trying to communicate the importance of psychology. Thus, the main idea is stated in the first sentence: *Psychology is relevant to our daily lives.*

STRATEGY 2

Another strategy for identifying a main idea explicitly stated in a paragraph is to visualize the possible locations of the main-idea sentence. Very often the main-idea sentence may be at the beginning of the paragraph, followed by the supporting information. You could think of the paragraph as information presented in the shape of an upside-down triangle: ▼

Or the supporting information may be presented first, with the concluding sentence stating the main idea. Picture the paragraph as a right-side up triangle: ▲

A paragraph may also present information, state the main idea in the middle of the paragraph, and then present additional information. Of course, a diamond shape would best represent this paragraph: ◆

Finally, both the introduction and concluding sentence of a paragraph may state the main idea. Visualize this format: ▼▲

Exercise 2

Read the following paragraphs and locate the main-idea sentences. Underline these sentences and then draw the shape (▼, ▲, ◆, ▼▲) that best fits the paragraph.

A.   Foods that supply "empty calories"—calories without many nutrients—are not considered nutrient-dense. Soft-drinks, potato chips, candy bars, and cookies are not very nutrient-dense and are sometimes called "junk foods." However, many foods labeled as junk foods supply more than calories even if they are not considered traditional sources of nutrients. For instance, cookies are made with flour, usually enriched, which provides some nutrients. Also, some people need calories, just as some people need to limit calories. Foods that supply just calories are not inherently bad. It is the overeating of these foods, precluding or limiting the intake of more nutritionally valuable foods, that can create problems. Within the framework of sound nutritional practices, the consumption of these so-called junk foods is, and should be, permitted. Therefore, the term junk food is considered by most nutritionists to be inappropriate. All foods supply some nutrients, albeit sometimes in limited amounts.[2]

Shape that best fits this paragraph: _____

(*Answers* to exercises in Chapter Ten are found on pp. 263-264.)

B.   Sounds are heard not only through the outer and middle ear, but also through the direct conduction of vibrations through the bones in the head. The clicking of one's teeth and chewing sounds from the mouth may be heard in this way. If a vibrating tuning fork is placed on the teeth, some of the vibrations are conducted directly to the cochlea of the inner ear. This kind of conductive hearing is very important when trying to determine whether a person has a hearing loss in the middle ear or has nerve damage in the inner ear. If a person has experienced a hearing loss and can hear a tuning fork placed on the teeth, the hearing loss has probably occurred in the outer or middle ear. If the tuning fork cannot be heard well using this method, the hearing loss is probably located in the inner ear. [3]

Shape that best fits this paragraph: _____

C.   Within eight years after Moliere's death, Louis XIV combined all French companies in one troupe, calling it the Comedie-Francais to differentiate it from the Comedie-Italian (commedia dell'arte). In 1689, a playhouse, the Theatre Francais, was built for the Comedie-Francais and the first national theatre in modern Europe was born. Sometimes known as the House of Moliere, the Theatre Francais was a symbol, in two important ways, of the emerging dominance of the middle class in the upcoming century. First, the repertoire of the Theatre Francais was based heavily on the comedies of Moliere, peopled with middle-class characters and their concerns. Second, the architectural shape of the Theatre Francais was more of a horseshoe than a semicircle. This subtle change commenced the process of eliminating the worst seats in the proscenium theatre and making more good seats available for the general public. That general public was the middle class who came to see themselves in Moliere's plays.[4]

Shape that best fits this paragraph: _____

D.   Before assessing someone's nutritional status, his family's medical history must be known. A history of heart disease, diabetes, obesity, or high blood pressure in a family can all be indicators of an increased risk for these diseases. Of course if an individual has problems such as diabetes, hypertension, kidney problems, and heart disease, nutritional status could be affected. A person's drug history is also important because many prescription drugs interfere with nutrient absorption, metabolism and excretion. The average elderly person takes three to eight prescription medicines per day. Many antibiotics such as penicillin interfere with the absorption of certain vitamins. A person may have an adequate intake of a nutrient, but because of interactions with a prescription drug, still develop symptoms of deficiency of that nutrient. For such reasons, you can fully evaluate someone's nutritional status only after assessing the complete medical history of that person.[5]

Shape that best fits this paragraph: _____

Another strategy for identifying the main idea is to consider "directional" words. For example, *in general, generally, above all,* and *of great importance* are "directional" words that direct you to the main idea of the paragraph. The author may come out and explicitly say, *the main idea is, the main point* or *the main feature is, the key point is*, etc.

Exercise 3

Read the following paragraphs and circle the directional words that point you to the main-idea sentence.

A.　　　Structure begins when one enters a classroom. As soon as people get together, even under a tree, structure begins. When they start talking we have even more structure. If it rains and we build a shelter to get in out of the rain even more structure emerges. And if there are too many people to meet all in the same room then other kinds of structure arise. Structure starts as soon as two people get together and continues as people continue. The crucial point is that some people persist in talking about unstructured education when they ought to be thinking about how much and what kind of structure.[6]

B.　　　Techniques for aging skeletons rely on the appearance and structure of the skeleton and teeth. For aging young individuals, anthropologists rely on changes in the skeleton and teeth during growth and development, such as the age of tooth development and eruption, and the closure of epiphyses. Skeletal aging is generally less accurate in adults than in children, but there are a number of reliable methods available. These include the extent of wear or attrition of the teeth, the fusion of sutures of the skull, and appearance of the pubic symphysis. In general, the best approach to adult skeletal aging is to use as many indicators of age from a skeleton as are available for estimating age at death. A single indicator will not be as accurate as the combination of a number of age indicators or sites.[7]

C.　　　It is clear that much of technology does come from the discoveries of science. It is also clear that a lot of technology doesn't. New "superconducting" materials are being made today. They conduct electricity with no resistance at relatively high temperatures, but we don't know how they work. The point is that it is technology that changes our lives, with the changes coming faster and faster. Given this tremendous impact, is it the case that students study technology in school? Do well educated people understand how microwave ovens work? Televisions? Automobile transmissions?[8]

MAIN IDEA OF A PASSAGE

DEFINITION

The main idea of a passage is an expanded version of the main idea of a paragraph. The main idea of a passage is the central or most important thought in the passage. Every other sentence and idea is related to the main idea.

STRATEGY 1

The same strategies you learned for determining the main idea for a paragraph can be applied for determining the main idea of a passage. Again, know the difference between topic and main idea. With a passage, the topic is sometimes referred to as the "general subject" and the main idea is sometimes referred to as the "central thought." The general subject would answer the question "Who or what the passage is about?" The central thought would answer the question "What is the author trying to communicate to me about the who or what?" Don't forget to answer these questions (in your mind) with complete sentences!

Exercise 4

Read the following passage, and answer the questions for identifying a main idea (or central thought) explicitly stated in a passage.

A.   A recent general theory of attitude change claims that there are two factors, or routes, involved in changing one's attitudes (Petty & Checkup, 1986; Teaser & Staffer, 1990). One factor of concern is the central route: the nature and quality of the message itself. The other factor is the peripheral route: issues above and beyond the content of the message, or its source. There are several factors involved in source credibility (e.g., such factors as vocal pleasantness and facial expressiveness) (Burgeon, Birk, & Pfau, 1990), but the two that seem especially important are expertise and trustworthiness.

Several studies (e.g., Aronson et al., 1963; Hovland & Weiss, 1951) suggest that the greater the perceived expertise of the communicator, the greater the persuasion. People convinced that they are listening to an expert are much more likely to be persuaded than they would be if they thought the speaker knew little about the subject matter—even if the messages were exactly the same.

Another factor that enhances a communicator's credibility is a high degree of trustworthiness (Cooper & Croyle, 1984). Studies by Walster and Festinger (1962), for example, demonstrated that more aided change resulted when subjects overheard a persuasive communication than when they believed the communication was directed at them. Trustworthiness and credibility were enhanced by a perceived lack of intent to persuade ("Why should they lie; they don't even know I can hear them?").[9]

1. Who or what is this passage about? _____

2. What is the author trying to communicate to me about this who or what?

_____

Again, these questions may help to structure your thinking. The passage is about communication. The author is trying to communicate to the reader that: "There are several factors involved in source credibility, . . . but the two that seem especially important are expertise and trustworthiness."

STRATEGY 2

The strategy for visualizing the possible locations of a main-idea sentence is helpful for determining the main idea of a passage. Remember, the main-idea sentence can be at the beginning, at the end, in the middle, or at the beginning and at the end of the passage.

Exercise 5

Read the following passage, underline the main-idea sentence, and then draw the shape that best fits the passage.

A.　　　The word science is derived from the Latin word scientia meaning knowledge, and, indeed, science is a way of understanding that leads to a particular type of knowledge. Much of our world is understandable as a sequence of causes and effects. For example, we see a broken egg on the kitchen floor and several eggs near the edge of the kitchen counter. The broken egg can be seen as an effect, and we surmise that the cause was the egg rolling off the counter. The placement of the egg near the edge of the counter may also be seen as an effect, and its cause may be some one placing it there. Thus causes and effects occur in sequential chains of events. Science is our way of understanding such causal relationships.

　　　Science should be contrasted with the humanities, which is a way of understanding aspects of the world that are not necessarily related to cause and effect. Judging the beauty of a picture or the morality of war are questions properly addressed within the humanities, but not through science. Both types of understanding are integral parts of our lives. A painter understands the science of pigments and light and the aesthetics of the painting being created. Both ways of understanding are necessary for human fulfillment.[10]

Shape that best fits the passage: _____

DETELS

DEFINITION

The details of a passage are the information provided by the author as proof, explanation, or support of the main idea. The details can be described as the evidence provided to support the argument.

STRATEGY 1

The strategy for answering detail items is to shuttle back to the passage to find the information. Remember that detail items are explicitly stated information in the passage. It may help to tell yourself that the answer to a detail item is in the passage; all you have to do is locate it. It may be stated somewhat differently in the passage than in the question, but the material is substantively the same.

Exercise 6

Read the paragraph below and underline the details provided to support the main idea.

A.   Teachers use a wide array of rewards. Some give students candy or toys to reward desirable behaviors. Others use films, free time, extra outdoor periods, permitting a child to be first in the lunch line and other such positive actions as rewards to reinforce desirable behaviors. Frequently tokens, or paper "chips" are given to students that may later be redeemed for physical rewards or favors.[11]

STRATEGY 2

Another strategy for answering detail items correctly is to recognize directional words. In the same way that directional words can "direct" you to the main idea, they can "direct" you to the details and help you distinguish between major details and minor details. Major details provide proof, explanation, or support of the main ideas, and minor details provide proof, explanation, or support of the major details. In other words, the major details contribute directly to the main idea, and the minor details usually elaborate on some other detail that supports the main idea. Some directional words for major details are *one, first, another, further, also, finally,* etc. Some directional words for minor details are *for example, to be specific, that, this means*, etc.

Exercise 7

Read the following paragraphs, circle the directional words, and note on the blank line whether the directional words point you to a major or minor detail.

A.   It seems that the need to achieve is learned, usually in childhood. Children who show high levels of achievement motivation are generally those who have been encouraged in a positive way to excel ("Leslie, that grade of B is very good. You must be proud of yourself" as opposed to, "What! Only a B?"). High-nAch (need to achieve) children are generally encouraged to work things out for themselves, independently, perhaps with parental support and encouragement ("Here, Leslie, you see if you can do this" as opposed to "Here, dummy, let me do it; you'll never get it right!"). Further, McClelland is convinced that achievement motivation can be specifically taught and acquired by almost anyone, of any age, and he has developed training programs designed to increase achievement motivation levels (e.g., McClelland & Winter, 1969).[12]

(continued on next page)

Exercise 7 (continued)

B.   During and after the 1950's, physical anthropologists became more concerned with hypothesis testing and understanding evolutionary processes. Measurement, therefore, became a method by which to test hypotheses rather than the primary objective of research. Accurate measurements of skeletal material are still necessary today for (1) describing skeletons from archaeological sites, (2) comparing primate fossil remains with extant primates, and (3) investigating cases in forensic anthropology. For example, accurate measurements allow the physical anthropologist to estimate stature. This information is useful to both the description of skeletons from an archaeological site and in the investigation of skeletal material involved in a criminal case.[13]

RELATIONSHIPS

COMPASS includes items that test your skill in recognizing three different types of relationships: sequential relationships, cause and effect relationships, and comparative relationships.

DEFINITION

Sequential relationships are relationships in which the order is important and changing that order changes the meaning.

STRATEGY

A strategy for recognizing sequential relationships is to recognize signal words often used to indicate order. Some of these signal words include: *first, second, third, after, before, when, until, at last, next, later,* etc.

Exercise 8

Read the following paragraph and circle the signal word or words that indicate a sequential relationship.

A.   Experimental design begins with the difficult problem of asking the right question from which a testable hypothesis can be derived. Predictions are made based on the hypothesis, and methods for testing those predictions are designed. The experiment is conducted and data (sing. datum) are gathered. Finally, data are interpreted with respect to the perceived "correctness" of the explanation offered through the hypothesis.[14]

DEFINITION

    Cause and effect relationships are patterns where one element is seen as producing another element.

STRATEGY

    A reader can recognize cause and effect relationships by understanding signal words and phrases often used to indicate this type of relationship. Following are cause and effect signal words and phrases to be on the lookout for: *for this reason, consequently, on that account, therefore, because, hence,* etc.

Exercise 9

Read the following paragraph and circle the signal word or words that indicate a cause and effect relationship.

A.   One possible mechanism for triggering star formation from gas clouds has been recently suggested on theoretical grounds. Violent explosive events are not unusual in the universe. Stars can literally explode, sending off up to about ten percent of their mass into space along with a great deal of radiation. One consequence of such an explosion is a shock wave, which is a rapid change in pressure traveling as a pulse through space in much the same way that a "sonic boom" would travel. There are many of these shock waves traveling through space and observations have found stars forming at the edges of these waves.[15]

DEFINITION

Recognizing **comparative** relationships involves an ability to see how two elements are similiar.

STRATEGY

    Again, look for key words that may indicate a comparative relationship. Signal words that are often used in this type of comparison are *greater than, less than, bigger than, similar, parallels,* etc.

Exercise 10

Read the following paragraph and circle the signal word or words that indicate a comparative relationship.

A.   Mars, midway in size between the Earth and the Moon, is also midway in many characteristics. It has an older surface with less activity than the Earth, but a younger and a more active surface than the Moon does. Martian lithosphere is thicker than the Earth's, indicating more rapid cooling, but not as thick as the Moon's. The Martian atmosphere is thin, but the Moon has none. But there does not seem to be intermediate life on Mars. Apparently physical conditions may once have been favorable for the beginning of life, but tests performed by the Viking Landers have not given results indicating life there today. The results do indicate a complex chemistry on the Martian surface so life on Mars is perhaps best left as an unanswered question.[16]

CRITICAL THINKING

Thinking critically may be described as an effort to make sense of our world by carefully examining our thinking and the thinking of others. Two types of items on COMPASS assess your ability to evaluate the thinking of others. These items are designed to determine your ability to recognize explicit evidence presented in support of a claim and your ability to recognize stated assumptions.

DEFINITION

Recognizing **explicit evidence** involves identifying the author's support for the idea or issue in question.

STRATEGY

A strategy for recognizing explicit evidence presented by the author is to be aware that evidence can be presented in a variety of forms. The author may provide evidence by relating a personal experience, describing observations, providing statistical data, discussing analogies (comparisons with similar situations), providing historical documentation, or explaining experimental evidence.

Exercise 11

Read the following paragraphs and write on the blank line the form of the evidence provided by the author to support the main idea.

A.   The world's petroleum use . . . is growing. While the growth rate varies somewhat, it is instructive to consider what will happen if we look at a simple calculation. From 1948 to 1973 oil consumption doubled in the U.S. In 1974 the world was consuming 56 million barrels of oil daily. Using these figures as a guide, a calculation can be made based on exponential growth. Starting in 1974, using 2×10^{10} barrels of oil and doubling every 22 years, in 784 years the earth would consume in one year a volume of oil equal to the volume of the earth![17]

_____

B.   When he was an MIT graduate student in industrial management, James Stoner gave subjects in his research a series of dilemmas to grapple with (Stoner, 1961). The result of each decision was to be a statement of how much risk the fictitious character in the dilemma should take. Much to his surprise, Stoner found that the decisions rendered by groups were much riskier than those individual group members had made prior to the group decision. Stoner called this move away from conservative solutions a risky shift. For example, doctors, if they were asked individually, might express the opinion that a patient's problem (whatever it might be) could be handled with medication and a change in diet. If these very same doctors were to get together to discuss the patient's situation, they might very well end up concluding that what was called for here was a new and potentially dangerous (risky) surgical procedure.[18]

_____

C.   Two flank eruptions of Kilauea volcano covered the village of Kapoho with lava. Between March 1 and 6, 1955, 36 million cubic yards of lava and cinders were erupted from vents west of the Kapoho prehistoric cone. Lavas covered 1,100 acres south of Kapoho. Between January 13 and February 20, 1960, 156 million cubic yards of lava flowed from vents north and east of Kapoho. Lavas covered 2,000 acres of land and formed 500 acres of new land when it flowed into the sea.[19]

D.   For hundreds of years, well into the eighteenth century, the attitude toward the mentally ill continued to be that they were in league with the devil or that they were being punished by God for sinful thoughts and deeds. They were witches who could not be cured except by confession and a denunciation of their evilness. When such confessions were not forthcoming, the prescribed treatment was torture. If torture failed to evoke a confession, death was the only recourse, often death by being burned at the stake. It has been estimated that between the fourteenth and mid-seventeenth centuries, nearly 200,000 to 500,000 "witches" were put to death (Ben-Yehuda, 1980).[20]

E.   I have attempted only one experiment that involved young children: a study of word associations. The procedure was simple: present a stimulus word and have a child respond with the first thing that came to mind. My first discovery was that 8 percent of the children simply did not want to play. They just walked away, back to the sandbox or some other activity. When children did agree to "play," they did some peculiar things. "I'm going to say a word, and then you tell me the first word you think of when you hear my word. Okay? My first word is black." After a moment's pause, a child looked up and responded, "My Mommy has a black dress and she wears it to church sometimes." The word association procedure is one of the most straightforward techniques in all of psychology. But "playing the game" is a task that some children may do with their own set of rules, and some may not be ready to play the game at all. I had failed to take into account the cognitive level of my "research participants."[21]

DEFINITION

Recognizing stated assumptions involves identifying an idea or principle that the writer states as true with no effort to prove the idea. When the author states an assumption with no proof or evidence, he assumes the reader will agree with what is being said. A critical reader does not believe something is true simply because it is in print or simply because it is in a textbook. However, a critical reader may decide to accept a statement without evidence, based on the author's qualifications or the quality of the publication.

STRATEGY

A strategy for recognizing stated assumptions is to identify any proof or evidence provided by the author to support what is being said. If proof or evidence is lacking, ask yourself questions such as, "Who wrote the article?" "What are the author's qualifications?" "Where was the article published?" "What seems to be the purpose of the publication?"

Exercise 12

Read the following paragraphs. Which paragraphs have stated assumptions by the author with no proof or evidence?

A.   Sadly enough, phobic disorders are far from uncommon. Estimates place prevalence rates at between 7 and 20 percent of the population; that's tens of millions of people (Marks, 1986; Robins et al., 1984). Phobias seldom extinguish on their own. Why don't they? There are many reasons, but one is that someone with a phobia is usually successful at avoiding the conditioned stimulus that elicits the fear. Someone with a fear of flying may get by driving or taking a bus or train.[22]

B.   Family therapy is based on the assumptions that (1) family members can be seen as a part of a system in which one member (and one member's problem) affects all of the others, and that (2) many psychological problems arise because of faulty communication, and that this is particularly critical within a family.[23]

C.   There are several potential advantages to group therapy. (1) The basic problem may be an interpersonal one and thus will be better understood and dealt with in an interpersonal situation. (2) There is value in realizing that one is not the only person in the world with a problem and that there are others who may have an even more difficult problem of the same nature. (3) There is therapeutic value in providing support for someone else. (4) The dynamics of intragroup communication can be analyzed and changed in a group setting.[24]

Which paragraphs have stated assumptions?_____

CHAPTER ELEVEN

REASONING ITEMS

As mentioned before, two of the five comprehension items following the passage will be reasoning items. Reasoning items test your skill level in making appropriate inferences about the main idea, thinking critically about the information in the passage, and determining meanings of words based on context. A definition for each of these subcategories of reasoning items, along with strategies for answering items correctly and exercises that allow you to practice these strategies, are presented below.

INFERENCES

DEFINITION

A basic level of reading comprehension is the literal level, where information is explicitly or directly stated in the passage. Chapter 10 provides strategies and exercises for the literal level of comprehension, or what we call referring items. You can go back to the passage and refer to what is actually stated in the passage to answer referring items. This is sometimes called "reading the lines." This chapter addresses a more advanced level of reading comprehension, the inference level. Rather than finding information directly stated in the passage, reading at the inferential level requires inferring the correct information from what the author suggests in his/her writing. This is sometimes called "reading between the lines."

Making appropriate inferences is a two-step process: first, you must be aware of the clues, or suggestions provided, and second, you must consider what you already know about the subject, or your background knowledge. For instance, imagine that you are walking down the street, and you notice a man walking toward you on the sidewalk. You realize certain things about this individual: he is walking in an unsteady manner and carrying a small brown bag that looks like it may contain a bottle of some kind. He is mumbling something to himself, and he looks unkempt with dirty, torn clothing. You decide, based on these clues or evidence, that this man is most likely drunk. He has not directly told you this, but because of his clothes, manner of walking, appearance, etc., you infer that he is drunk. You also make this inference based on what you know about behavior of individuals who are intoxicated. You have either experienced being intoxicated yourself, been around other individuals who were intoxicated, or you have read about behavior of individuals under the influence of alcohol. So, based on the evidence provided and your background knowledge, you make an inference. However, there could be other explanations for his behavior: perhaps this individual is sick, and that is why he is walking in an unsteady manner, or perhaps this person is playing a joke on you and trying to make you think he is intoxicated. You may consider these alternative explanations and discard them, or you may adjust your inference.

This same process is employed to make correct inferences with written material. Consider the clues, or evidence, provided by the author. These clues, together with your background knowledge, lead you to the appropriate inference. If your background knowledge about the subject is limited, you must rely more heavily on your reading skills, or your ability to understand the clues or evidence provided by the author.

STRATEGY 1

The following process is helpful in considering the clues or evidence provided by the author:

1) Understand the information on the literal level first. Before a reader can make correct inferences he has to understand what the author is directly telling him.

2) Become conscious of the connotative meaning of words, or the emotions surrounding words. Authors select words very carefully with a great deal of thought in an effort to make a reader feel or think a certain way. For instance, describing where one lives as "a home" creates different feelings than describing where one lives as a "house" or "shack." A reader feels differently toward a character described as a "guest" versus one described as a "boarder." Describing sleepwear as "lingerie" makes one feel more positive than does a description of "pajamas." The connotative meaning of words is important evidence to support an inference.

3) Consider the author's tone. Word choice and the connotative meaning of words will determine if the author is generally positive, negative, or neutral regarding the issues. Have you ever had anyone tell you, "Don't use that tone of voice with me!" Perhaps you were communicating more with your tone than with your actual words. The same may be true of written text. From word choice, one can determine whether the author is being sarcastic, angry, sympathetic, funny, etc.

4) Understand the author's point of view. Word choice, along with the general manner of description, will help the reader know "where the author is coming from." A student may describe a recent tuition increase in a different manner than a university official. It is perfectly acceptable for one's point of view to influence the manner in which information is presented. It is the reader's responsibility to be sensitive to various points of view and to decide for himself where he stands on the issue.

5) Determine the author's purpose. If the author's purpose is to explain or inform, which is often the case with textbook material, the author will likely present factual material. If the author's purpose is to persuade, the material may be presented in a more subjective, opinionated manner. A sophisticated reader is sensitive to the difference between facts (something that can be proven true or false) and opinions (that which cannot be proven true or false) and realizes that the author's purpose influences how the information is presented.

Exercise 1

Read the following paragraphs, and, in your own words, write the main idea in a complete sentence in the space provided. Write the clues or suggestions provided by the author as the support for inferring this main idea.

A.   Overpraise tends to create an environment in which student actions are largely designed to please the teacher and are less likely to be products of student judgment. Students who are given a high level of overt praise are less adventurous in their thinking, choosing the safe answer over the creative one. A pattern of frequent overt teacher praise also reduces subject matter related interactions among students. Students tend to guard their responses so they can acquire the praise. In a high praise classroom, students listen less to one another and seldom react to another student's statement except to disagree. The use of overt praise can result in discipline problems as students compete to be called on by the teacher.[1]

Main Idea: _____

Clues:_____

_____

_____

_____

B.   Industrial production creates air and water pollution. Acid rain has been killing trees and the life in lakes in Europe since the 1800s. The smog from burning coal in London in the nineteenth century was so thick that sunlight couldn't get through. Human skin needs some sunshine to produce vitamin D. Unless the skin produces this, or it is present in the diet (many foods are fortified with vitamins today), a deficiency disease called rickets occurs. Rickets results in a softening and bending of growing bones, and children in London were often found to have it.

      Conditions in early factories were often horrible. People worked fourteen hours a day or more, in ill lit and poorly ventilated factories. The equipment was dangerous, and there were no provisions for injury. Children had to work as much as adults. In some cases, such as with weaving machines, children were preferred over adults because they were smaller and were able to reach into the machines and make repairs. (The machines were usually not stopped to do this.)[2]

Main Idea: _____

Clues: _____

_____

_____

_____

CRITICAL THINKING

Thinking critically about what you are reading involves actively examining the validity of the information presented by the author. **COMPASS** determines if you have a critical understanding of the text with reasoning items that focus on recognizing assumptions made by the author and recognizing logical fallacies.

DEFINITION

Assumptions by the author are ideas, beliefs, or information recognized by the author as valid. A critical reader is sensitive to the assumptions made by the author, and a critical reader questions information presented to support a particular position.

STRATEGY 1

The critical reader asks, "What is left unstated?" and "What are the underlying assumptions?" The author is assuming certain things are true, but has the author presented actual evidence to support what is being said? One strategy is to evaluate whether the author is presenting facts (information that can be proven to be true or false) or opinions (information that can not be proven to be true or false).

Exercise 2

Read the following paragraphs and write the assumptions made by the author.

A.   The complaint journalism teachers hear most often from employers is that graduates cannot spell. "Why don't you teach them how to spell?" is the universal question. The answer possibly is that no one can teach students how to spell. All that can be taught is the necessity of spelling words correctly. Correct spelling is achieved as other journalistic demands are achieved—by diligent attention to detail. Spelling correctly is just a matter of accuracy, as are other areas of reporting and writing.[3]

Assumptions:

_____

_____

_____

B.   Effective teaching takes much practice. Similar to other pursuits in life, the rewards of teaching seem both proportional to, and contingent on, thoughtful involvement, structured action, and continuous learning and evaluation. Hopefully, the end product of this teaching will be a person who is informed, who is individually productive and socially responsible, who has the ability to analyze, criticize, and choose alternatives, and who has a compelling system of values whereby he may actualize his life in a manner consistent with ever-increasing knowledge—in a word, a person who evidences discipline.[4]

Assumptions:

_____

_____

_____

DEFINITION

An author may present **fallacious arguments** that appeal for support to factors that have little or nothing to do with the argument. A critical reader is able to recognize fallacious thinking even though the material may sound quite convincing.

STRATEGY 1

The best strategy for recognizing fallacious thinking is to become aware of the more commonly used arguments. The following represent different false appeals that often substitute for sound reasoning:

Appeal to authority: The author attempts to persuade the reader of the value of a product, or position on an issue, through the appeal of an authority figure. A critical reader considers whether these authorities offer any legitimate expertise about the issue or product.

Appeal to pity: The author provides irrelevant reasons to support a conclusion. The reasons may be true and they are often effective in eliciting sympathy, but the reasons do not support the conclusions, and therefore the argument is not sound. A critical reader is aware that evidence must be relevant to the argument.

Appeal to fear: The author more or less threatens an unpleasant consequence if the reader does not agree with his position. A critical reader recognizes that appeals to fear do not provide support for conclusions.

Appeal to ignorance: The author takes the position that if you cannot disprove what is being said, then the conclusion is true. A critical reader realizes that the inability to disprove a conclusion is not evidence that the conclusion is in fact justified.

Appeal to personal attack: The author ignores the issues of the argument and focuses instead on the personal qualities of the person with whom he is arguing. A critical reader understands that discrediting the person does not discredit the argument.

Exercise 3

Read the following paragraphs and write in the space provided the type of fallacious arguments presented by the author.

A.	At present rates of consumption we have enough coal to last for thousands of years. The problem with this is that we don't continue to consume at our present rate. If we continue to increase our consumption, then sooner or later, we will be in the "last minute." The consequences of running low on petroleum, natural gas, and coal would be devastating.[5]

Appeal to _____

B.	I admit that my client embezzled money from the company, your honor. However, I would like to bring several facts to your attention. He is a family man, with a wonderful wife and two terrific children. He is an important member of the community. He is active in the church, coaches a little league baseball team, and has worked very hard to be a good person who cares about people. I think that you should take these things into consideration in handing down your sentence.[6]

Appeal to _____

C.	"With me, abortion is not a problem of religion. It's a problem of the Constitution. I believe that until and unless someone can establish that the unborn child is not a living human being, then that child is already protected by the Constitution, which guarantees life, liberty, and the pursuit of happiness to all of us." Ronald Reagan, October 8, 1984.[7]

Appeal to _____

D.	Hi. You've probably seen me out on the football field. After a hard day's work crushing halfbacks and sacking quarterbacks, I like to settle down with a cold, smooth Maltz beer.[8]

Appeal to _____

E.	"Well, I guess I'm reminded a little bit of what Will Rogers once said about Hoover. He said it's not what he doesn't know that bothers me, it's what he knows for sure just ain't so." Walter Mondale characterizing Ronald Reagan, Oct. 8, 1984.[9]

Appeal to _____

WORD MEANINGS

COMPASS includes vocabulary items to assess your ability to determine, based on context, the specific meaning of difficult, unfamiliar, or ambiguous words.

DEFINITION

The **context** of a word refers to the sentence or paragraph in which the word appears. The information offered in the context helps the reader determine the word's definition. There are limitations in relying on the context for determining the meaning of a word, since often the context does not provide enough information. Also, the context will provide information only on the meaning of the word as used in this setting, and often words have several different meanings.

STRATEGY 1

The strategy for using the context to determine word meaning is to be aware of the typical manner in which this information is presented. Often called "context clues," the different types are as follows:

Definition or Synonym Clues - A writer may give a brief definition or synonym for a word. A synonym is another word with the same meaning. The definition or synonym usually appears in the same sentence as the word being defined, and it may be set apart from the key idea with commas, dashes, or parentheses. Some directional words for recognizing definitions or synonyms are *such as, including, for instance, to illustrate,* and *for example.*

Contrast Clues - A writer may use a word opposite in meaning of the word being defined. A writer may also present a word or phrase indicating that the opposite or contrasting situation exists. Some direction words for recognizing contrast clues are *rather than, but, however, despite, rather, while, yet,* and *nevertheless.*

Inference Clues - A writer may rely on the logical reasoning of the reader or expect the reader to draw on his or her own knowledge and experience. In other words, the general sense of the paragraph or passage, or the main idea, may provide clues to the meaning of the word.

Exercise 4

Read the following paragraphs and answer the vocabulary item based on the surrounding context of the word. In the space provided, identify the type of clue provided by the surrounding context.

A.   As waves approach the shore, they begin to "feel bottom," which causes an increase in height and steepness. If the offshore zone is of variable depth, the section of a wave passing over shallow water will be retarded more than the section in deeper water. As a result, the wave front will be bent, or **refracted**. Shallow water in front of rocky headlands and deeper water in adjacent bays cause refraction and concentrate wave energy on the headlands, which are rapidly eroded.[10]

Refracted means _____

Type of context clue _____

(continued on next page)

Exercise 4 (continued)

B.   So, exactly how does the process of genetic transmission work in humans? You probably recognize that the process is very complex, even though the basics are straight-forward. The nuclei of all human cells normally contain 23 pairs of chromosomes, except for the sex cells (the sperm in males, the ovum in females), which hold only half of each of the 23 possible pairs. At **conception**, the male and female sex cells unite to form a new cell, producing a new mixture of 23 chromosome pairs (and genes), half from the father and half from the mother.[11]

Conception means _____

Type of context clue _____

C.   Wegener proposed that the supercontinent, which he called Pangaea, was made up of all the present continents and had existed about 200 million years ago. Pangaea broke apart, and the pieces, which form today's continents, moved apart, creating new oceans between them. Wegener cited a variety of evidence for his theory, including similarities of rocks, fossils, and geological structures on separate continents. The evidence wasn't bad, but it was not **compelling**, especially since no one could come up with a plausible mechanism for the motion of huge continents. There didn't seem to be any force large enough to do this. While some scientists speculated on the possibility of "continental drift," most ignored it. There simply wasn't enough hard evidence.[12]

Compelling means _____

Type of context clue _____

D.   One could say that vicarious learning is not only important but also represents the future hope for our civilization. Certainly we hope that a child does not need to participate in violence to learn that it is destructive, nor be prejudiced in order to learn about racial, religious, or sexual discrimination, nor engage in war to learn of desolation and death. Many things, because of their permanence or harmfulness, are better learned vicariously.[13]

Vicarious means _____

Type of context clue _____

CHAPTER TWELVE

PRACTICE TEST ONE

PASSAGE ONE

You may use the following question to help you focus your reading:

How did the use of tokens influence the development of writing?

(The following text is adapted from R. A. Roy, <u>Physical Science: An Integrated Approach</u> © 1991 by Contemporary Publishing.)

One scenario for the development of writing uses four stages. In the first stage merchants used the tokens to represent commodities such as sheep, jugs of oil, or clothing materials. This allowed them to keep track of their "inventory." In the second stage merchants began to use the tokens in actual trading. When they shipped goods, they would enclose the appropriate tokens in sealed clay balls called bullae. When the goods arrived, the recipient would break the bullae open and check the shipment against the tokens which acted as an invoice. Thus the bullae were the first bills of lading. In the next stage, merchants made token marks on the outside of the bullae before firing them so there was a record inside and outside. Finally merchants realized they could more easily just make all the token marks on a clay tablet and dispense with lots of tokens and sealed balls. Thus, "pictographs," the shapes and marks on the tokens began to represent real objects. Then the pictographs would easily represent, in a more abstract way, a work, the name of the object. As symbols began to represent sounds, which could be put together to make words, alphabets were developed. Because writing was tied in with trade, it developed and spread rapidly. (Using symbols to represent objects also led to another useful invention: money.)[1]

---

1. The best title for the above passage is

   ○ A. Trade and The Development of Writing.

   ○ B. Tokens, Bullae, and Pictographs.

   ○ C. The Invention of Writing and Money.

   ○ D. Writing.

   ○ E. Trade and Inventory.

2. At what stage in the development of writing did merchants make token marks on the outside of the bullae before firing them so there was a record inside and outside?

   ○ A. the second stage

   ○ B. the third stage

   ○ C. the final stage

   ○ D. the stage where symbols represent sounds

   ○ E. the first stage

3. Bullae were used by merchants for what purpose?

   ○ A. The bullae held the tokens, which acted as the merchant's invoice.

   ○ B. Pictographs, the shapes and marks that began to represent real objects, were written on the bullae.

   ○ C. The bullae represented commodities such as sheep, jugs of oil, or clothing materials.

   ○ D. Bullae was the name given to the clay tablet used as the invoice for shipment of goods.

   ○ E. Bullae were used by merchants in place of tokens.

4. The best statement of the main idea of the above passage is:

   ○ A. writing developed as merchants of trade began using symbols to represent objects.

   ○ B. bullae and tokens were the base of our alphabet.

   ○ C. marks on a clay tablet, bullae, and tokens played important roles in the trade process.

   ○ D. the inventions of writing and money were based on using symbols to represent objects.

   ○ E. bullae were the first bills of trading.

5. The author discusses the four stages in the development of writing through

   ○ A. cause and effect.

   ○ B. demonstrating a comparative relationship among the stages.

   ○ C. sequential order of the stages.

   ○ D. a pattern where one element is seen as causing another element.

   ○ E. comparison and contrast.

PASSAGE TWO

You may use the following question to help you focus your reading:

What are the two different methods used by anthropologists to determine the sex of a skull?

(The following passage is adapted from L.D. Wolfe, L.S. Lieberman & d.L. Hutchinson, Laboratory Textbook for Physical Anthroplogy. © 1994 by Contemporary Publishing.)

There are differences in the male and female human skeleton. In general, the skeletons of males are larger and more **robust** than the skeletons of females. There are also specific differences between women and men in skulls and pelves, which can be used to determine sex. Physical anthropologists and forensic anthropologists use two different methods to determine the sex of a skull. One method, which is qualitative, depends on a visual inspection of the skull. That is, the skull is inspected and its traits noted. Subsequently, the observed traits are compared to those of skulls of known sex.

There is also a quantitative method to sex skulls. This method involves measuring skulls of known sex from anatomical collections and generating discriminant function scores that best characterize the samples. Giles and Elliott (1963) examined crania from American Blacks and American Whites in order to identify the discriminant functions that could be used to determine the sex of a skull. Giles (1970) later incorporated a similar study of the Japanese by Hanihara (1959).[2]

---

6.   From the above passage, one can conclude that

  ○ A. the quantitative method to sex skulls involves numerical analysis.

  ○ B. the skulls of men are more pristine than the skulls of women.

  ○ C. it is more difficult to sex skulls by the qualitative method.

  ○ D. it is necessary to use both qualitative and quantitative methods to sex skulls accurately.

  ○ E. the skeletons of females are more robust than the skeletons of males.

7.   The main idea of the above passage is:

  ○ A. there are no differences in the male and female human skeleton.

  ○ B. there is a qualitative and quantitative method for determining the sex of a skull.

  ○ C. studies by Giles (1970) and Hanihara (1959) determined that the ethnic origin of the skull was important in determining sex.

  ○ D. qualitative research methods rely on observations and quantitative research methods rely on measurement.

  ○ E. there are specific differences between women and men in skulls.

8. As it is used in the passage, the word **robust** most nearly means

○ A.　more delicate.

○ B.　smaller.

○ C.　stronger.

○ D.　masculine.

○ E.　feminine.

9. The quantitative method to sex skulls involves

○ A.　a visual inspection of the skull.

○ B.　measuring skulls of known sex from anatomical collections and generating discriminant function scores that best characterize the samples.

○ C.　a determination that the skeletons of males are larger and more robust than the skeletons of females.

○ D.　measurement of specific differences between pelves of women and men.

○ E.　notation of typical traits.

10. Both qualitative and quantitative methods for determining the sex of skulls

○ A.　were used in studies by Giles and Elliot (1963).

○ B.　are used by physical and forensic anthropologists.

○ C.　involve measuring skulls.

○ D.　involve the statistical procedure of discriminant function.

○ E.　were used in a study of the Japanesse by Hanihara (1959).

PASSAGE THREE

You may use the following question to help you focus your reading:

Why are sedimentary rocks important to Historical Geology?

(The following passage is adapted from R.A. Gastaldo, C.E. Savrda, & R.D. Lewis, Deciphering Earth History. © 1996 by Contemporary Publishing.)

Rocks of all types—igneous, metamorphic, and sedimentary—have stories to tell about Earth history. Sedimentary rocks, however, are most important to Historical Geology. Sedimentary rocks have grossly similar origins; most are born at the Earth's surface by weathering of pre-existing rock, the transport of solid or dissolved weathering products by various agents (e.g., water, wind, ice), and eventual deposition or precipitation in one of a multitude of settings ranging from glaciated mountain peaks to the deepest ocean basins. Despite their general genetic similarities, sediments and sedimentary rocks differ broadly in composition, texture, and other features. These differences reflect **variations** in physical and chemical conditions at the Earth's surface and help us recognize temporal and spatial changes in the magnitude of weathering, mechanisms of transport, and environments in which sediments accumulated. This type of information, in turn, allows us to reconstruct aspects of the geologic past, including ancient climates, geographies, and tectonic events. Moreover, sedimentary rocks contain the great majority of fossils, and hence, provide the basis for our understanding of the history of life on Earth.[3]

11. Although sedimentary rocks are similar in genetic origin, they differ broadly in

- ○ A. tectonic events.
- ○ B. fossil density.
- ○ C. composition.
- ○ D. environmental sediments.
- ○ E. geologic past.

12. The author believes that rocks of all types—igneous, metamorphic, and sedimentary—

- ○ A. are important to Historical Geology.
- ○ B. allow us to reconstruct aspects of the geologic past.
- ○ C. have stories to tell about Earth history, but sedimentary rocks are the most important to Historical Geology.
- ○ D. are born at the Earth's surface by weathering of pre-existing rock.
- ○ E. differ broadly in composition.

13. The best statement of the main idea of the above passage is

 ○ A. sedimentary rocks are important for understanding historical geology.
 ○ B. rocks of all types have stories to tell about Earth history.
 ○ C. differences in composition and texture help us to understand sedimentary rocks.
 ○ D. sedimentary rocks reflect differences in chemical conditions at the Earth's surface.
 ○ E. sedimentary rocks contain the great majorigy of fossils.

14. The author supports his position on the importance of sedimentary rock through

 ○ A. objective facts.
 ○ B. subjective experience.
 ○ C. comparisons of the three types of rocks.
 ○ D. experimental evidence.
 ○ E. anecdotal evidence

15. In the above passage, **variations** means

 ○ A. similarities.
 ○ B. consistencies.
 ○ C. viscosity.
 ○ D. dissimilarities.
 ○ E. conditions.

PASSAGE FOUR

You may use the following question to help you focus your reading:

How is the brightness of a variable star different than a comparison star?

(The following passage is adapted from J.W. Wilson, Astronomy: A laboratory Textbook. © 1996 by Contemporary Publishing.)

In general, most stars have a constant brightness. However, certain very young stars and some aging stars become unstable and vary in brightness and are known as variable stars. The oldest observations of variable stars come from China. The star Omicron Ceti was discovered in 1596 as the first periodic variable star. It was named Mira, The Wonderful, and has been studied by astronomers ever since.

Modern day astronomers know that many stars are variable and have classified them into groups. One type is called the Mira variables because they exhibit the same characteristics as Mira. These Mira variables are known to be red giant stars near the end of their evolutionary lives. Their amplitudes vary over several stellar magnitudes and over hundreds of days.

When astronomers observe a variable star they usually compare the brightness of the variable to the brightness of a nearby star which has a constant brightness, the "comparison star." A comparison star may be chosen **at random**, and it is possible that, by chance, it is also some type of variable star. In this case, the astronomer is comparing one variable star to another variable star and the observations are meaningless. In order to make sure the comparison star is constant, its brightness is compared to yet another star called the "check star" (because it is used to check for variations of the comparison star).[4]

16. According to the author, variable stars

   ○ A. have the same brightness as the "comparison star."
   ○ B. are very young stars and aging stars that have become unstable and vary in brightness.
   ○ C. may be chosen at random, which makes observations of variable stars a meaningless process.
   ○ D. originated in China in 1596.
   ○ E. have a constant brightness.

17. In paragraph three, the author is describing

   ○ A. the process involved in observing a variable star.
   ○ B. how the science of astronomy is based on chance.
   ○ C. how and why variable stars are at the end of their evolutionary lives.
   ○ D. the role played by the comparison star when observing the variable star.
   ○ E. the star called Omicron Ceti, discovered in 1596.

18. According to the author, the star Omicron Ceti

◯ A. is periodically different than a variable star.

◯ B. has a constant brightness and is often used as a "comparison star."

◯ C. was discovered in 1596 as the first variable star.

◯ D. was named Mira, The Wonderful, by modern-day astronomers.

◯ E. is often called the "check star."

19. According to the passage, the "check star" is

◯ A. more important than the variable or comparison star for understanding constellations and brightness.

◯ B. used to check for variations of the comparison star.

◯ C. used to check for variations of the variable star.

◯ D. one type of red giant star.

◯ E. was named Mira, the Wonderful.

20. In the above passage, **"at random"** means

◯ A. by design.

◯ B. according to a plan.

◯ C. with certainty.

◯ D. arbitrarily.

◯ E. purposefully.

PASSAGE FIVE

You may use the following question to help you focus your reading:

What is one explanation for phobic disorders?

(The following passage is adapted from R. Gerow, Psychology: An Introduction. © 1995 by Addison-Wesley Educational Publishers.)

Some people are intensely afraid of flying, of elevators, of heights, of small closed-in areas, of spiders, or of the dark. Psychologists say that these people are suffering from a phobic disorder—an intense, irrational fear of an object or event that leads a person to avoid contact with it. There are many explanations for how phobic disorders, or phobias, occur, but one clear possibility is classical conditioning.

This explanation goes as follows: a person experiences an intense, natural emotional response to a powerful, emotion-producing stimulus—perhaps a traumatic event, such as a severe injury or an accident. When an emotion-producing stimulus occurs in the presence of another, neutral stimulus, the pairing may result in the formation of a conditioned fear response to the originally neutral stimulus. A child at a local carnival becomes separated from his parents and gets swept away by a large crowd into a tent where clowns are performing. The youngster is (sensibly) frightened by the separation from his parents, and after they are reunited, requires considerable reassurance before he settles down. Should we be terribly surprised if this child—even much later, as an adolescent or an adult—appears to be irrationally afraid of carnivals, circuses, or clowns? Not if one believes that classical conditioning can account for the formation of phobias.[5]

---

21. According to the author, classical conditioning is

○ A. the only logical explanation for fear of flying.

○ B. one explanation for phobic disorders.

○ C. when an emotion-producing stimulus occurs in the presence of another emotion-producing stimulus.

○ D. involves the separation of certain stimuli.

○ E. unrelated to the formation of phobias.

22. According to the passage, a phobic disorder is

○ A. when an emotion-producing stimulus occurs in the presence of a neutral stimulus.

○ B. an intense, irrational fear of an object or event that leads a person to avoid contact with it.

○ C. experienced by most first-time airplane passengers.

○ D. a traumatic event, such as a severe injury or an accident.

○ E. when a child becomes separated from his parents.

23. The author explains classical conditioning and phobic disorders through

⭘ A. personal experience.

⭘ B. psychological experiments.

⭘ C. examples.

⭘ D. scientific data.

⭘ E. historical evidence.

24. From the above passage, one can conclude that

⭘ A. there is only one explanation for phobic disorders.

⭘ B. classical conditioning is one explanation of phobic disorders.

⭘ C. many children experience phobic disorders.

⭘ D. phobic disorders are treatable.

⭘ E. most people are afraid of heights.

25. According to the above passage, a conditioned fear response may be evoked by an originally

⭘ A. emotion-producing stimulus.

⭘ B. natural emotional response.

⭘ C. neutral stimulus.

⭘ D. intense emotional response.

⭘ E. positive stimulus.

PASSAGE SIX

You may use the following question to help you focus your reading:

What are Francie's feelings about the librarian?

(The following passage is adapted from B. Smith, A Tree Grows in Brooklyn. © 1943 by Harper Collins Publishers.)

She stood at the desk a long time before the librarian **deigned** to attend to her.

"Yes?" inquired the lady pettishly.

"This book. I want it." Francie pushed the book forward opened at the back with the little card pushed out of the envelope. The librarians had trained the children to present the books that way. It saved them the trouble of opening several hundred books a day and pulling several hundred cards from as many envelopes.

She took the card, stamped it, pushed it down a slot in the desk. She stamped Francie's card and pushed it at her. Francie picked it up, but she did not go away.

"Yes?" The librarian did not bother to look up.

"Could you recommend a good book for a girl?"

"How old?"

"She is eleven."

Each week Francie made the same request and each week the librarian asked the same question. A name on a card meant nothing to her and since she never looked up into a child's face, she never did get to know the little girl who took a book out every day and two on Saturday. A smile would have meant a lot to Francie and a friendly comment would have made her so happy. She loved the library and was anxious to worship the lady in charge. But the librarian had other things on her mind. She hated children anyhow.

Francie trembled in anticipation as the woman reached under the desk. She saw the title as the book came up: <u>If I Were King</u> by McCarthy. Wonderful! Last week it had been <u>Beverly of Graustark</u> and the same two weeks before that. She had the McCarthy book only twice. The librarian recommended these two books over and over again. Maybe they were the only ones she herself had read; maybe they were on a recommended list; maybe she had discovered that they were surefire as far as eleven-year old girls were concerned.[6]

---

26. **Deigned**, as used in the above passage, most likely means

○ A. designed.

○ B. decided.

○ C. condescended.

○ D. deliberately.

○ E. with kindness.

27. The above passage indicates that Francie

    ◯ A. wanted to please the librarian.

    ◯ B. found reading very tedious and boring.

    ◯ C. had an excellent rapport with the librarian.

    ◯ D. often misbehaved in the library.

    ◯ E. was often disrespectful to her elders.

28. Francie is requesting the library book for

    ◯ A. her friend.

    ◯ B. herself.

    ◯ C. the librarian.

    ◯ D. the lady in charge.

    ◯ E. a twenty-year-old girl.

29. The librarians trained the children to present their books in a certain way because

    ◯ A. there was a good amount of book theft.

    ◯ B. the same books were requested each week.

    ◯ C. they checked out hundreds of books.

    ◯ D. they wanted children to respect them.

    ◯ E. the children did not respect books.

30. The explanations for why the librarian recommends the same books over and over again indicate Francie's

    ◯ A. desire to think well of others.

    ◯ B. sarcastic nature.

    ◯ C. caustic wit.

    ◯ D. ability to see people for what they are.

    ◯ E. negative outlook.

PASSAGE SEVEN

You may use the following question to help you focus your reading:

Would speaking more than one language help Americans in foreign trade?

(The following passage is adapted from L. Lauder, "The Language of Foreign Trade." © 1985 by The New York Times Co.)

Why has no one raised the fact that so many Americans engaged in foreign trade can speak no language but their own? It's getting late in the day to realize that the language of international trade is not English. The language of international trade is the language of the customer.

It is self-evident that you can't sell unless there is a demand for the product. It is also self-evident that you can't begin to understand what a people demand if you can't talk to them on their own terms. Their own terms, of course, means their own language.

As far as business is concerned, our national **parochialism** is growing worse. A study commissioned by the National Council on Foreign Language and International Studies questioned 1,690 young men and women in 564 business schools working toward their doctoral degrees in business in the spring of 1984. The study found only 17 percent of these students were taking one or more courses in international affairs and foreign languages. In 1976, that figure was 25 percent.[7]

31.   **Parochialism**, as used in the above passage, most likely means

    ○ A. provincialism.

    ○ B. openness.

    ○ C. perspective.

    ○ D. viewpoint.

    ○ E. attitude.

32.   "It's getting late in the day" as used in the above passage most likely means it is

    ○ A. late afternoon or early evening.

    ○ B. long past overdue.

    ○ C. late in the year.

    ○ D. insulting.

    ○ E. inappropriate.

33. The author states that the language of internal trade is

○ A. not entirely practical.
○ B. speaking English.
○ C. most prevalent in doctoral programs.
○ D. essential for success.
○ E. the language of the customer.

34. The passage indicates that the study of foreign language in business schools

○ A. is on the decline.
○ B. will increase in the future.
○ C. is more important in foreign trade schools.
○ D. is the responsibility of the faculty.
○ E. rose from 17 to 25 percent.

35. According to the author, understanding what a people demand

○ A. depends on the product you are selling.
○ B. requires proficiency in English.
○ C. is self-evident.
○ D. is taught in business schools.
○ E. requires talking to them in their own language.

PASSAGE EIGHT

You may use the following question to help you focus your reading:

How do the Agricultural and Industrial Revolution differ in terms of energy used?

*(The following passage is adapted from R.A. Roy, <u>Physical Science: An Integrated Approach.</u>
© 1991 by Contemporary Publishing.)*

> After the Agricultural Revolution, growth and change took place, but at a slower pace. One way to describe this growth is by the energy available for work. At the beginning of the Agricultural Revolution, human energy was used, along with fire. As people learned how to make hotter fires, **pyrotechnology** led to fired clay, to smelted metals, and to cooking and preserving foods. The domestication of large animals like horses and oxen allowed more work to be done like plowing larger fields and transporting more goods. Early sailboats harnessed the wind.
>
> As the Dark and Middle Ages proceeded, larger, more powerful animals were bred. (This development, as today, was often tied to war. Large horses were used to carry armored knights, the military "tanks" of their day.) Wind was used more effectively by "fore and aft" rigs on sailboats, allowing a vessel to tack into the wind. Windmills and waterwheels were also developed. Around 1750 in England, however, changes began to occur that led to revolutionary changes in energy use. The changes, termed the Industrial Revolution, involve using mechanical devices, machines, which can apply energy to perform useful work. We are still in this revolution. Machines are used in agriculture, mining, commerce, and other areas, even in the home. Large factories, by concentrating machines, raw materials, labor, and energy can mass produce huge amounts of manufactured goods: automobiles, clothes, steel chemicals, and the rest of the modern cornucopia of technology.[8]

36. **Pyrotechnology**, as used in the above passage, means

   - ❍ A. pottery.
   - ❍ B. clay work.
   - ❍ C. art of fire.
   - ❍ D. fireworks.
   - ❍ E. smelted metals

37. The time frame discussed in the above passage is

   - ❍ A. the Agricultural Revolution to the Industrial Revolution.
   - ❍ B. the Dark Ages.
   - ❍ C. around 1750 in England.
   - ❍ D. the Industrial Revolution.
   - ❍ E. the Middle Ages.

38. The author states that the military "tanks" of their day were the

⭘ A. large horses.

⭘ B. rigs on sailboats.

⭘ C. windmills and waterwheels.

⭘ D. oxen.

⭘ E. armored knights.

39. The Industrial Revolution occurred

⭘ A. before the Agricultural Revolution.

⭘ B. at the same time as the Dark Ages.

⭘ C. during the Middle Ages.

⭘ D. around 1750.

⭘ E. only in England.

40. According to the passages, the Industrial Revolution involved

⭘ A. machines that could apply energy to perform useful work.

⭘ B. human energy and pyrotechnology.

⭘ C. harnessing the wind.

⭘ D. the domestication of large animals like horses and oxen that allowed more work to be done.

⭘ E. the "fore" and "aft" rigs on sailboats.

PASSAGE NINE

You may use the following question to help you focus your reading:

What are dramatic artists trying to achieve through "entertaining"?

(The following passage is adapted from a.W. Staub, Varieties of Theatrical Art. © 1994 by Contemporary Publishing.)

The verb "to entertain" comes from the Latin words meaning "to hold between," and that is what entertainment attempts to do: hold someone's attention from a beginning to an end. But there are many ways to hold a person's attention between two points in time or space. Most people, for instance, are attentive when threatened with a weapon, though most will not feel entertained. **Coercion** is not entertaining. Entertainment is agreeable; coercion is not. "Let me entertain you" means "let me hold your attention in an agreeable manner from the moment I take hold until the moment I let go." Why should anyone want to hold another's attention agreeably? Because it is satisfying to be the center of attention. To be so placed is like being loved. Indeed, many entertainers have been literally adored. Moreover, persons being entertained often find the experience so pleasant that they are willing to pay the entertainer well, sometimes extravagantly. For many performers, however, a third motivation is equally important; the entertainment arts provide performers a means to create beauty and communicate ideas about the human experience. In fact, the theatrical arts are an ideal medium of communication, for when people are in an agreeable mood they are more likely to be receptive to another's thoughts and feelings. That is why dramatic artists are first and foremost communicators; they create beauty and express ideas and attitudes about life while holding an audience's attention within an agreeable form or artistic metaphor.[9]

41. According to the passage, people entertain

- ○ A. to be the center of attention.
- ○ B. for money.
- ○ C. to create beauty and communicate ideas.
- ○ D. to hold someone's attention.
- ○ E. for all of the above reasons.

42. The author describes dramatic artists as first and foremost

- ○ A. attention seekers.
- ○ B. mercenaries.
- ○ C. individuals seeking love.
- ○ D. communicators.
- ○ E. attention givers.

43. **Coercion**, as used in the above passage, means

   ○ A. volition.

   ○ B. freedom.

   ○ C. free will.

   ○ D. force.

   ○ E. threatening.

44. The author states that dramatic arts are an ideal medium of communication because

   ○ A. people are agreeable when they are being entertained and therefore open to ideas.

   ○ B. people communicate more effectively when they have paid a great deal of money to be entertained.

   ○ C. the theater is the best place to discuss ideas and attitudes about life.

   ○ D. people will listen more to individuals they adore.

   ○ E. the theater often intimidates people.

45. What is the author's central point about entertainment?

   ○ A. Artists entertain primarily for attention.

   ○ B. There is no clear definition of what it means "to entertain."

   ○ C. The opportunity to make money is not important to artists.

   ○ D. Artists are communicators that create beauty and express ideas about life.

   ○ E. Most artists expect to be paid extravagantly well.

PASSAGE TEN

You may use the following question to help you focus your reading:

Is information from an "authority" more readily accepted?

The following passage is adapted from R.A. Roy, Physical Science: An Integrated Approach. © 1991 by Contemporary Publishing.)

Ordinary people accept most of their information from an "authority." We accept what we read in the newspapers, what our teachers and friends tell us; rarely are we skeptical. Many human activities are based on authority. Law is one example. In a criminal or civil proceeding, the outcome is determined by what statutes say and by the outcomes of earlier, similar cases. The judges, juries, and attorneys do not make up new laws for the specific case, but accept the authority of preceding cases.

Religion is also based on authority. This might be found in a document such as the Bible or the Koran, or in a hierarchy of church officers such as the College of Cardinals or a presbytery.

Scientists do not accept information from authority. In our everyday lives we are usually not skeptical; but, when doing science, skepticism is required. No matter how carefully the information is collected, scientists check it rigorously before accepting it.[10]

---

46.   The above passage focuses on the relationship between

    ❍ A. ordinary people and scientists.

    ❍ B. law and religion.

    ❍ C. religion and scientists.

    ❍ D. authority and science.

    ❍ E. criminal and civil.

47.   The author states that the outcome of a criminal or civil proceeding is determined by

    ❍ A. new laws made up for specific cases.

    ❍ B. the hierarchy of church officers.

    ❍ C. the authority of documents such as the Bible.

    ❍ D. the Koran.

    ❍ E. what statutes say.

48. All of the following accept information from authority except

    ○ A. ordinary people.

    ○ B. lawyers.

    ○ C. scientists.

    ○ D. priests.

    ○ E. teachers.

49. As it is used in the passage, the word **skeptical** most nearly means

    ○ A. silly.

    ○ B. made up.

    ○ C. unaccepting.

    ○ D. accepting.

    ○ E. smart.

50. When doing science, according to the passage,

    ○ A. most information comes from an "authority."

    ○ B. we accept what we read in the newspaper.

    ○ C. we rely heavily on teachers, family, and friends.

    ○ D. skepticism is required.

    ○ E. reference is made to the College of Cardinals.

PRACTICE TEST TWO

PASSAGE ONE

You may use the following question to help you focus your reading:

Do individuals have the right to decide when to die?

(The following passage is adapted from N. Cousins, "The Right to Die," The Saturday Review. © 1975 by General Media International.)

The world of religion and philosophy was shocked recently when Henry P. Van Dusen and his wife ended their lives by their own hands. Dr. Van Dusen had been president of Union Theological Seminary; for more than a quarter-century he had been one of the **luminous** names in Protestant theology. He enjoyed world status as a spiritual leader. News of the self-inflicted death of the Van Dusens, therefore, was profoundly disturbing to all those who attach a moral stigma to suicide and regard it as a violation of God's laws.

Henry and Elizabeth Van Dusen had lived full lives. In recent years, they had become increasingly ill, requiring almost continual medical care. Their infirmities were worsening, and they realized they would soon become completely dependent for even the most elementary needs and functions. Under these circumstances, little dignity would have been left in life. They didn't like the idea of taking up space in a world with too many mouths and too little food. They believed it was a misuse of medical science to keep them technically alive.

They therefore believed they had the right to decide when to die. In making that decision, they weren't turning against life as the highest value; what they were turning against was the notion that there were no circumstances under which life should be discontinued.

An important aspect of human uniqueness is the power of free will. In his books and lectures, Dr. Van Dusen frequently spoke about the exercise of this uniqueness. The fact that he used his free will to prevent life from becoming a caricature of itself was completely in character. In their letter, the Van Dusens sought to convince family and friends that they were not acting solely out of despair or pain.[11]

---

1.   The author of the above passage probably

   ○ A. agrees with the moral stigma attached to suicide.

   ○ B. regards suicide as a violation of God's life.

   ○ C. believes suicide is turning against life as the highest value.

   ○ D. supports the Van Dusens' decision to end their lives.

   ○ E. believes life should continue under any circumstances.

2. The passage states that Dr. Van Dusen's position in the world of theology was

○ A. that of a world spiritual leader.

○ B. undeserved since he committed suicide.

○ C. profoundly disturbing.

○ D. a hardship as his medical problems worsened.

○ E. controversial.

3. **Luminous**, as used in the above passage, means

○ A. recognized.

○ B. obscure.

○ C. little known.

○ D. infamous.

○ E. enlightened.

4. The author states that Dr. Van Dusen's books and lectures revealed his belief that

○ A. humans are unique in their ability to exercise free will.

○ B. humans need to avoid becoming dependent on others.

○ C. family and friends should support their decision.

○ D. theology and philosophy are unique disciplines.

○ E. life should be valued above everything.

5. The statement that Van Dusen used "his free will to prevent life from becoming a caricature of itself" most likely means he committed suicide

○ A. to avoid people taking advantage of his illness.

○ B. so that others would not belittle him.

○ C. so that his status as a spiritual leader would not be threatened.

○ D. so that his illness would not make a mockery of his life.

○ E. to avoid dependency on family and friends.

PASSAGE TWO

You may use the following question to help you focus your reading:

What evidence supports the Big Bang theory on how the universe began?

(The following passage is adapted from P.G. Hewitt, "The Origin of the Universe and Solar System," Conceptual Physics. © 1985 by Scott, Foresman, and Company.)

No one knows how the universe began. Evidence suggests that about 15 to 20 billion years ago most of the matter-energy of the universe was highly concentrated at an unimaginably high temperature and underwent a primordial explosion, usually referred to as the **Big Bang**, which was accompanied by a high-powered blast of high-frequency radiation that we call the primeval fireball. The universe is the remnant of this explosion, and we view it as still expanding. Radiation from the dying embers of the primeval fireball now permeate all space in the form of the presently observed long-wavelength microwaves, which have been lengthened by the expansion of the universe. The present expansion of the universe is evident in a Doppler red shift in the light from other galaxies, which is greater than gravitation would account for. This red shift indicates a recession of the galaxies. All galaxies are getting farther away from our own. This does not, as a first thought may indicate, place our own galaxy in a central position. Consider a balloon with ants on it: as the balloon is inflated, every ant will see every neighboring ant getting farther away, which certainly doesn't suggest a central position for each ant. In an expanding universe, every observer sees clusters of all other galaxies receding.

If you throw a rock skyward, it slows down due to its gravitational attraction to the earth below. Similarly, matter blown away in the primordial explosion is gravitationally attracted to every other bit of matter, which results in a continual slowing down of the overall expansion.[12]

6.   The best title for the above passage is

   ○ A. The Expanding Balloon.
   ○ B. The Big Bang and The Expanding Universe.
   ○ C. The Big Bang.
   ○ D. Recession of the Galaxies.
   ○ E. The Doppler Red Shift.

7.   The author provides the example of the balloon with ants on it to explain

   ○ A. how you throw a rock skyward.
   ○ B. how the Earth can be compared to the balloon.
   ○ C. that matter in the explosion is centrally located.
   ○ D. that although galaxies are getting further away, it does not place our galaxy in a central position.
   ○ E. the gravitational attraction of the Earth.

8. The author states that the Big Bang was, in essence,

   ❍ A. high-frequency radiation.

   ❍ B. an explosion.

   ❍ C. a Doppler red shift.

   ❍ D. a primeval fireball.

   ❍ E. long-wavelength microwaves.

9. The author most likely views the Big Bang Theory as

   ❍ A. the only explanation for the beginning of the universe.

   ❍ B. an incorrect explanation for the beginning of the universe.

   ❍ C. a theory on the beginning of the universe proven by evidence.

   ❍ D. a theory on the beginning of the universe suggested by evidence.

   ❍ E. a ridiculous theory.

10. The author states that the present expansion of the universe is evident in a(n)

   ❍ A. Doppler red shift in the light from other galaxies.

   ❍ B. Doppler red shift being less than gravitation would account for.

   ❍ C. primeval fireball.

   ❍ D. presently observed long-wavelength microwaves.

   ❍ E. inflated balloon with ants on it.

PASSAGE THREE

You may use the following question to help you focus your reading:

What has delayed industrialization of certain regions in the world?

(The following passage is adapted from R.A. Roy, Pysical Science: An Integrated Approach.
© 1991 by Contemporary Publishing.)

Why haven't all regions in the world undergone industrialization? Agriculture occurs everywhere; why not industry? Various answers have been given for this, many of them **invidious**. People are described as lazy, or unintelligent, or lacking in the cultural values required to run industries. The real answer is that large amounts of energy are simply not available to all countries. Not everyone is lucky enough to have deposits of petroleum, oil, coal, and natural gas, to say nothing of ore deposits, rich soils, and good weather. There is another reason also, which goes back to the early days of the Industrial Revolution. In Europe there arose an economic policy called mercantilism. This emphasized the economic development of the home country at the expense of trading partners such as colonies. By passing laws and regulations, a home country, such as England or Spain, could benefit greatly. England imported raw materials from its colonies, made the finished goods in its factories and sold them back to the colonies at a profit. The colonies were forbidden by law to make their own finished products, or even to make factories. The colonies were also forbidden to trade with other countries, so that they were economic "captives." It is asserted, with some justification, that this system greatly delayed industrialization in many areas. Needless to say, these repressive economic policies led to real revolutions, the American Revolution being the first of several.[13]

---

11.   From the above passage, one can conclude that the author

  ○   A.   supports the economic policy of mercantilism.

  ○   B.   believes people delayed industrialization in many countries.

  ○   C.   believes mercantilism is an unjust economic policy.

  ○   D.   supported home countries' efforts to control colonies.

  ○   E.   believes mercantilism promoted industrialization.

12.   The purpose of the above passage is to

  ○   A.   discuss the importation of raw materials from colonies.

  ○   B.   discuss the reasons industrialization was delayed in many areas.

  ○   C.   explain the process of colonization.

  ○   D.   support people in nonindustrialized nations.

  ○   E.   note the importance of petroleum, oil, coal, and natural gas for industrialization.

13. The passage attributes delayed industrialization to

    ○ A. the lack of motivation of the people.

    ○ B. the abundance of energy.

    ○ C. the amount of coal and petroleum.

    ○ D. revolutions.

    ○ E. mercantilism.

14. **Invidious**, as used in the above passage, means

    ○ A. industrious.

    ○ B. insulting.

    ○ C. divisive.

    ○ D. insubstantial.

    ○ E. substantial.

15. Home countries enforced mercantilism by

    ○ A. laws and regulations making colonies "economic captives."

    ○ B. preventing cultural values.

    ○ C. teaching cultural values.

    ○ D. preaching motivation and ambition.

    ○ E. using large amounts of energy.

PASSAGE FOUR

You may use the following question to help you focus your reading:

What factors affect an individual's basal metabolic rate (BMR)?

(The following passage is adapted from W.A. Forsythe, Nutrition and You With Readings. © 1995 by Contemporary Publishing.)

Much of the energy you use each day maintains the basal metabolic rate (BMR). Energy used for basal metabolism is the minimum energy used to keep a person alive. Some of the body processes that use energy for BMR are...[those] that would continue if you are to stay alive. Think of them as the processes that would continue if a person were in a coma. Any activity or movement above this is not truly basal.

Your BMR is directly affected by your body size. The larger a person is, the greater the BMR. A larger body size means more tissue to keep functioning and therefore more energy expended in the BMR. Men, on average, have a higher BMR than women, in part because men are bigger than women. BMR also increases as lean body mass increases. Lean body mass is a person's weight minus the weight of his adipose (fat) tissue. The more bone and muscle you have, the greater the amount of energy needed to maintain the BMR. Again, because men generally have more lean body mass than women, their BMR will be greater. It is easy to understand that a 230-pound person would have a higher BMR than a 150-pound person. However, if a man and a woman each weigh 150 pounds, the man, having a greater lean body mass than the woman, would have a higher BMR. It takes much more energy to keep muscle and bone functioning than it does to keep adipose (fat) tissue functioning.

A last factor that affects one's BMR is age. The BMR decreases as one gets older. It is estimated that a person's BMR decreases by about 10% per decade of life after age forty. That means that a person at age 75 needs only about one-half as much energy to support the BMR as when he was 25 years old.[14]

---

16.   Examples of body processes that use energy for basal metabolic rate are

    ◯ A. beating of the heart.

    ◯ B. body-temperature regulation.

    ◯ C. liver and kidney function.

    ◯ D. pumping of blood.

    ◯ E. all of the above.

17. According to the passage, if a man and a women each weigh 150 pounds, the one with a lower BMR is the

    ○ A. person with the greater lean body mass.

    ○ B. man.

    ○ C. woman.

    ○ D. person with less fat.

    ○ E. person with more bone and muscle.

18. According to the passage, lean body mass

    ○ A. is the same as the weight of fat tissue.

    ○ B. is the opposite of bone and muscle.

    ○ C. needs less energy.

    ○ D. is a person's weight minus the weight of fat tissue.

    ○ E. is adipose tissue.

19. The factors, according to the passage, that affect one's BMR are

    ○ A. body size, lean body mass, and age.

    ○ B. activities or movements that are not truly basal.

    ○ C. body processes and age.

    ○ D. sex and energy level.

    ○ E. age and metabolism.

20. According to the passage, BMR increases as

    ○ A. lean body mass increases.

    ○ B. one gets older.

    ○ C. the weight of fat tissue increases.

    ○ D. body size decreases.

    ○ E. bone and muscle decreases.

PASSAGE FIVE

You may use the following question to help you focus your reading:

What is the explanation for the Doppler phenomenon?

(The following passage is adapted from J. Wagner, Introductory Musical Acoustics. *© 1994 by Contemporary Publishing.)*

When a police car or ambulance approaches and passes, the frequency and the amplitude of the siren increase as the vehicle approaches, reach a peak level at the closest point, and then decrease as the vehicle passes. This seemingly odd acoustical phenomenon is called the Doppler effect.

It may seem that the nearer we are to a sound, the higher its pitch. Although we know this is not true, if either the sound source or the listener is moving at a sufficient rate, the Doppler phenomenon will be perceived.

The explanation is quite simple. Pitch depends upon the number of vibrations per second that reach the ear. If one moves rapidly toward a sound source or it toward us, the rate at which those vibrations reach us increases. That is, more vibrations reach the ear per second than if both sound source and listener were stationary. The natural consequence of this phenomenon is that a higher pitch is perceived, i.e., one with more vibrations per second.

As the sound source moves away from the listener (or the listener from the sound source), fewer vibrations reach the listener per second and the pitch becomes lower. The relative speed of the sound source or listener is all-important. The distance between the two is not a factor. Distance may seem to play a part because as the sound source and listener get closer and closer, amplitude increases.

To review, the faster the speed that the sound source and listener travel toward or away from each other, the greater the rise or fall in pitch. The rate of movement toward or away from the source of sound is all-important. Distance has only to do with the amplitude of the sound.[15]

---

21. According to the passage, the rise or fall in pitch depends on the

- ○ A. speed that the sound source and listener travel toward or away from each other.
- ○ B. distance between the sound source and listener.
- ○ C. increase in amplitude of the sound.
- ○ D. increase in frequency of the sound.
- ○ E. decrease in frequency of the sound.

22. According to the passage, the Doppler effect explains why it may seem that the nearer we are to a sound,

○ A. the lower its pitch.

○ B. the higher its pitch.

○ C. the fewer vibrations reach the ear per second.

○ D. the lower its amplitude.

○ E. the fewer vibrations reach the listener.

23. The best title for the above passage is

○ A. Acoustical Phenomena.

○ B. Sound Effects.

○ C. Frequency and Amplitude of Sound.

○ D. Pitch and The Doppler Effect.

○ E. Sound Vibrations and the Ear.

24. The author explains the Doppler effect through

○ A. objective facts.

○ B. comparison and contrast.

○ C. scientific experiments.

○ D. analogies.

○ E. historical evidence.

25. The best statement of the main idea of the above passage is:

○ A. the Doppler phenomenon is explained by the speed that the sound source and listener travel toward or away from each other.

○ B. amplitude is as important as pitch in the Doppler effect.

○ C. amplitude depends upon the number of vibrations per second that reach the ear.

○ D. more vibrations reach the ear per second when sound source and listener are moving than when they are stationary.

○ E. sound vibrations cause pitch to be higher.

PASSAGE SIX

You may use the following question to help you focus your reading:

What kinds of thoughts and actions are controlled by the cerebral cortex?

(The following passage is adapted from J. Wagner, Introductory Musical Acoustics. © 1994 by Contemporary Publishing.)

The cerebral cortex (covering of the cerebrum) or "grey matter" is possibly the most interesting of the brain's components because it contains distinctive electrical properties, which can be monitored to give clues about sensory input and thought processes. The cortex contains over ten billion nerve cells and, through synaptic routing, there are more possible combinations of neural pathways than there are atoms in the universe! This intricate organ shows both a continuous and rhythmic alteration of electrical potential and a variety of more localized, larger microvoltage responses. The continuous flow of electrical output is called "spontaneous" activity because it is always present in living organisms. The localized responses are called "evoked" because their presence seems closely associated with the input of the senses.

A closer examination of the physical makeup of the cerebral cortex will reveal the nature of these brainwaves. The cortex of the cerebrum is divided into two hemispheres (halves)—a right hemisphere and a left hemisphere. Each hemisphere is divided into four lobes—frontal, parietal, temporal and occipital. Together, these four lobes make up one hemisphere of the cerebral cortex. Each of the brain's hemispheres is nearly a mirror of the other, yet the brain hemispheres seem to specialize in controlling certain kinds of thoughts and actions.

To state accurately all the functions of each of the four lobes would be impossible, since the human brain is still in the early stages of being mapped. It may generally be said that areas of the occipital lobes are associated with the input of visual stimuli, parts of the parietal lobes with speech and motor activities, and portions of the frontal lobes with complex thought processes.[16]

26. The number of lobes in the cerebral cortex is

   ○ A. two.

   ○ B. four.

   ○ C. eight.

   ○ D. impossible to state accurately.

   ○ E. six.

27.　The author believes the cerebral cortex is probably the most interesting of the brain's components because of the

　○　A.　information it provides about sensory input and thought processes.
　○　B.　number of atoms in the brain.
　○　C.　ten billion nerve cells.
　○　D.　possibilities of electrical potential.
　○　E.　larger microvoltage responses.

28.　The author refers to localized "evoked" responses as

　○　A.　electrical responses closely associated with the input of the senses.
　○　B.　the continuous flow of electrical output.
　○　C.　very similar to the spontaneous activity.
　○　D.　continuous alteration of electrical potential.
　○　E.　rhythmic alteration of electrical potential.

29.　The best title for the above passage is

　○　A.　The Cerebral Cortex.
　○　B.　Input and Output of Electrical Activity.
　○　C.　The Right Hemisphere of the Brain.
　○　D.　Frontal, Parietal, Temporal and Occipital Lobes.
　○　E.　Occipital Lobes and Visual Stimuli.

30.　By stating that "the human brain is still in the early stages of being mapped" the author means

　○　A.　there is more to be learned about the functions of the brain.
　○　B.　each lobe of the brain has a specific job to do.
　○　C.　we have yet to distinguish between "spontaneous" and "evoked" electrical output.
　○　D.　we need a closer examination of the physical makeup of the cerebral cortex.
　○　E.　it is extremely difficult to monitor electrical properties.

PASSAGE SEVEN

You may use the following question to help you focus your reading:

What are the beliefs of Hinduism?

(The following passage is adapted from R. Eshleman & B.G. Cashion, Sociology: An Introduction. © 1985 by Scott Foresman and Company.)

The great majority of the 457 million Hindus in the world live in India and Pakistan. In India, approximately 85 percent of the population is Hindu. Hinduism has evolved over about 4,000 years and comprises an enormous variety of beliefs and practices. It hardly corresponds to most Western conceptions of religion since organization is minimal and there is no religious hierarchy.

Hinduism is so closely intertwined with other aspects of the society that it is difficult to describe it clearly, especially in the case of castes. Hindus sometimes refer to the ideal way of life as fulfilling the duties of one's class and station, which means obeying the rules of the four great castes of India: the Brahmins, or priests; the Ksatriyas, warriors and rulers; the Vaisyas, merchants and farmers; and the Sudras, peasants and laborers. A fifth class, the Untouchables, includes those whose occupations require them to handle "unclean" objects.

To Hindus, the word "dharma" means the cosmos or the social order. Hindus practice rituals that uphold the great cosmic order. They believe that, to be righteous, one must strive to behave in accordance with the way things are. In a sense, the Hindu sees life as a ritual. The world is regarded as a great dance determined by one's Karma, or personal destiny, and the final goal of the believer is liberation from this cosmic dance. Hindus also believe in transmigration of souls. After one dies one is born again in another form, as either a higher or lower being, depending on whether the person was righteous or evil in the previous life. If one becomes righteous enough, one will cease to be reborn.[17]

---

31. An example of a member of the fifth class would be a

- ○ A. priest in a respected holy order.
- ○ B. carpenter in a small village.
- ○ C. shop owner in India.
- ○ D. nurse in a leper colony.
- ○ E. great warrior.

32. Transmigration of souls, according to Hindus, involves

- ○ A. reincarnation.
- ○ B. one's Karma.
- ○ C. one's personal destiny.
- ○ D. striving to behave in accordance with the way things are.
- ○ E. the social order.

33. The author states that Hinduism "hardly corresponds" to most Western religions. He most likely means

  ○ A. it is difficult to write about with Western influences.
  ○ B. there is a great deal of similarity between Hinduism and Christianity.
  ○ C. the two religions have many followers.
  ○ D. there are very few similarities between Hinduism and Western religions.
  ○ E. that Hinduism and Western religions need stronger leadership.

34. The author of the above passage

  ○ A. is most likely Jewish.
  ○ B. has little respect for Hinduism.
  ○ C. presents the information in an objective manner.
  ○ D. thinks the beliefs of Hinduism are very strange.
  ○ E. is most likely Christian.

35. According to the above passage, Hindus

  ○ A. should strive for upward social mobility.
  ○ B. will achieve Karma if they better themselves.
  ○ C. achieve righteousness through acceptance.
  ○ D. strive to be continually reborn.
  ○ E. strive for transmigration of souls.

PASSAGE EIGHT

You may use the following question to help you focus your reading:

How did Helen Keller discover the meaning of language?

(The following passage is adapted from H. Keller, The Story of My Life. © 1976 by Buccaneer Books.)

> She brought me my hat and I knew I was going out into the warm sunshine. This thought, if a wordless sensation may be called a thought, made me hop and skip with pleasure.
>
> We walked down the path to the well-house, attracted by the fragrance of the honeysuckle with which it was covered. Some one was drawing water and my teacher placed my hand under the spout. As the cool stream gushed over one hand she spelled into the other the word water, first slowly, then rapidly. I stood still, my whole attention fixed upon the motion of her fingers. Suddenly I felt a misty consciousness as of something forgotten—a thrill of returning thought; and somehow the mystery of language was revealed to me. I knew then that w-a-t-e-r meant the wonderful cool something that was flowing over my hand. That living word awakened my soul, gave it light, hope, joy, set it free! There were barriers still, it is true, but barriers that could in time be swept away.
>
> I left the well-house eager to learn. Everything had a name, and each name gave birth to a new thought. As we returned to the house every object which I touched seemed to quiver with life. That was because I saw everything with the strange, new sight that had come to me.[18]

36. After her experience at the well, Helen

   ○ A. was aware that her eyesight was greatly improved.

   ○ B. was extremely discouraged.

   ○ C. worried about the barriers she had yet to overcome.

   ○ D. connected language and thought.

   ○ E. experienced deep depression.

37. The experience by the well most likely occurred

   ○ A. during spring or summer.

   ○ B. after school.

   ○ C. during winter.

   ○ D. before school.

   ○ E. during a rainstorm.

38.   Helen's attitude toward learning could best be described as

○ A. enthusiastic.

○ B. discouraged.

○ C. realistic.

○ D. cynical.

○ E. critical.

39.   The above passage is describing

○ A. how the mystery of language was revealed to Helen Keller.

○ B. the relationship between Helen and her teacher.

○ C. how Helen Keller overcame barriers.

○ D. how we all connect language and objects.

○ E. Helen's relationship with her family.

40.   The author makes her point about the importance of language through

○ A. description.

○ B. analogy.

○ C. critical analysis.

○ D. sequential events.

○ E. comparison and contrast.

PASSAGE NINE

You may use the following question to help you focus your reading:

What skills are important for an education?

(The following passage is adapted from R.A. Roy, Physical Science: An Integrated Approach. © 1991 by Contemporary Publishing.)

In school we learn two kinds of things. One kind of thing is learning to read and write. (Yesterday's new technology is today's basic skill.) We learn arithmetic and algebra, how to write a business letter and how do to chemistry. These skills certainly help us with jobs and with life. But there is another kind of learning. It is more basic and more important. It is the skill of learning itself. We learn how to learn. If we are good learners, we will be able to keep up. If we are poor learners, we will be passed by.

Most of us realize that there are some skills, like algebra perhaps, that we won't need very much. "Why bother?" we ask ourselves. The answer is that if we can learn how to master new and difficult material, then we will be able to master the new skills necessary to get a better job and to have a richer life. (It will probably also turn out that the algebra was useful after all.)

One big part of making the American Dream a reality is to get an education. Our economic and political way of life depends so much on educated citizens that educational opportunity is guaranteed to everyone through high school; and, most can go to college with some individual effort. No one is forced to learn, but the opportunity is there for everyone.[19]

41.   The two kinds of things learned in school, according to the author, are

○   A.   reading and writing.

○   B.   reading and algebra.

○   C.   algebra and arithmetic.

○   D.   basic skills and the skill of learning itself.

○   E.   writing and listening.

42.   The author believes

○   A.   algebra is an impractical skill.

○   B.   educational opportunity is readily available.

○   C.   basic skills are unimportant.

○   D.   the American Dream is far from reality.

○   E.   reading and writing are the most important skills

43. Statements in the above passage are primarily

○ A. facts.

○ B. opinions.

○ C. supported by data.

○ D. common sense.

○ E. backed by scientific evidence.

44. The best title for the above passage is

○ A. The Importance of Learning to Learn.

○ B. Writing and Education.

○ C. Education.

○ D. Basic Skills.

○ E. Algebra.

45. The author believes the American Dream

○ A. is difficult to achieve.

○ B. can be achieved through education.

○ C. is only possible for a select few.

○ D. is a hoax.

○ E. will pass us by.

PASSAGE TEN

You may use the following question to help you focus your reading:

How is the theme of an advertisement related to the theme of a news story?

(The following passage is adapted from E.D. Yates, The Writing Craft. © 1985 by Contemporary Publishing.)

Just as in a news story, the advertisement must have a theme, a unity provided by using only material that will reflect the theme. You arrive at a theme in an ad usually by choosing a specific benefit that the particular product will provide for the reader/listener/ viewer. Once you have selected a theme, the material you select to use in the ad must advance and enhance that theme. You should put nothing in the ad that would detract from the theme or divert the attention of the consumer from the theme.

The theme can be anything that is likely to persuade the reader/listener/viewer to purchase the product being advertised or to use the service being advertised. The benefit can be anything that appeals to the reader/listener/viewer's need or desire for amusement, good health, recognition, food or drink, security, comfort, approval of the opposite sex and friends of the same sex, a chance to make or save money, a chance to save time, a chance to gain relief from labor, etc. In other words, anything that will improve life or the perception of life.

The theme of an advertisement, unlike the theme of a news story, is more likely to be an appeal to an emotional response than it is an intellectual response. Thus, the need to create a desire for the item or service advertised and the need to move the reader/ listener/viewer to action often will take precedence in determining the theme than the need to attract attention and gain interest.[20]

46. The author discusses advertisements by

- ❍ A. comparing an advertisement to a news story.
- ❍ B. chronological events.
- ❍ C. sequential developments.
- ❍ D. description.
- ❍ E. scientific evidence.

47. According to the author, the theme of a news story

- ❍ A. is less likely to be an appeal to an emotional response.
- ❍ B. is unrelated to an advertisement.
- ❍ C. has less of a theme than an advertisement.
- ❍ D. may detract from the theme of an advertisement.
- ❍ E. may enhance advertisements.

48. The author believes that the benefit of what is being advertised can be

○ A. security.

○ B. desire or need for amusement.

○ C. need for recognition.

○ D. comfort.

○ E. any or all of the above.

49. According to the author, an advertisement and news story must both

○ A. have a theme.

○ B. appeal to an emotional response.

○ C. have benefits that improve life.

○ D. create a need for action.

○ E. offer a chance to make or save money.

50. According to the author, in determining the theme in an advertisement, the need to create a desire for the item is

○ A. more important than the need to attract attention.

○ B. less important than the need to gain interest.

○ C. less important than the need to take action.

○ D. impossible without a strong interest.

○ E. less important than the need to attract attention.

ANSWERS KEY FOR THE READING SKILLS SECTION

Chapter 10 *Answers*

EXERCISE 2

Paragraph A
Main idea sentence: All foods supply some nutrients, albeit sometimes in limited amounts.
Shape: ▲

Paragraph B
Main idea sentence: Sounds are heard not only through the outer and middle ear, but also through the direct conduction of vibrations through the bones in the head.
Shape: ▼

Paragraph C
Main idea sentence: Sometimes known as the House of Moliere, the Theatre Francais was a symbol, in two important ways, of the emerging dominance of the middle class in the up-coming century.
Shape: ◆

Paragraph D
Main idea sentences: Before assessing someone's nutritional status, his family's medical history must be known. For such reasons, you can fully evaluate someone's nutritional status only after assessing the complete medical history of that person.
Shape: ▼

EXERCISE 3

Paragraph A
Directional words: The crucial point is
Paragraph B
Directional words: In general
Paragraph C
Directional words: The point is

EXERCISE 5

Paragraph A
Main idea sentence: Both ways of understanding are necessary for human fulfillment.
Shape: ▲

EXERCISE 6

Paragraph A
Details: candy, toys, films, free time, extra outdoor periods, first in the lunch line, tokens, "chips"

EXERCISE 7

Paragraph A
Directional word: Further, major
Paragraph B
Directional words: therefore, major; For example, minor

EXERCISE 8

Paragraph A
Signal word(s): Finally

EXERCISE 9

Paragraph A
Signal word(s): One consequence of

EXERCISE 10

Paragraph A
Signal word(s): older, younger, thicker

EXERCISE 11

Paragraph A
Form: providing data
Paragraph B
Form: explaining experimental evidence
Paragraph C
Form: providing data
Paragraph D
Form: providing historical documentation
Paragraph E
Form: describing observations

EXERCISE 12

Stated assumptions in Paragraph B and C

Chapter 11 *Answers*

EXERCISE 1

Paragraph A
   Main idea: Overpraise may have negative effects on students.
   Clues: Author's tone is negative.
Paragraph B
   Main idea: There are many negative results of industrial production.
   Clues: Author's tone is negative.

EXERCISE 2

Paragraph A
   Assumptions: Author assumes that spelling cannot be taught and that attention to detail will lead to correct spelling.
Paragraph B
   Assumptions: Author assumes rewards of teaching are proportional to effort.

EXERCISE 3

Paragraph A
   Appeal to fear
Paragraph B
   Appeal to pity
Paragraph C
   Appeal to ignorance
Paragraph D
   Appeal to authority
Paragraph E
   Appeal to personal attack

EXERCISE 4

Paragraph A
   Refracted means bent
   Type of context clue: synonym
Paragraph B
   Conception means male and female sex cells unite
   Type of context clue: definition
Paragraph C
   Compelling means strong
   Type of context clue: contrast
Paragraph D
   Vicarious means indirect
   Type of context clue: inference

ANSWERS FOR THE READING SKILLS
PRACTICE TESTS

Practice Test One

1. A	26. C		
2. B	27. A		
3. A	28. B		
4. A	29. C		
5. C	30. A		
6. A	31. A		
7. B	32. B		
8. C	33. E		
9. B	34. A		
10. B	35. E		
11. C	36. C		
12. C	37. A		
13. A	38. E		
14. A	39. D		
15. D	40. A		
16. B	41. E		
17. D	42. D		
18. C	43. D		
19. B	44. A		
20. D	45. D		
21. B	46. D		
22. B	47. E		
23. C	48. C		
24. B	49. C		
25. C	50. D		

Practice Test Two

1. D	26. C
2. A	27. A
3. A	28. A
4. A	29. A
5. D	30. A
6. B	31. D
7. D	32. A
8. B	33. D
9. D	34. C
10. A	35. C
11. C	36. D
12. B	37. A
13. B	38. A
14. B	39. A
15. A	40. A
16. E	41. B
17. C	42. B
18. D	43. B
19. A	44. A
20. A	45. B
21. A	46. A
22. B	47. A
23. D	48. E
24. A	49. A
25. A	50. A

ACKNOWLEDGEMENTS

Chapter 10

1 Gerow, R. *Psychology: An Introduction*, 4th Edition. Addison-Wesley Educational Publishers, Inc., Reading, MA, (1995). p. 42.

2 Forsythe, W.A., III. *Nutrition and You With Readings*, 3rd Edition. Contemporary Publishing Company of Raleigh, Inc., Raleigh, NC, (1995). p. 7.

3 Wagner, J. *Introductory Musical Acoustics*, 3rd Edition. Contemporary Publishing Company of Raleigh, Inc., Raleigh, NC, (1994). p. 62.

4 Staub, A.W. *Varieties Of Theatrical Art*, 3rd Edition. Contemporary Publishing Company of Raleigh, Inc., Raleigh, NC, (1994). p. 212.

5 Forsythe, W.A., III. *Nutrition and You With Readings*, 3rd Edition. Contemporary Publishing Company of Raleigh, Inc., Raleigh, NC, (1995). p. 41.

6 Madsen, C.K. & Kuhn, R.L. *Contemporary Music Eduction*, 2nd Edition. Contemporary Publishing Company of Raleigh, Inc., Raleigh, NC, (1994). p. 70.

7 Wolfe, L.D., Lieberman, L.S. & Hutchinson, D.L. *Laboratory Textbook for Physical Anthropology*, 4th Edition. Contemporary Publishing Company of Raleigh, Inc., Raleigh, NC, (1994). p. 10-35.

8 Roy, R.A. *Physical Science: An Integrated Approach*. Contemporary Publishing Company of Raleigh, Inc., Raleigh, NC, (1991). p. 369.

9 Gerow, R. *Psychology: An Introduction*, 4th Edition. Addison-Wesley Educational Publishers, Inc., Reading, MA, (1995). p. 690–691.

10 Curry, K.J. *Biology Experience*, 2nd Edition. Contemporary Publishing Company of Raleigh, Inc., Raleigh, NC, (1995). p. 1.

11 Esler, W.K. & Sciortino, P. *Methods for Teaching: An Overview of Current Practices*, 2nd Edition. Contemporary Publishing Company of Raleigh, Inc., Raleigh, NC, (1991). p. 72.

12 Gerow, R. *Psychology: An Introduction*, 4th Edition. Addison-Wesley Educational Publishers, Inc., Reading, MA, (1995). p. 514.

13 Wolfe, L.D., Lieberman, L.S. & Hutchinson, D.L. *Laboratory Textbook for Physical Anthropology*, 4th Edition. Contemporary Publishing Company of Raleigh, Inc., Raleigh, NC, (1994). p. 10-1.

14 Curry, K.J. *Biology Experience*, 2nd Edition. Contemporary Publishing Company of Raleigh, Inc., Raleigh, NC, (1995). p. 5.

15 Roy, R.A. *Physical Science: An Integrated Approach*. Contemporary Publishing Company of Raleigh, Inc., Raleigh, NC, (1991). p. 250.

16 Roy, R.A. *Physical Science: An Integrated Approach*. Contemporary Publishing Company of Raleigh, Inc., Raleigh, NC, (1991). p. 186.

17 Roy, R.A. *Physical Science: An Integrated Approach*. Contemporary Publishing Company of Raleigh, Inc., Raleigh, NC, (1991). p. 380.

18 Gerow, R. *Psychology: An Introduction*, 4th Edition. Addison-Wesley Educational Publishers, Inc., Reading, MA, (1995). p. 714.

19 Brook, G. & Heyl, R.J. *Introduction to Landforms*, 3rd Edition. Contemporary Publishing Company of Raleigh, Inc., Raleigh, NC, (1993). p. A-7.

20 Gerow, R. *Psychology: An Introduction*, 4th Edition. Addison-Wesley Educational Publishers, Inc., Reading, MA, (1995). p. 637.

21 Gerow, R. *Psychology: An Introduction*, 4th Edition. Addison-Wesley Educational Publishers, Inc., Reading, MA, (1995). p. 353.

22 Gerow, R. *Psychology: An Introduction*, 4th Edition. Addison-Wesley Educational Publishers, Inc., Reading, MA, (1995). p. 216–217.

23 Gerow, R. *Psychology: An Introduction*, 4th Edition. Addison-Wesley Educational Publishers, Inc., Reading, MA, (1995). p. 674–675.

24 Gerow, R. *Psychology: An Introduction*, 4th Edition. Addison-Wesley Educational Publishers, Inc., Reading, MA, (1995). p. 674.

Chapter 11

1 Esler, W.K. & Sciortino, P. *Methods for Teaching: An Overview of Current Practices*, 2nd Edition. Contemporary Publishing Company of Raleigh, Inc., Raleigh, NC, (1991). p. 72.

2 Roy, R.A. *Physical Science: An Integrated Approach*. Contemporary Publishing Company of Raleigh, Inc., Raleigh, NC, (1991). p. 377.

3 Yates, E.D. *The Writing Craft*, 2nd Edition. Contemporary Publishing Company of Raleigh, Inc., Raleigh, NC, (1985). p. 122.

4 Madsen, C.H., III & Madsen, C.K. *Teaching/Discipline: A Positive Approach For Educational Development*, 3rd Edition. Contemporary Publishing Company of Raleigh, Inc., Raleigh, NC, (1983). p. 77.

5 Roy, R.A. *Physical Science: An Integrated Approach*. Contemporary Publishing Company of Raleigh, Inc., Raleigh, NC, (1991). p. 381.

6 Chaffee, J. *Thinking Critically*, 3rd Edition. Copyright © 1991 by John Chaffee. Reprinted with permission of Houghton Mifflin Company, Boston, MA. p. 571.

7 Chaffee, J. *Thinking Critically*, 3rd Edition. Copyright © 1991 by John Chaffee. Reprinted with permission of Houghton Mifflin Company, Boston, MA. p. 571.

8 Chaffee, J. *Thinking Critically*, 3rd Edition. Copyright © 1991 by John Chaffee. Reprinted with permission of Houghton Mifflin Company, Boston, MA. p. 570.

9 Chaffee, J. *Thinking Critically*, 3rd Edition. Copyright © 1991 by John Chaffee. Reprinted with permission of Houghton Mifflin Company, Boston, MA. p. 572.

10 Brook, G. & Heyl, R.J. *Introduction to Landforms*, 3rd Edition. Contemporary Publishing Company of Raleigh, Inc., Raleigh, NC, (1993). p. 14-2.

11 Gerow, R. *Psychology: An Introduction*, 4th Edition. Addison-Wesley Educational Publishers, Inc., Reading, MA, (1995). p. 355.

12 Roy, R.A. *Physical Science: An Integrated Approach*. Contemporary Publishing Company of Raleigh, Inc., Raleigh, NC, (1991). p. 356.

13 Madsen, C.K. & Kuhn, R.L. *Contemporary Music Eduction*, 2nd Edition. Contemporary Publishing Company of Raleigh, Inc., Raleigh, NC, (1994). p. 17.

Chapter 12

1   Roy, R.A. *Physical Science: An Integrated Approach.* Contemporary Publishing Company of Raleigh, Inc., Raleigh, NC, (1991). p. 374.

2   Wolfe, L.D., Lieberman, L.S. & Hutchinson, D.L. *Laboratory Textbook for Physical Anthropology*, 4th Edition. Contemporary Publishing Company of Raleigh, Inc., Raleigh, NC, (1994). p. 10-47.

3   Gastaldo, R.A., Savrda, C.E. & Lewis, R.D. *Deciphering Earth History.* Contemporary Publishing Company of Raleigh, Inc., Raleigh, NC, (1996). p. 1-1.

4   Wilson, J.W., *Astronomy: A Laboratory Textbook*, 2nd Edition. Contemporary Publishing Company of Raleigh, Inc., Raleigh, NC, (1996). p. 25.1.

5   Gerow, R. *Psychology: An Introduction*, 4th Edition. Addison Wesley Educational Publishers, Inc., Reading, MA, (1995). p. 216.

6   Smith, B. *A Tree Grows In Brooklyn.* HarperCollins Publishers, Inc., New York, NY, (1943). p. 25.

7   Lauder, L. "The Language of Foreign Trade," © 1985 by *The New York Times Co.*, New York, NY, (October 7, 1985). p. 136–137.

8   Roy, R.A. *Physical Science: An Integrated Approach.* Contemporary Publishing Company of Raleigh, Inc., Raleigh, NC, (1991). p. 375.

9   Staub, A.W. *Varieties of Theatrical Art*, 3rd Edition. Contemporary Publishing Company of Raleigh, Inc., Raleigh, NC, (1994). p. 19.

10   Roy, R.A. *Physical Science: An Integrated Approach.* Contemporary Publishing Company of Raleigh, Inc., Raleigh, NC, (1991). p. 3.

11   Cousins, N. "The Right To Die," *The Saturday Review*, © 1975, General Media International, Inc., New York, NY, (June 14, 1975). p. 258–260.

12   Hewitt, P.G. "The Origin of the Universe and Solar System," in *Conceptual Physics*, 5th Edition, Scott, Foresman and Company, Glenview, IL, p. 591, from *Academic Reading*, Scott, Foresman/Little, Brown Higher Education, Glenview, IL, (1985).

13   Roy, R.A. *Physical Science: An Integrated Approach.* Contemporary Publishing Company of Raleigh, Inc., Raleigh, NC, (1991). p. 375.

14   Forsythe, W.A., III. *Nutrition and You With Readings*, 3rd Edition. Contemporary Publishing Company of Raleigh, Inc., Raleigh, NC, (1995). p. 46.

15   Wagner, J. *Introductory Musical Acoustics*, 3rd Edition. Contemporary Publishing Company of Raleigh, Inc., Raleigh, NC, (1994). p. 48.

16   Wagner, J. *Introductory Musical Acoustics*, 3rd Edition. Contemporary Publishing Company of Raleigh, Inc., Raleigh, NC, (1994). p. 82.

17   Eshleman, R. & Cashion, B.G. Adapted from *Sociology: An Introduction*, 2nd Edition. Scott Foresman, and Company, p. 353–4 from *Academic Reading*, Scott, Foresman/Little, Brown Higher Education, Glenview, IL (1985).

18   Keller, H. *The Story Of My Life.* Buccaneer Books, New York, 1976. Ed. by John Albert Macy, Cambridge, Mass. (1903). p. 36.

19   Roy, R.A. *Physical Science: An Integrated Approach.* Contemporary Publishing Company of Raleigh, Inc., Raleigh, NC, (1991). p. 382.

20   Yates, E.D. *The Writing Craft*, 2nd Edition. Contemporary Publishing Company of Raleigh, Inc., Raleigh, NC, (1985). p. 71.